CONFRONTING COMPLEXITY

CONFRONTING COMPLEXITY

X-EVENTS, RESILIENCE, AND HUMAN PROGRESS

JOHN L. CASTI,
ROGER D. JONES,
AND MICHAEL J. PENNOCK

The X Press

First printing 2016

Cataloging-in-Publication data is available from the Library of Congress. A catalog record for this book is available from the British Library.

ISBN 978-0-9972557-5-1 paperback
ISBN 978-0-9972557-6-8 e-book

Text design by Under|Over. Typeset by AarkMany Media, Chennai, India. Printed by Book-Mobile in the United States and CPI Books Ltd in the United Kingdom. The U.S. printed edition of this book comes on Forest Stewardship Council-certified, 30% recycled paper.

CONTENTS

PREFACE   13

ACKNOWLEDGMENTS   15

1   HERE IN THE REAL WORLD   17

   1.1   It Came from Outer Space   18
       1.1.1   Cancelling Armageddon   21
       1.1.2   Exercises: Potential Energy   22
       1.1.3   Just a Little Shove   23
       1.1.4   Exercises: Kinetic Energy   25
       1.1.5   Don't Blow Your Top   25
       1.1.6   Exercises: Internal Energy   28
       1.1.7   Exercises: Power and Energy Flux   29
       1.1.8   Not-So-Extreme Events   29

   1.2   The Context and the Trigger   31
       1.2.1   Complexity Gaps   33
       1.2.2   Exercises: Complexity Measurement   36
       1.2.3   Exercises: Complexity of Social Mood   38
       1.2.4   Social Mood   39
       1.2.5   Exercises: Is Shannon Entropy Right?   44
       1.2.6   Measuring Social Mood   46
       1.2.7   US Presidential Elections and Social Mood   47
       1.2.8   Exercises: Systems   49

   1.3   Resilience: The Good, the Bad, and
       the Absolutely Essential   50

   1.4   Hurricanes as Complexity Metaphors   56
       1.4.1   Scientifically Accurate Poetry   57
       1.4.2   Spiral of Complexity   58
       1.4.3   Thermal Conduction   59
       1.4.4   Emergence of Order: Rayleigh-Bénard Instability   60
       1.4.5   Sudden Complexity Shifts   61
       1.4.6   Hadley, Ferrel, and Polar Cells   61
       1.4.7   Effect of Earth's Rotation   63

1.4.8   Sudden Creation of Hurricanes   65
1.4.9   But . . . Hurricanes Rotate in the Wrong Direction 66
1.4.10 Heat Transfer to the Poles   66

1.5   Discussion and Research Questions   71
1.5.1   Extreme Value Theory   71
1.5.2   Feedback   72
1.5.3   Extreme Value Theory Redux   73
1.5.4   Undulating Landscape   75
1.5.5   Feedback and Social Mood   76
1.5.6   Resilience of Social Systems   77

2. DRIVERS OF CHANGE   81

2.1   Trends and Transitions   82
2.1.1   Ferguson's Drivers of Historical Change   83

2.2   Five Stages of Collapse   85

2.3   Mood and Complexity as Leading Drivers   87

**2.4   Discussion Questions: Complexity
       Mismatch and Mood   100**
2.4.1   Why Is the Trend "Normal" Behavior?   100
2.4.2   Why Is It Difficult to Assign a Probability
        to an X-event?   101
2.4.3   Is Social Mood an Aggregation of Everyone's
        Subjective Probability of the Future?   102
2.4.4   How Does Herding Affect Social Mood?   102
2.4.5   Why Are Shifts in the Trend a Surprise?   104
2.4.6   Shifts in Social Mood Are Different in Going
        from Optimistic to Pessimistic Than
        Pessimistic to Optimistic   105

2.5   Demographic Transition   106
2.5.1   What Do We Mean By a Model?   107
2.5.2   Irrigation System: Flows   109
2.5.3   Irrigation System: Distribution of Water   113
2.5.4   Irrigation System: System Behavior   115
2.5.5   Irrigation System: Controlling the Flow of Water 116
2.5.6   Irrigation System: Dynamics of the Irrigation System 117
2.5.7   Exercises: Dynamics of the Irrigation System   119
2.5.8   Hey! . . . What About Women's Education and
        Economic Drivers of Fertility?   119

2.5.9   Effects of Controller Responsiveness   120
2.5.10   Core Model   122
2.5.11   Vital Demographic Variables   124
2.5.12   Statics of the Demographic Transition   127
2.5.13   Clustering of World Populations   128
2.5.14   Dynamics of the Demographic Transition   131
2.5.15   Exercises: Population Explosion   133
2.5.16   Discussion Questions: Population Explosion   134
2.5.17   Exercises: Demographic Transition   135
2.5.18   Discussion Questions: Demographic Transition   139
2.5.19   Exercises: Aging and Economics   142

3. **UP CLOSE AND PERSONAL**   **147**

3.1   **The One and the Many**   **148**
3.1.1   Exercise: X-Events at the Personal Level   150
3.1.2   Discussion Question: Ashby's Law   150
3.1.3   Discussion Question: Hamlet   150

3.2   **"Middle" Crises**   **151**

3.3   **Discussion Question: Hero's Journey**   **156**
3.3.1   Stages of the Journey   157

3.4   **Inequality Kills Everything**   **158**

3.5   **Discussion Questions: Productivity, Income Inequality, and the Jobless Recovery**   **165**
3.5.1   Productivity   165
3.5.2   Income Inequality   166
3.5.3   The Jobless Economic Recovery   167

3.6   **Polarization and Social Mood**   **168**
3.6.1   Examples: Stable States   169
3.6.2   Examples: Mixing of Optimists and Pessimists   170
3.6.3   Examples: Competition Between Uniform and Mixed Domains   172
3.6.4   Discussion Question: Red Counties and Blue Counties   172
3.6.5   The Model   173
3.6.6   Simulation Results   174
3.6.7   Fixed Points of the System   174

	3.6.8	Fixed Points Solutions	175
	3.6.9	Exercise: Character of Fixed Points	177
	3.6.10	Stability of Fixed Points	177
	3.6.11	Exercises: Modeling Inequality	179

3.7 Discussion Questions: Personal X-Events   **179**

	3.7.1	Bipolar Disorder	180
	3.7.2	Nature vs. Nurture	180
	3.7.3	Evidence-Based Beliefs	181
	3.7.4	Changing Religious Demographics in the United States	181

3.8 Discussion Questions: Political X-Events   **182**

	3.8.1	Political Leaders	182
	3.8.2	Social Mood and the 2014 US Midterm Election	183
	3.8.3	Texas Politics	184

3.9 Discussion Questions: Utility   **186**

	3.9.1	Risk Aversion	187
	3.9.2	Prospect Theory	187
	3.9.3	Probability Adjustment	188

4 STAYIN' ALIVE   **191**

4.1 Time for a Change   **192**

4.2 Failure is Always An Option   **193**

4.3 Out of the Ashes   **197**

| | 4.3.1 | Discussion Question: Bailouts | 198 |

4.4 Mirror Vision and Complexity Overload   **199**

| | 4.4.1 | Discussion Question: Swiss-Cheese Model | 201 |

4.5 Over the Edge of the Technology Cliff   **201**

| | 4.5.1 | Exercises: Complexity Mismatch in Business and Politics | 202 |

4.6 How Mood Affects the Nature of Products   **203**

	4.6.1	Commodities	204
	4.6.2	Risk in Commodity Production	204
	4.6.3	Product Quality	205
	4.6.4	Mood and Compound Products	205
	4.6.5	Meta-Products	206

4.6.6   Discussion Questions: Risk,
         Mood, and Commodities   207

4.7   **How Stability of Companies Leads to Instability
       of Companies**   **208**
       4.7.1   Stability and Middle Management   208
       4.7.2   Negative Feedback   209
       4.7.3   The Example of Kodak   210
       4.7.4   Discussion Questions: Stability of Companies 211
       4.7.5   Discussion Questions: Photography and Visual Arts 212

4.8   **The Beer Game**   **212**
       4.8.1   The Beer Supply Chain   213
       4.8.2   Playing the Beer Game Live   213
       4.8.3   Stable Operation of the Live Beer Game   216
       4.8.4   Simulation of the Beer Game   217
       4.8.5   Simulation Parameters and Contextual Drivers 218
       4.8.6   Analysis of a Beer Game Simulation
                with Variable Chain Length   219
       4.8.7   Discussion Question: Communication Delay   223
       4.8.8   Exercises: The Beer Game   223
       4.8.9   Discussion Questions: The Beer Game   224

4.9   **The Business of US Healthcare**   **224**
       4.9.1   US Healthcare is Poised for an X-Event   225
       4.9.2   Why is Healthcare Not a Commodity?   227
       4.9.3   Two Visions   229
       4.9.4   Discussion Question: Physician Compensation 231
       4.9.5   Technology-Driven Complexity Mismatch   232
       4.9.6   Patents Affect Complexity Mismatch   234
       4.9.7   Regulation of the Pharmaceutical Industry   235
       4.9.8   Discussion Question: Forces on
                the Pharmaceutical Industry   237
       4.9.9   Personalized Medicine and Information
                Management for Treatment   238
       4.9.10   Personalized Medicine and Clinical Trials   241
       4.9.11   Insurance-Driven Healthcare Cost Inflation   242
       4.9.12   Discussion Question: Employer-Funded Insurance 243
       4.9.13   Discussion Question: Affordable Care Act of 2010 244
       4.9.14   Discussion Question: Complexity, Mood,
                and Random Triggers in Healthcare   244

4.10   **Discussion and Research Questions**   **245**

5   EXPECTING THE UNKNOWN UNKNOWNS   **251**

5.1   The Resilience of "Resilience"   **252**
5.1.1   Discussion Question: Resilience on All Scales   255

5.2   Resilient Against What?   **255**
5.2.1   Exercise: Insurance World   261

5.3   Planning for the Unimaginable   **261**
5.3.1   Discussion Question: Oregon Healthcare   265

5.4   How Resilient Are You?   **265**
5.4.1   Exercise: Measuring the Four As   267

**5.5   Climate Change: An Example of
Managing the Four As**   **267**
5.5.1   Building on the Hurricane Example   268
5.5.2   Beliefs and Mood on Climate Change   269

5.6   Climate Change: Awareness   **269**
5.6.1   Is the Climate Warming?   272
5.6.2   Discussion Question: Measuring
Ancient Temperatures   273
5.6.3   How Do Scientists Know That Recent Climate
Change Is Caused by Human Activities?   273
5.6.4   Discussion Question: CO_2 275
5.6.5 CO_2 Is Already in the Atmosphere Naturally, so Why
Are Emissions from Human Activity Significant?   276
5.6.6   Discussion Question: Hydrocarbons and Much More   277
5.6.7   What Role Has the Sun Played in
Climate Change in Recent Decades?   278
5.6.8   Exercises: Sunspot Cycle   279
5.6.9   Climate Is Always Changing. Why Is
Climate Change of Concern Now?   280
5.6.10 Exercise: Ice Ages   280
5.6.11 Discussion Question: Time Scales   281
5.6.12 Is the Current Level of CO_2 Concentration
Unprecedented in Earth's History?   281
5.6.13 Is There a Point at Which Adding More CO_2
Will Not Cause Further Warming?   282
5.6.14 Exercise: Absorption Bands   282
5.6.15 Does the Rate of Warming Vary
from One Decade to Another?   282
5.6.16 Exercise: Modulations   283
5.6.17 Discussion Question: Frogs in a Pot   283

5.6.18   Does the Recent Slowdown of Warming Mean
         That Climate Change Is No Longer Happening?   284
5.6.19   Exercise: Warming Over the Last Decade   284
5.6.20   If the World is Warming, Why Are Some
         Winters and Summers Still Very Cold?   285
5.6.21   Discussion Question: Second
         Law of Thermodynamics   285
5.6.22   Exercise: Autocatalytic Reactions   286
5.6.23   Why Is Arctic Sea Ice Decreasing
         While Antarctic Sea Ice Is Not?   287
5.6.24   Exercise: Ice Melt in the Antarctic   287
5.6.25   How Does Climate Change Affect the
         Strength and Frequency of Floods,
         Droughts, Hurricanes, and Tornadoes?   288
5.6.26   How Fast Is Sea Level Rising?   288
5.6.27   Exercise: Florida   289
5.6.28   What Is Ocean Acidification
         and Why Does It Matter?   289
5.6.29   How Confident Are Scientists That Earth Will
         Warm Further over the Coming Century?   290
5.6.30   Discussion Question: There Is Time, but So What?   290
5.6.31   Are Climate Changes of a Few
         Degrees a Cause for Concern?   291
5.6.32   What Are Scientists Doing to Address
         Key Uncertainties in Our Understanding
         of the Climate System?   291
5.6.33   Are Disaster Scenarios about Tipping Points Like
         'Turning off the Gulf Stream' and Release of
         Methane from the Arctic a Cause for Concern?   292
5.6.34   If Emissions of Greenhouse Gases Were
         Stopped, Would the Climate Return to
         the Conditions of 200 Years Ago?   292

5.7   **What About Other X-Events Simultaneous to
      Climate Change?**   **293**

5.8   **Climate Change: Assimilation**   **293**
5.8.1   Discussion Question: How Bad Is It Likely To Be?   294
5.8.2   Discussion Question: How Do We Identify Our
        Options for Survival?   295
5.8.3   Discussion Question: How Do We Evaluate Our
        Options for Survival?   295
5.8.4   Discussion Question: How Do We Implement Our
        Options for Survival?   296

5.9   Climate Change: Agility   **297**

5.9.1   Discussion Question: What are the
          Opportunities That Might Arise?   297

5.9.2   Discussion Question: What Resources Do We
          Have to Take Advantage of the Opportunities?   298

5.10   Climate Change: Adaptivity   **298**

5.11   Discussion Question: Venice, Italy   **299**

5.12   Discussion Question: Punctuated Equilibrium   **300**

5.13   Discussion Question: Human Progress   **301**

5.14   Discussion Question: Path Dependence   **302**

5.15   Discussion Question: Simulation   **303**

5.16   Discussion Question: Controlled X-Events   **304**

5.17   The Burkian Game   **305**

5.17.1   Connections   305

5.17.2   Germ Theory of Disease   307

5.17.3   Childhood Deaths and Fertility   308

5.17.4   Economic Response   309

5.17.5   Climate Change   310

5.17.6   Discussion Question: Are
          Human Brains Big Enough?   311

INDEX   **313**

PREFACE

A philosopher who is not taking part in discussions is like a boxer who never goes into the ring.
Ludwig Wittgenstein

I wanted to write that my work consists of two parts: of the one which is here, and of everything which I have not written. And precisely this second part is the important one.
Ludwig Wittgenstein

Things are much more marvelous than the scientific method allows us to conceive.
Barbara McClintock

THE CONVERSATION

The book you are holding or seeing on your screen may look like a normal book; it is not. It is a conversation in which you are a participant. The book does not offer pat answers to hard questions. In fact, it barely even gives definition to hard questions. Rather, this book presents that stage in which science is most challenging and, arguably, most interesting—the period of identifying just what the problems and issues are. That is why we solicit your help in writing this story—the story of extreme events in social systems.

The participants in this book-writing enterprise are independent thinkers who wish to understand the forces impinging on social systems and the systems' often dramatic and extreme responses to those forces. Extreme events, the sudden and discontinuous response of social systems to these forces, are what we for shorthand term *X-Events*. We imagine the reader to be a person who wants to intelligently manage his or her actions and behaviors in the midst of an X-event—in short, to manage an organization in chaos. And not only manage, but be a beneficiary of that event. Explicitly, we understand that there are no simple answers to social questions. But there is at least a *gestalt* that can help an individual anticipate and manage X-events. The program outlined here is to build the gestalt by total immersion in the topic—by examining the issues from many perspectives.

Here we look at X-events from the following points of view or frames of reference:

- case studies
- mythology
- academic sociology
- natural analogs
- English literature
- engineering risk management
- mathematical modeling

No one perspective is sufficient to capture the entire picture. But patterns begin to emerge when questions are asked from several points of view. What seems to be emerging is that X-events are a fundamental property of social systems, and that if human progress is to be made it depends intimately on X-events for propelling it forward.

GRAY BOXES

You will see that the book is divided into two formats: a normal black-on-white part and a part that is presented in gray boxes. As the spirit of the book is a conversation, different authors are responsible for each part. One of the authors (JC) is responsible for the initial introductions to the material, the black-on-white part. The other authors (RDJ and MP) then respond to JC's text with questions and different points of view. The reader who doesn't want to dig deeper can get the gist of the book by reading JC's part. A reader who also wants to *participate* in the conversation will want to read and respond to the material in gray boxes.

The goal of the gray track is not to answer questions, but to identify that part that is not being said. As Wittgenstein noted, this is the important part. Content, exercises, and discussion questions populate the boxes. The authors have not worked out the exercises, nor do they have pat answers to the discussion questions. There is supplemental material as well as blog conversations on a companion blog site for the book. We hope this site will serve as a vehicle to explore the ideas presented here in deeper and more specific contexts. Google *xeventsblog.com* to locate the site.

ACKNOWLEDGMENTS

We would like to thank good friends, old and new, who have given their time and effort to review and criticize portions of this book. In particular David Lane, Doug Craft, Bill Rouse, and Tom Burch who made noble attempts to keep us from embarrassing ourselves. If we did anyway, it is not their fault.

1
HERE IN THE REAL WORLD

1.1
IT CAME FROM OUTER SPACE

TIME: *65 million years ago.*
PLACE: *What is now the Yucatan Peninsula in eastern Mexico.*
EVENT: *The crash of an asteroid 20 kilometers across.*
EFFECT: *The end of the dinosaurs and most other life forms on Earth at the time.*

Suppose you were a lumbering triceratops. What would your walnut-sized brain have registered when this fiery crash occurred? Answer: Basically, almost nothing beyond an unbelievably intense light in the sky before you were instantaneously reduced to a heap of ashes, or even obliterated entirely if you happened to be in the impact zone. Here's the scenario.

A huge fireball suddenly appears in the sky—for a second or two—followed by an ear-splitting impact. For thousands of miles around, animals like our friend the triceratops are incinerated, and those in the immediate vicinity of the impact simply vanish. The Earth seems to be ablaze, as a gigantic column of dust and fire extends miles up into the stratosphere.

The asteroid impact sends a massive shock wave cycling to the other side of the planet, the wave moving both on the surface via massive tsunamis and beneath the ground as a wave in the Earth's crust. This ground wave generates huge earthquakes, as well as activating numerous volcanoes. As the two shock waves traveling around the Earth in opposite directions collide, the Earth's crust is forced up into a mountain ridge of Himalayan proportions. And this is just what's going on in the first few *hours* following the impact!

The seas soon calm down and the fires go out. But the dust and smoke don't clear away. Instead, the massive amount of debris thrown up into the atmosphere by the impact encircles the Earth in a dense black cloud, blocking out the Sun for months—or possibly even years. It is literally midnight in winter—everywhere. Temperatures drop by more than 20 degrees centigrade worldwide and the surface of the Earth freezes solid. Photosynthesis by plants is stopped dead in its tracks and virtually all plant life dies. Animals quickly die too, at least those relying on plants for their sustenance, which means just about everything larger than a bacterium. Basically, the only thing left alive after a few months are bacteria, mosses, and perhaps a few insects, rat-like rodents, and fish.

Oddly enough, a strike by an asteroid or one of its cousins, a meteor or comet, didn't raise much attention and was not regarded as a threat to life on

Earth until the work of Nobel-prize winning physicist Luis Alvarez and his son, Walter, both professors at the University of California, Berkeley. In Gubbio, Italy in 1978, they discovered a thin layer of the rare mineral iridium in the soil. Iridium is not an element found in abundance in Earthly nature. But it does make up a very visible fraction of the material in the type of rock making up asteroids and meteorites. So it was a huge surprise to find this layer in the geologic record at just the point on the timeline where the dinosaurs departed and the age of mammals began.

Later, the same iridium layer was found at the very same place in the soil record in other parts of the world, leading paleobiologists to conjecture that the huge cloud of debris from the shattered asteroid impact at that time settled from the stratosphere to form that iridium layer. From here it was but a small step to conclude that this asteroid strike was the causal agent for the demise of the dinosaurs. The only missing element was the "smoking gun," geologic evidence of the crater created by the impact.

The controversy as to whether or not there was an asteroid of the right size that struck and left a trace of iridium raged on for a decade or more until 1991 when a NASA satellite spotted the crater. What the satellite saw was a huge indentation underneath the Yucatan Peninsula, near the town of Chicxulub, which had been covered over by millions of years of weather erosion, shifts in the Earth, continental drifts, and other such phenomena that unfold only on a geologic timescale.

From the size of the crater, scientists estimated that the asteroid creating it must have been about 30 thousand feet in diameter—just about the height of Mount Everest. In short, the Earth was hit by a massive *mountain*. And the asteroid struck with a force of about 100 million megatons. That's right, 100 million million tons of TNT. This amounts to five *trillion* atomic bombs the size of the one that leveled Hiroshima during World War II. Now *that's* an explosion!

So ended the reign of the dinosaurs when this asteroid strike created the Chicxulub crater on the Yucatan Peninsula 65 million years ago. Or, at least, this is the conventional wisdom today for how the dinosaurs departed this Earth after ruling it for more than 150 million years. And thus opened an econiche for our distant ancestors to slip into. But things are never simple in science, and regardless of what the current fashion happens to be, there is always a counter faction arguing something different.

In this case, the counterargument is that it was not the Chicxulub impact that leveled the dinosaurs, but one that took place in India about 300,000 years later. This counterclaim says that the Yucatan strike just weakened the dinosaurs, and it took the second strike to actually finish them off. For our purposes, such academic quibbling is meaningless. Either strike serves admirably to illustrate how human life and society as it exists today can be wiped away in an instant by an indifferent cosmos.

One might wonder if perhaps the dinosaurs were just unlucky, and that the asteroid strike ending their reign (Mexican or Indian version) was a fluke. But as Goldfinger phrased it in the famous eponymous film, "No, Mr. Bond. I expect you to die." The Chicxulub strike was neither the first, nor the biggest, nor the last such strike from outer space. Many believe that in the very early days of the Earth, over four billion years ago, a massive object struck the planet breaking it apart, one of the parts becoming what we now see as the Moon, while what remained is the planet we now call home. The next major strike, about 500 million years later, was most likely a cluster of asteroids so dense that the Earth's crust actually melted, destroying all geologic evidence of the planet up to that time.

Similar strikes from the blue seem to have taken place every 200–300 million years, recycling the flora and fauna much like a Las Vegas dealer recycles the cards at the blackjack table, each "shuffle" removing dominant species, thus opening up opportunities for others to take their place. And the beat goes on even in modern times.

Among the most celebrated of all cosmic fireworks displays took place on June 30, 1908, when a huge explosion shook up the village of Tunguska in central Siberia. Observers reported seeing the sky light up in a blast of fire, followed by an instantaneous rise in temperature and the ignition of surrounding forests for many tens of kilometers. Later, investigators from Moscow found more than four thousand square kilometers of forest simply flattened, as if a huge iron had run through and laid out all the tress in a circular pattern. Initial speculation as to the cause of this gigantic explosion ranged from a mini-black hole exploding to an engine meltdown in an alien spacecraft. Today, we know that the cause was a meteor fifty meters across that exploded that day in an airburst at eight kilometers over the remote region. It's estimated that the energy released in the Tunguska event was the equivalent of one thousand Hiroshima-strength nuclear bombs.

On the basis of these and many other known extraterrestrial interventions into Earthly affairs, scientists now estimate that an "exterminator"-type asteroid or comet like the Chicxulub event occurs about once every 100–200 million years. But smaller events like that over Tunguska happen every 300 years or so. Imagine such an explosion over Tokyo or London or New York. This is very far from impossible, especially since about ten percent of the surface area of the Earth is inhabited. Statistically, then, we should expect destruction of an inhabited area about once every 3,000 years. By this analysis we're long overdue!

But why worry? NASA assures us that they're keeping a watchful eye on all things aeronautical, spatial, and cosmic. So if an asteroid comes into our part of the solar system it will be observed and either destroyed or deflected. Can this government-sponsored PR fluff be taken seriously? How easy do you think it is to "deflect" a rock the size of Mount Everest moving at a speed of 20–50 *thousand* miles per hour? When humans confront nature, do the humans always (ever?) win? Can we stop an onrushing tornado? Can we extinguish a volcano ready to erupt? And what about a hurricane like Katrina? Can humans muster the means needed to divert such a storm? Well, you know the answers to these questions as well as we do. So what about an asteroid intent on wiping humankind out as it did for the dinosaurs? Is there any realistic way to avert such a disaster? Let's look a little closer at the facts of the matter.

1.1.1
CANCELLING ARMAGEDDON

The 1998 film *Armageddon*, starring Bruce Willis and Billy Bob Thornton (do people really name their children "Billy Bob"?), is a quintessential example of Hollywood-style science of the sort that leaves practicing scientists grinding their teeth. The story is an action-packed adventure in which a space-age group of oil drillers led by Willis saves the world from extinction by an asteroid "the size of Texas."

Even though the film's producers supposedly consulted former NASA scientists on the physics of the situation, the number of major scientific gaffes presented as facts in the film is impressive even by Hollywood standards. For example, it's truly difficult for our puny human minds to comprehend the destruction that would follow if an asteroid the size of Texas impacted the Earth. The energy would be 100,000 times greater than that released by the asteroid that undid the dinosaurs. The impact crater would be larger than the continental United States, and virtually all life forms other than microbes and deep-sea organisms would be "disappeared" instantly. Moreover, not a single plant would be left alive. The explosive power of such an asteroid is equivalent to ten *trillion* Hiroshimas!

The film creates one scientific faux pas after another of this sort, leading one reviewer to comment, "Mother Nature would have a heart attack if she saw this movie, and Isaac Newton is probably tossing and turning in his grave right now." The producers have created an asteroid that will truly revolutionize our conception of such objects. For instance, their asteroid is the first ever noted that has an atmosphere and rock slides. There is also a gravitational force holding the drillers to the asteroid that defies anything known to the physics of today, since a 200-pound man on the asteroid would weigh only about 10 pounds and certainly float off into space without the aid of this magical "fifth" force. In short, the science in this film is total rubbish. And it would be a pity if viewers took it at all seriously—but they do!

As for the way the film addresses the problem of deflecting the asteroid, the movie at least gets one part correct when someone states that detonating 150 nuclear bombs would hardly have an effect on an object as mammoth as this. So what is their plan? It's to drill a hole in the asteroid (hence the need for drillers!) 800 feet deep, and insert a hydrogen bomb into the hole to split the asteroid into two pieces that will travel around the Earth, one on each side. As a reviewer also noted, if 150 bombs won't do the job, neither will one bomb regardless of whether it's detonated at the center of the asteroid or not. Can one nuclear bomb detonated underground create a crack that will stretch across the state of Texas? And so it goes.

Is there really a point to this scientific nonsense (besides infantile entertainment)? At least for our purposes here there actually is a point. The point is that there is no conceivable way to modify the orbit of a huge asteroid by any known human means. And there are a couple of asteroids right now in the asteroid belt between Mars and Jupiter that *are* the size of Texas. These are *Pallas* and *Vesta*. And there's one, *Ceres*, that's twice that size. So if one of these objects somehow got on a course for Earth, we can all kiss our ***** goodbye.

But what about smaller asteroids and meteors of the Tunguska variety? As noted earlier, there are many objects of this size that have struck the Earth in the past and we can expect them to strike again. Their potential for devastation is also great. But perhaps we could at least protect against such intruders. Let's see.

1.1.2
EXERCISES: POTENTIAL ENERGY

"Conservation" (the conservation law) means this . . . that there is a number, which you can calculate, at one moment— and as nature undergoes its multitude of changes, this number doesn't change. That is, if you calculate again, this quantity, it'll be the same as it was before. An example is the conservation of energy: there's a quantity that you can calculate according to a certain rule, and it comes out the same answer after, no matter what happens.

Richard P. Feynman

In many places in this book, the unit of energy for comparison purposes is the amount of energy released in the nuclear detonation in Hiroshima. This is a large number and difficult to get one's head around. We introduce here a smaller unit of energy, the amount of energy released when a one-ton boulder is released from a height of one meter. One can imagine this boulder cracking sidewalks and smashing small objects. In Exercise 1.1.6 we compare the energy with the energy in the Hiroshima bomb.

1. Imagine we have a boulder that weighs one metric ton (1000 kg), and that we are holding the boulder one meter above the surface of the Earth. If we drop the boulder, what total energy is released to the Earth, atmosphere, and to heat in the boulder? Let's go ahead and walk through the answer to this question. The amount of energy V in joules (J) stored as gravitational potential energy is

$$V = mgh$$

where h is the height above the surface in meters (m), g is the acceleration due to gravity (9.8 m/s^2) in meters per second squared, and m is the mass of the boulder in kilograms (kg). The amount of energy released is then

$$V = mgh = 1000\,\text{kg} \times 9.8\,\text{m/s}^2 \times 1\,m = 9800\,\text{J} \approx 10\,\text{kJ},$$

which is about 10 kilojoules. Let's give this amount of energy a name. Let's call it a "bump." Suppose a bump of energy was applied over about 1/2 second to a square meter of concrete sidewalk. What would happen to the sidewalk? Suppose the energy was applied evenly over 100 square meters of sidewalk over a period of a week. What would happen to the sidewalk?

2. How much energy would be required to raise the boulder back up to a meter above the ground?

3. Suppose an asteroid with the diameter equal to the distance across Texas was dropped from one kilometer above the surface of the Earth. How many bumps of gravitational energy is stored in the asteroid? Assume the density of an asteroid is about $2\,\text{g/cm}^3 = 200\,\text{kg/m}^3$.

1.1.3
JUST A LITTLE SHOVE

First of all, forget any ideas about deflecting or destroying an asteroid by a nuclear explosion. As Dr. Keith A. Holsapple of the University of Washington points out, a nuclear detonation might just break the asteroid up into several pieces, thus *increasing* the threat, not reducing it. Or the asteroid might simply soak up the energy in the explosion like a sponge soaks up water. So one big "shove" is not the way to go.

Most alternatives to a nuclear blast involve gradually nudging the asteroid into a new orbit by applying a constant force acting over a period of time.

One of the methods suggested for generating the needed force is a mass driver, which is a kind of conveyor belt placed on the asteroid that throws rocks and dirt from its surface continually. Newton's Third Law, stating that for every force there is an equal and opposite force, would then apply, the momentum arising from the discarded surface material then creating numerous tiny pushes that could shift the asteroid's orbit enough over time to avoid an Earthly collision.

Another possibility would be to place a huge parabolic mirror in orbit around the asteroid, using the mirror to concentrate sunlight onto the asteroid's surface. This would generate a plume of vaporized surface material, the escaping plume creating a small, continual force on the asteroid by the same Newtonian principle.

Yet a third approach suggested by Joseph Spitale of the University of Arizona is to follow the dictates of the 1966 Rolling Stones song and "paint it black." This would change the amount of sunlight the asteroid absorbs, thus changing how hot it gets. The heat coming off an asteroid would then create a small force in the opposite direction. Changing the amount of heat would then change the force and thus modify the asteroid's orbit.

It's clear, though, that implementing any of these ideas involves huge logistical problems and enormous expense. Most scientists agree that given the very low odds of a strike anytime soon, development of an asteroid deflection system today is a poor investment. Rather, they argue that we should be putting our money into improved detection systems that would enable us to identify more potential "impactors" and better understand the threat they pose.

At present, effort is focused on detection of asteroids larger than one kilometer in size. Best estimates today say there are about 1,100 such objects, half of which have already been identified and deemed to be no threat. Odds are very high that the other half pose no threat either. But to say that with the kind of conviction we'd like (for example, greater than 90 percent), we need to be able to find these objects and calculate their orbits.

Unfortunately, at present there are no detection systems for smaller asteroids a la Tunguska. It's estimated that there are about half a million such objects greater than fifty meters in diameter in our solar system, which is the minimal size capable of getting through the Earth's atmosphere. Moreover, there is no detection system for identifying potentially threatening comets either. So the situation seems to be that either we'll get a lot of advance warning of a threat (if it's a large asteroid) or virtually no warning at all (if it's the type that devastated central Siberia). Feast or famine and no in-between.

But if you think an asteroid strike is literally and figuratively a hopelessly remote possibility, let's look at something a lot closer to home that carries the same fatal wallop.

1.1.4
EXERCISES: KINETIC ENERGY

1. The kinetic energy of an asteroid is

$$K = \frac{1}{2}mv^2$$

   where v is the speed of the asteroid. What is the typical speed of an asteroid with respect to Earth? Suppose we wished to slow the speed of the asteroid by 10 percent. How much energy does this require in terms of bumps? How does this compare with dropping the asteroid one kilometer? The *total energy* is the sum of the various kinds of energy of a system. If a system is composed of potential and kinetic energy the total energy is the sum $E = K + V$.
2. Estimate how many bumps there are in a landslide—in a volcanic eruption?
3. The density of water is 1 g/cm^3 = 1000 kg/m^3. How many bumps are in a wave two meters high, two meters thick, and 100 meters long?
4. The density of air at sea level is about 1.225 kg/m^3. Assume this density is constant to an altitude of 10 km. Suppose that the entire atmosphere of the Earth taken at this density and height is moving at 1 m/s. How much kinetic energy is in the wind?

1.1.5
DON'T BLOW YOUR TOP

Contrary to popular belief, the biggest natural disaster in history was not the asteroid impact that killed off the dinosaurs. It wasn't even close. About 180 million years earlier an event happened that exterminated over 90 percent of all species living at the time. This event, now called the *Permian-Triassic extinction*, set the stage for the *appearance* of the dinosaurs, just as the asteroid that struck them down opened the evolutionary door for mammals (including humans!) to step through.

Presently, no one really knows the nature of the event that sparked off the Permian-Triassic extinction. The betting odds, though, are that it did not come from outer space, but rather came from the part of "inner" space we now know as Siberia. That scenario holds that a massive Siberian volcano erupted, spewing enough lava, dust and gas into the atmosphere to destroy the Earth's climate and set the evolutionary clock back to time zero. But volcanoes come in all sizes, shapes, and magnitudes. And not all of them are capable of extinguishing life as we know it. For that, we need super-volcanoes, rarities that show up only once every few hundred thousand years.

A super volcano is by far the most destructive force on Earth. Note that we're not talking here about "normal" volcanoes of the Mount St. Helens or Vesuvius type. Those are destructive enough. But they pale by a factor of tens of thousands in comparison with a super volcano. Super volcanoes differ from normal ones in several other ways besides just in the energy of the eruption. The standard image of a volcano is something that looks like Mount Fuji outside Tokyo: a towering cone from which smoke, fire, and lava burst forth from time to time, burying places like Pompeii, but for the most part only doing damage in the local vicinity.

First of all, super volcanoes are not cones; they form in huge depressions in the ground termed calderas. When a normal volcano erupts, lava builds up gradually before finally coming out the top of the cone. In the case of a super volcano, the magma in the Earth's crust is blocked from reaching the surface. Instead it fills huge underground reservoirs, melting the nearby rock to form a very thick, viscous magma. In fact, the magma is so heavy that the volcanic gases that would normally set off an eruption cannot get through it. So huge, almost unbelievable pressures build up. These pressures steadily increase for hundreds of thousands of years before the volcano simply blows its top (if it had a top!), blasting away massive amounts of surface matter that then forms a new caldera.

The last super volcano that erupted seems to have been one that left humanity hanging on by its fingertips in its wake. This was a blast from the past that took place 75,000 years ago on the island of Sumatra near the village of Toba. The eruption was ten thousand times greater than Mount St. Helens, shooting thousands of cubic kilometers of dirt and dust into the atmosphere. The debris blocked sunlight over the entire planet. More than four thousand kilometers from Sumatra, ash covered the ground to a depth of nearly one foot. Temperatures dropped worldwide by over twenty degrees (centigrade), and rain fell that was so contaminated by gases from the volcano that it was almost pure sulfuric acid.

In the aftermath of the Toba eruption, humankind was driven to near extinction. Scientists estimate that not more than two *thousand* humans were left. And three out of four plant species in the Northern Hemisphere also died out.

Probably the biggest hazard from such an eruption is the ash spit out into the atmosphere. A bit after the Toba blast, another super volcano made a mess out of what is now the continental United States, covering more than 21 states with a layer of ash that in some places was more than twenty meters thick! Just to be clear about it, this was not the sort of ash you see in your fireplace. Rather, it was ash composed of tiny pieces of solid rock. So if this type of ash falls onto your car or your house they will literally collapse as the weight adds up. Moreover, if you breathe in this sort of ash, a kind of cement will form in your lungs leading ultimately to suffocation.

So a super volcano explosion is no fun. No fun at all. And even if you did manage to survive the ash, the sulfuric rain, tsunamis, nuclear winter, and myriad other hazards inevitably lead to a totally devastated planet. Basically, all the plants and animals that humans depend upon for survival would be wiped away. All that would be left is the same barren, bleak world that we spoke of earlier in connection with the aftermath of an asteroid impact.

Potentially the worst part of this story is that the next super eruption may be brewing beneath the surface in the United States right now. Perhaps the loveliest national park in the country is the first one, Yellowstone National Park, located mostly in the state of Wyoming. A comparatively little-known aspect of the park is that it harbors one of the few super volcanoes on the planet, one that erupts about every 600,000 years. When scientists began to search for the caldera in the park they couldn't find it because it was so gigantic. Only satellite images revealed the extent of the caldera. It turns out that it constitutes the *entire park*, a region measuring 85 kilometers by 45 kilometers.

The scary part of the Yellowstone volcano is that the last time it erupted was around 640,000 years ago, making it already overdue for an encore. To add yet a bit more spice to the situation, the ground in Yellowstone has risen more than seventy centimeters (over two feet) during the past century, a strong, not-so-early warning sign of pressure building beneath the surface. Although no one will or can say for sure, this is an ominous indicator telling us that *something* is happening in Yellowstone. And if that something is the eruption of the super volcano, well . . .

Extinction in the cold and the dark. That's the take-home message from either the asteroid-impact or the super-volcano scenarios for ushering humankind off center-stage in the evolutionary derby. Fire from below or above, take your choice. It's a bit like the way capital punishment used to be carried out in the American state of Utah, where the condemned prisoner was given his or her choice of method: death by firing squad or death by hanging. But death in either case.

Regardless of the actual agent of extinction—asteroid or volcano—the end result is the same. After the initial fireball and explosive effects die down, the planet is covered by a massive cloud of debris that blots out the Sun for months, if not years. Moreover, the gases liberated from the interior of the Earth give rise to acid rain of biblical proportions, corroding and eating away at anything it touches. As the planet suffocates from a lack of energy input from the Sun, plant and animal species die off. And since humans depend on these species for their own survival, humankind quickly follows suit. End result: a barren planet, where the evolutionary tape has run out (at least for the human species). On such an Earth, a new tape must then be inserted into the evolutionary machine, and the long, slow process of repopulating the planet begun anew after the smoke finally clears away.

What can humans do about either of these scenarios? The short answer is not much. Or, more colloquially, *nada, zilch, nichevo.* A somewhat more thoughtful answer is to rebuild and reenergize the space program. The only hope for humankind in the long run is to abandon our planet altogether. Space colonization is really the only game in town.

But while we're waiting for human thought and initiative to catch up to reality and the space colonization program to finally gain some much-needed traction, let's go back and look at these asteroid and volcanic activities within the broader context of extreme events. Generally, when people use the term "extreme event" they have in mind something like a major earthquake, hurricane, or even volcano. That is, they're thinking about a rare, surprising, and generally damaging event thrown our way by nature. But, in fact, most extreme events (or what we'll term in this book "X-events") do not arise from nature at all. Rather, they come from *human nature.* They are events caused by human miscalculation, misunderstanding, miscommunication, malevolent intent, or just plain stupidity (quite a lot of that, actually!). So in the chapters to follow, we'll take a look at how and why such events occur, as well as what we might do to build-in a bit of protection beforehand rather than simply waiting until the event takes place and then start worrying about how to clean up the mess.

Killer asteroids and super volcanoes are the sorts of multi-millennial events that we can comfortably term "extreme." In fact, they are about as extreme as any event can possibly be. It's difficult to imagine what type of event us puny humans could construct that would have the devastating impact of these sorts of concoctions whipped-up by a not-so-benign Mother Nature. But that is the real story of this book. How bad can we make things for ourselves, even without a helping hand from nature? Let's start with a perennial favorite, a nice, little war.

1.1.6
EXERCISES: INTERNAL ENERGY

The internal energy is energy that is stored as kinetic or potential energy inside matter: the nuclear energy inside the nucleus of atoms, the chemical energy stored in atoms that produces fire, the heat energy stored in the kinetic energy of the random motion of molecules.

1. The amount of energy released by an explosion of one ton of TNT is about 4.184 gJ (1 gJ = 10^9 J), which is one gigacalorie. How many bumps is that? The chemical energy in one barrel of oil is 6 gJ. How does this relate to the chemical energy of a ton of TNT? Estimate which has the higher chemical energy density in J/kg, oil or TNT?

2. The Hiroshima bomb released about 15 kilotons of energy. How many bumps is that?
3. How much heat is released when water vapor turns into liquid water? When liquid water turns into ice?
4. What is the difference between heat and temperature?

The total energy of a system is the sum of kinetic, potential, and internal energies $E = K + V + I$ where I is the internal energy. The total energy remains constant, but the kinetic, potential, and internal energies can convert to each other. For example, the kinetic energy of a car is converted to internal heat energy when the car is braked. A ball rolling down a hill converts potential energy to kinetic energy.

1.1.7
EXERCISES: POWER AND ENERGY FLUX

1. The world power usage is about 15 terawatts or 15×10^{12} J/s. How many bumps of energy are used each second? How many Hiroshima bomb equivalents are used each second? Suppose the Texas-sized asteroid collision with the ground took place over a period of 10 seconds. How does the energy transfer of the asteroid to the earth compare with the world's power usage?
2. Energy flux is the amount of energy per second that is flowing into a given area. Which is more likely to affect an individual, a large amount of energy transferred in one second over a square kilometer around the individual, or the same energy applied in the same time over 100 square kilometers around the individual?

1.1.8
NOT-SO-EXTREME EVENTS

As far as archaeologists and historians know, continuing conflict has marked the course of human history. Border skirmishes, tribal disputes, national conflicts, global wars, take your pick. The history books are full of these sorts of battles fought over everything from territory to natural resources to political and/or religious ideologies and a lot more. It's fair to say then that war in one form or another is the most common form of human interaction throughout recorded history. And from a quick scan of the headlines today, this doesn't seem likely to change anytime soon. Here's an everyday example just to fix the point.

On August 26, 1999, the Russian Federation launched what is now known as the Second Chechen War, following the invasion of Dagestan by Islamic forces from Chechnya. The Russian invasion of Chechnya on October 1 restored Russian control of the "independent" Chechen Republic of Ichkeria. On the surface, this looked like a form of Russian civil war. But given the large number of foreign fighters involved on the Chechen side, it cannot be so easily dismissed as simply an internal Russian affair. The battle phase of this war was short, lasting only a few months. But the insurgency that followed dragged on interminably, only being closed out with a decisive Russian victory in April 2009, over nine years after the war began.

As wars go, the Second Chechen War was not particularly notable. The total number of military and civilians killed over the entire span of the war is estimated to be 50,000–70,000, or a few thousand per year. Moreover, there was nothing especially surprising about the outbreak of the war either, since the Russians made it clear long beforehand that they would not tolerate an independent state in Chechnya. Nevertheless, the war was in some ways "rare," at least to the extent that the act of declaring a war as opposed to being in a state of an undeclared uprising, insurgency or other societal activity, especially the state of no conflict at all, was (and is) not a typical event in Chechnya or anywhere else on any particular day. In other words, if you pick a day at random in Chechnya, the likelihood is small that a declared war will begin on that day.

So what can we conclude about the "extremeness" of the Second Chechnyan War? Mostly, that while the outbreak of war on August 26 was rare, there was nothing especially surprising about it. Nor was the human damage caused by the war in any way unusual as wars go. Admittedly, it was greater than if there had been no war at all. But in the spectrum of damages and deaths from a war, it was quite ordinary. All in all, then, the extremeness of this war was pretty low, maybe something like 2 or 3 on a scale of 0–10—but still greater than zero.

It's worth noting here that while we speak about X-events as if they are always negative, giving rise to destruction, death, damage, and collective psychological angst, that is just one side of the coin. Of course, it's the side that gets all the attention in the press, mostly because negative X-events like financial crashes, the outbreak of jungle fevers, a collapse of the electric power grid, and the like are events that generally unfold quickly and do a lot of damage. As a result, we are conditioned to fear them and make Herculean efforts to anticipate and prevent them. Hence, they make news.

But every coin has two sides, regardless of how thinly it's sliced. And so it is with X-events, too. The negative side emphasizes short-term, destructive events that we would prefer to avoid. The other side of the coin represents opportunities, not problems. There we find the constructive events that come about as a result of the "eco-niches" opened up by the destruction arising from the negative side. We will tell this story in detail later. For now, it suffices to say that no such constructive events can possibly take place *without* the destructive side of the coin acting first. In other words, the complete story of collective human affairs calls for both sides of the coin to show themselves in sequence, starting with the destruction. Later, the innovation and revival of society can rise up out of the ashes of the social structures destroyed by the damaging X-events.

With these preliminary definitions out of the way, let's dig a bit deeper into the actual subject matter of this book, namely, X-events. What are the drivers of such events? How do they actually happen? How can we measure the risk of such events, especially those for which we have little or no historical data? Can we forecast such events? Answers to these and other questions surrounding X-events will unfold throughout the course of this book. For now, let's take a high-level overflight of the general territory.

1.2
THE CONTEXT AND THE TRIGGER

To understand X-events and how they occur, we first have to understand the way events, in general, take place. A good picture for this process is to imagine that you are walking in the mountains, where the landscape consists of hills, valleys, mountain peaks, plateaus, and flat, lowland terrain. At any moment, you occupy a position in this landscape. The event of immediate concern is where you will be at the next moment. Unless you happen to be standing on the edge of a cliff or on the top of a sharp mountain peak, your next step will not change your position much. But if you *are* near the edge of a cliff or on a mountain peak, even the smallest step in the wrong direction will change your life dramatically and very likely not for the better. In fact, such a small step for a man (or woman) may well be the last step. So there are two kinds of locations, or points, here in this mountainous terrain: an ordinary point, from which a small step doesn't change your situation much at all, and a *critical* point, where even a minor step in the wrong direction can lead to a major discontinuity in your life.

To bring this landscape metaphor into closer contact with the realities of human life, imagine now that the landscape is not static, but is dynamically shifting and undulating at every moment. This means that you might think that you're standing in the middle of a plateau, but while you're contemplating your next step from there the plateau may morph into a mountain peak—without you even noticing. Now if you don't recognize this shift and take it into account in deciding which direction to step next, well . . .

The dynamically changing landscape of events is what we'll term the *context* of events. It is this geometry that defines the space of possible events and the likelihood of which one will actually be realized at the next moment. Since the context is continually changing, so is the set of possibilities and likelihoods. So what is it that picks out one of those possibilities and turns it into the reality that you actually experience at the next moment? That catalyst is what we call a *random trigger*. This trigger is like that famous butterfly in the Amazonian rain forest, flapping its wings today and giving rise to a tornado in Topeka tomorrow.

Think of the beginning of the so-called Arab Spring in 2011. At that time, North African countries were poised for major social change. In our geometric terms, they were sitting on a mountaintop waiting for a random trigger to push them into one of the valleys below. The bigger valleys represented revolutionary changes involving ouster of long-standing, repressive political regimes. Smaller valleys represented harsh actions by the regimes to retain their power. Governments like the Mubarak regime in Egypt did things like totally shutting down the Internet to stifle communication among the demonstrators, in effect changing the context and trying to make the government's valleys larger (more likely). Who could have said that it would be the event of a fruit seller burning himself up on a street in Tunisia that would serve as the random shove sending that country into one of the valleys of regime change? Answer: No one. That immolation in Tunisia could not possibly have been predicted. And even if it could have been forecast, it would have been simply impossible to say that its consequences would lead to the major shift in political power that we still see unfolding today in Tunisia, Egypt, and elsewhere in the region. Such is the power of a random nudge of the right sort at the right time. As the old saying goes, timing is everything in life. And in death too, it seems.

Thus, we see that fortune's formula for any kind of event, ordinary or extreme, is

$$Event = Context + Random\ trigger$$

Since the trigger is random, this means it has no discernible pattern or structure. Therefore, it cannot be forecast. So any hope we have for predicting, or even anticipating, an event rests upon our being able to understand the context and how it shifts over the course of time. An important part of the argument of this book is to provide concepts and tools for doing just that.

The 800-pound gorilla in the room when it comes to forecasting X-events is not simply the random trigger. That randomness is a problem in forecasting any event, X- or otherwise. But in situations where we have a lot of data available on past occurrences of an event, it's often the case that the different random triggers acting each time one of the events takes place tend to cancel each other out over a sufficiently large number of occurrences. So the real problem with X-events is that by their very nature they are rare; in fact, we are often faced with trying to evaluate the likelihood of an event that may have never happened before. In that case, the standard tools of probability and statistics are powerless to help in assessing what is and is not likely and by how much. So what to do?

In what follows, instead of taking the top-down approach of looking at the events themselves as is the custom in conventional risk analysis, we take a bottom-up perspective and examine the context of the event and the situations where that context tells us we're in the yellow zone of impending danger of the occurrence of an X-event. In other words, we abandon the idea of actually forecasting the event and look to concepts and tools for *anticipating* it. For this, we need to understand the drivers that create the ever-changing landscape, which in turn tells us when we are near the edge of a cliff or on a mountain peak instead of resting on safe and solid ground.

Let's first be clear about the types of X-events we'll be focusing on in this book. Our concern is with collective human social events, not the kinds of events like the Toba super volcano or the Chicxulub asteroid thrown our way by nature. Stock market crashes, changing trends in popular culture like styles in fashion or films, shifts in political ideologies, or the outbreak of war are our concern. These are X-events that involve the collective action of groups of people, not the actions of a single person. And the impact of the occurrence of this type of X-event is felt throughout an entire group or society. Our goal will be to present ideas for how the context of these types of X-events changes over the course of time, and how those changes strongly bias the nature of the event itself. This disclaimer now being on the record, let's proceed to the business at hand.

Over the past years, we have discovered two principal drivers of the dynamics that shape the context of events. The first is a *structural* driver, what we will term the "complexity gaps" between subsystems in interaction. The second is a *behavioral* driver stemming from the collective "mood," or beliefs, of a group or society. In broad terms then the drivers of how context changes involve both systemic features, the complexity gaps, and mass psychological elements, associated with what we call the overall social mood. These two factors taken together create the shifting context.

1.2.1
COMPLEXITY GAPS

In 1988, American archaeologist Joseph Tainter published a path-breaking volume, *The Collapse of Complex Societies*. He noted that just as the vast majority of species that have ever existed are now extinct, the same is true of societies. Tainter's goal was to investigate the collapse of now defunct societies and ask: was the principal reason for the collapse essentially different in each case? Or could one point to a common cause for each of the collapses? His conclusion is that indeed there was a common cause, something he called "complexity overload." The basic idea is quite simple.

As time marches on, every society faces problems. These may be social, economic, or political but the default response is always the same. When the problem appears, governments create a new level of structure whose job is to solve that problem. For example, the attack on the World Trade Center in New York on September 11, 2001 created a problem for the US government: terrorist attacks on US soil. The government responded in the by-now-traditional manner and created a new layer of structure designed to combat this problem. This structure even has a name: The Department of Homeland Security. And if the past is prologue to the future, the solution will long outlast the problem, and the Department of Homeland Security will be with us long after the last terrorist has gone to terrorist heaven. Tainter then argues that when the next problem appears, the same process leads to yet another layer of structure and so on, until finally a point is reached when all the resources of the society are being consumed maintaining the existing governmental and social structures. In particular, no resources remain to deal with the next problem when it arises. What happens then?

What happens is that either the problem goes unattended, or what's often even worse, the problem is parceled out to one or another of the existing structures, one that was never created to deal with this sort of problem. In either case, as problems continue to appear at some point the entire structure (read: society) collapses from an overdose of structural complexity. In a nutshell, this is the argument Tainter explores and validates for virtually every social collapse in the historical record in his eye-opening book.

While Tainter presented his argument for the case of a single system, an entire society, the basic idea can be generalized to the case of two or more systems in interaction. This was done in the 2012 book *X-Events*. To make things simple, consider the case of two systems in interaction, say the US financial services sector and the government regulators. Each of these systems has a level of complexity, one that's dynamically changing. If the two levels are approximately equal, there is some measure of harmony between the two systems and everything works reasonably well. But as the complexity gap between the two systems widens as it did in the early 2000s, the size of the complexity gap creates stresses in the system that must be reduced. If these stresses are left unattended, ultimately the interaction between the two systems collapses just like one of Tainter's societies. We might think of this complexity gap as a measure of the risk of a collapse: the greater the gap, the greater the risk of collapse.

A good way to envision what's going on here is to think of what happens when you stretch a rubber band. Suppose the two ends represent the two systems in interaction, with the length of the band measuring the complexity gap between them. As you stretch the band, the gap widens and you can actually feel the tension in your muscles and arms as the band extends. As you continue to pull on the band, it ultimately reaches its limit of elasticity. If you attempt to stretch the band further it breaks, i.e., you have a crash.

The only way to avoid the crash is to voluntarily "downsize" the gap by decreasing the complexity of the more complex system or increasing the complexity of the less complex one. But humans are not generally in a downsizing frame of mind, so what typically happens is we continue to extend the gap until nature, or human nature, steps in and says if you won't voluntarily reduce the gap, I'll do it for you. And the way nature does it isn't pretty, as we're all aware.

The financial services-regulator example cited a moment ago shows how this process works. In the early 2000s, the complexity of the financial services sector was soaring off into the stratosphere, as firms were feverishly creating financial derivatives and products of a bewildering level of complexity. So complex, in fact, that many still feel today that not even their creators really understood them. At the same time, the complexity of the regulators, measured by the number of independent actions they had at their disposal to counteract or at least reign-in these instruments of financial destruction, was pretty much frozen in place. Thus, the complexity gap between these two systems grew to the point that the entire financial system went over the edge in 2007. Here is another example illustrating some of the same ideas in the setting of a corporation.

John Mariotti is the former president of the Rubbermaid Office Products Group and Huffy Bicycles. He is also a rarity in the US corporate hierarchy, a man who thinks long, hard, and deep about the role complexity plays in a corporation's success or lack thereof. In his hugely illuminating and insightful 2008 book *The Complexity Crisis*, Mariotti introduces what he terms the "complexity factor (CF)." This is a metric that he argues characterizes the level of complexity at which firms are most healthy. Here is how Mariotti calculates the CF. It consists of the following six quantities:

1. **The number of finished products** (the company's product line)
2. **The number of different markets served**
3. **The number of legal entities constituting the company** (the number of subsidiaries and legal elements forming the company)
4. **The number of facilities** (manufacturing sites, sales offices, etc.)
5. **The total number of employees, suppliers, and customers of the company**
6. **The company's total sales revenues**

The complexity factor is then simply the sum of elements 1–5, divided by element number 6. In other words, CF is the number of units of revenue needed to pay for all of the expenses incurred by the firm. Mariotti argues that if this number is small, say less than 1.0, the company is not very complex and has avoided most of the complexity overload mentioned earlier. Such a firm has a good chance of being profitable, assuming the products are of good quality and well designed.

A CF value over 50 suggests a firm that is unnecessarily complex, one that provides many opportunities for improvement (and increased profitability).

As in chess and many other activities in life, it is the middle range where CF is between 1 and 50 that is most interesting. This is where corporate management is supposed to earn its money. These are mid-range firms that could be quite profitable. But they have to make major decisions about whether to try to capitalize on their complexity or reduce it. Many more details and myriad real-world examples of the use of the CF to help with corporate decisions can be found in Mariotti's enlightening book cited in the Notes and References for this chapter.

The reader will note that the corporate story told by Mariotti is the story of a single system, a corporation, and says nothing about the complexity gap arising from the interaction of that firm with other organizations (competitors, regulators, customers, and the like). So in this sense his analysis is interesting in the very same way that Tainter's analysis of ancient civilizations is interesting: it serves as a starting point for a broader-based theory of corporate complexity, as well as provides a concrete suggestion about how to actually measure the complexity of a firm. That measure, incidentally, is of the same sort used by Tainter, who simply added up the number of levels of structure in a society. Mariotti's complexity factor does much the same thing for the number of layers of structure in a firm, and then normalizes it by the size of the firm's sales revenues.

With this notion of complexity and complexity gaps in hand, let's move to a consideration of the behavioral driver of context, the social mood of the group as a whole.

1.2.2
EXERCISES: COMPLEXITY MEASUREMENT

Human beings, viewed as behaving systems, are quite simple. The apparent complexity of our behavior over time is largely a reflection of the complexity of the environment in which we find ourselves.

Herbert Simon

This exercise is an introduction to measures of complexity. It will illustrate complexity mismatch in a few clearly defined cases. It will become apparent that complexity measurement is in the early stages of its development.

- We can divide types of complexity measures for a system into the answers to three questions:

1. How hard is the system to describe?
2. How hard is it to create the system?
3. What is the system's degree of organization?

The answer to the first question, "How hard is it to describe?" is usually measured in bits or bytes of information. An intuitive way to think about this is that the complexity of a system is equal to the number of words required for the shortest possible description. This is equivalent to the size of the smallest computer file that can describe the system.

- The answer to the second question, "How hard is it to create?" is usually measured in the time, energy, or money that it takes to create the system. This is a good measure for business and other social systems. The answer to the final question, "What is its degree of organization?" is again measured in bits or bytes. It can be the amount of information that is shared by the parts of the organization. In other words, it may be measured as the amount of information that flows among the various components of the organization. Suppose, for instance, the organization is an accounting firm. The complexity may be measured as the amount of information that flows to the organization from the clients plus the amount of information that flows among the various internal departments plus the information that flows to the Internal Revenue Service, the SEC, the states, and back to the clients.

- The intention of the observer is intimately associated with the measure of complexity. Take a rock as your example of a system. What is the complexity of the rock? What is the complexity of the rock if you intend to use the rock as a projectile? What is the complexity of the rock if it is your intention to extract gold from the rock? What is the complexity of the rock if you plan to shine x-rays through thin slices of the rock and look at the photographs the x-rays produce? This means the complexity is context-dependent, i.e. it depends on the observer more than it depends on the rock itself.

  Similarly, if the observer is the IRS, then the complexity of a firm being audited is mostly determined by the finance department of the organization. The details of the production line may be of little interest to the IRS. However, if the observer is a customer, the details of the production line and its reliability may determine the complexity of the organization to that observer.

- Complexity measures based on how hard a system is to create are more straightforward than those that describe the system. One projects the cost and time required to build the system. This is an accounting and forecasting exercise and forms the basis for most business planning in the world. It typically requires a great deal of domain expertise to estimate these numbers accurately. Again, complexity is a context-dependent measure.

- Finally, we use a simple example to illustrate complexity measures based on the degree of organization of the system. Consider a healthcare billing system. It is composed of various types of healthcare providers including physicians, hospitals, Medicare (in the US), insurance companies, and various support vendors. One measure of the system's complexity is to measure the number of bits that compose packets of information that are transferred among all the various parts of the system when patients have billable procedures.
- How can complexity mismatch be described by systems networks described in Exercise 1.2.8?
- Ashby's Law of Requisite Variety states that if a system is to be stable, the number of states of its control mechanism must be greater than or equal to the number of states in the system being controlled. How do efficiency and information gathering play off each other according to Ashby's Law to take a system to optimal complexity?

1.2.3
EXERCISES: COMPLEXITY OF SOCIAL MOOD

> There is no evidence that dogs have the kind of complex emotional lives and value systems that we do. It's one reason why we love them so much, in fact. They are neither "good" nor "bad." They don't hold grudges, act in petty ways, or seek revenge. They read our moods, but not our minds.

Jon Katz

1. Consider complexity measured by description. Let's consider the case of a polarized population in which some fraction of the population is optimistic and the remaining fraction is pessimistic. As a kind of shorthand, we will refer to optimists as *happy* and pessimists as *sad*. If everyone is happy, the complexity is very low. The same is true if everyone is sad. It takes very little information to specify the

state of each individual. However, if half the people are sad and half are happy, a great deal of information is required to specify who is happy and who is sad. The complexity of this population can be measured in bits with the Shannon entropy. The Shannon entropy is defined as the expected value of the information obtained from a sample.

$$H = E(I) = -\sum_i p_i \log_2(p_i)$$

where p_i is the probability of a measurement, and the sum over i is over all possible measurements. In the case of the polarized population, there are two possible states a person may be in, happy and sad. If the probability of a person being happy is p, then the probability of a person being sad is $q = 1 - p$. We can take p as the fraction of people who are happy. The Shannon entropy for the moody population is

$$H = -p\log_2(p) - q\log_2(q)$$

The entropy is 0 if all the people are happy

$$H = -p\log_2(p) - q\log_2(q) = -1 \times \log_2(1) - 0 \times \log_2(0) = 0$$

and 1 if half the population is happy

$$H = -p\log_2(p) - q\log_2(q) = \frac{1}{2}\log_2(2) + \frac{1}{2}\log_2(2) = 1.$$

The Shannon entropy and, consequently, the complexity is higher when the measurements are more evenly distributed.

2. $\log_2(0) \rightarrow -\infty$, so why is $0 \rightarrow \log_2(0)$ equal to 0?
3. What if the population had three moods: happy, sad, and indifferent. What is the Shannon entropy in the case in which everyone is happy and the case in which the population is evenly distributed among happy, sad, and indifferent?

1.2.4
SOCIAL MOOD

Everyone is familiar with the fact that when we are optimistic about our future and believe that tomorrow will be better than today, the type of actions we take today tend to be very different than if we were fearful rather than optimistic about tomorrow. For example, if your partner is angry with you and you believe he or she might decide to pack their suitcase and walk out the door (negative mood), you might volunteer to help with the house cleaning and take out the trash in order to try to smooth over the situation. On the other hand, if you're in a positive mood and believe that tomorrow may bring a more forgiving partner into your life, then your actions today might involve leaving both the dust on the shelves and the garbage under the sink just where they are and let your partner worry about them. The point here is that either set of actions, cleaning up or leaving things lay, are both possible. But your beliefs about tomorrow strongly bias which action you are likely to take today. So your mood, positive or negative, is a biasing factor, or driver, of the context of events shifting the odds from one course of action to another.

This very same idea of mood can be scaled up to an entire group rather than just for an individual, leading to what we'll call the *social mood* of a group or population. It's important to note here that what we're talking about are the *beliefs* of the group, not its feelings. The two are entirely different and even arise from entirely different parts of the brain. Beliefs come from the rational, logical, deductive part of the cognitive cortex; feelings stem from the primitive, reptilian part of the brainstem, which is responsible for emotions. Feelings come and go very quickly, while beliefs tend to stay fixed in place unless strong arguments and/or forceful experiences change them. So in what follows, whenever we speak about social mood bear in mind that what we're talking about is beliefs, not feelings. Now let's see how this all works in practice.

◆ ◆ ◆

In the autumn of 2001, the financial collapse of the Enron Corporation hit the front pages of virtually every newspaper in the world. At the time it was the largest bankruptcy in US corporate history. But as scandals go, it turned out to be just one of many accounting "irregularities" that numerous American corporations had been practicing for a decade or more during the runaway bull market that began in the early 1980s. By far the most interesting aspect of the Enron collapse though was the public's reaction to the event. Basically, both the financial and general press promoted the view that the Enron accounting revelations had deeply discouraged investors, thereby *causing* a crisis of confidence on Wall Street. In essence, the conventional wisdom of the chattering classes was that Enron's collapse *generated* a negative social mood, which in turn led to a lack of investor confidence in the market.

Notice the italicized words in the preceding paragraph, "causing" and "generated." They suggest a direction of causality in social events, one that is so deeply hardwired into the collective subconscious that to question it is akin to challenging our taken-for-granted reality as to the way the world works. It's useful to consider the Enron situation as an entry point into the fundamental questions of what constitutes the social mood and how that mood, whatever it is, influences social events and actions. Lets take a closer look at how these questions look in the specific setting of the Enron situation.

A headline in *USA Today* in the spring of 2002 captured succinctly the mainline view of Enron social dynamics when it proclaimed to the world, "Scandals Shred Investors' Faith." The implication of this headline is that the market was moving along just fine—until the Enron revelations shattered people's confidence in stocks. If this line of reasoning were even approximately correct, one would have expected the market to experience a precipitous sell-off following the revelation of Enron's accounting shenanigans and the company's consequent bankruptcy filing. If you're tempted to believe this fiction, have a look at Figure 1.1, showing the daily price movement of the Standard & Poors 500 Index (a bench-mark measure for overall US stock market performance) from the year 2000 onward:

The figure shows that in the 18 months preceding the Enron scandal, the market declined 39 percent. After the scandal broke in 2001, the market actually rose more than 10 percent—and stayed up at those levels for nearly a year afterwards. So the actual facts of the matter fly completely in the face of the notion that the Enron collapse "spooked" the market. In point of fact, the flow of events ran in just the opposite direction. Here's what actually happened.

The declining market from January 2000 onward put enormous pressure on Enron's ability to use its high-flying stock price as leverage to secure loans to support the firm's accounting legerdemains. The decline of the stock price and the consequent drying up of the firm's lines of credit then led to the

Figure 1.1 Enron Events and the S&P 500 Index from 2000 to late 2002 to late 2009.

collapse of the company—and the subsequent scandal—when regulators and creditors began digging into the company's books. The increasingly negative social mood also whetted the public's appetite for scandal, recrimination, and punishment. A scapegoat was needed and Enron was the perfect candidate.

So contrary to the wisdom of the time, a more viable line of reasoning is that it was the negative social mood, as reflected in the dramatically falling stock market, that led to the Enron collapse, not the other way around. In this view, investors were not depressed at all as a result of the Enron collapse; rather, they were already depressed for the preceding 18 months as Figure 1.1 so graphically illustrates. In a very definite sense then, it was this negative tone in investor psychology that led to Enron's collapse. And if it had not been Enron it would have been some other firm employing similar magical accounting procedures— which indeed turned out to be the case, as witnessed by the subsequent bankruptcies of WorldCom, US Air, Delta Airlines, General Motors, and numerous other firms that couldn't quite get it together over the past several years.

♦ ♦ ♦

The importance of timescale comes into play when we recognize that collective events have a natural unfolding time characteristic of the nature of the event. For example, an event involving some aspect of popular culture, such as the type of fashions that are in vogue or the sorts of books that are popular are short timescale phenomena, generally unfolding over a period of a few months to a year or so. On the other hand, a collective event like the shift in a dominant political ideology has a much longer unfolding time, normally several years to a decade or more. Finally, very slowly unfolding events like the decline of a global power may take a century or more. So if we want to argue that the social mood of a population is a driving factor in the type of events we can expect to see, we must match the timescale of the event with the timescale of the social mood that's biasing the event. For example, it would give no insight into the likelihood of a country like the United States leaving the world's center stage to look at the social mood in the US on a timescale of weeks or even months. That timescale is much too short to see the unfolding of a long timescale event like the collapse of global political and moral power. Such an event would require examining the shift in social mood on a timescale of decades, not weeks or months. We will see several examples of this timescale issue later in the book.

Our first order of business is to examine the connection, if any, linking a group's social mood M and the collective events E that arise from interactions among the people making up the group. Logically, there are four collectively exhaustive and mutually exclusive possibilities:

1. M and E are logically independent: In this case, M does not imply E or vice-versa. The two are totally independent of each other.

2. M and E are mutually dependent: In this situation M implies E and E implies M; there is a feedback loop from one to the other and vice-versa.
3. E implies M: Here an event impacts the social mood, but not vice-versa.
4. M implies E: In this case, the social mood implies the social event, but not vice-versa.

Conventional wisdom argues that hypothesis II must necessarily be the case. And, in fact, this is such a taken-for-granted background belief that it is almost never questioned. In this book, we will argue that the fact that everyone believes this hypothesis doesn't necessarily make it true. After all, a few centuries ago everyone believed the Earth was flat, too. But that universally-held belief did not make it so.

Notice what's involved here. The concept of logical implication is an all-or-nothing proposition: either M implies E or it doesn't. There is no room for "sometimes" or "partially." So either a feedback from E to M exists all the time or it doesn't exist at all. With this caveat in mind, the conventional-wisdom hypothesis II says that collective events always impact the social mood, and vice-versa. Hypothesis IV, on the other hand, states that a feedback from events to mood is never present for any collective event.

The airtight constraint of logical implication can be softened somewhat in the following way. We will certainly admit that in some cases there may actually be such a feedback from E to M, but it is not required. Its presence or absence depends on the interaction pattern of individuals composing the group, the timescale of the event, and other factors there is no room to discuss right now. The point is that the feedback is very seldom present, and certainly not for every collective event. We will see examples later of cases when such a feedback is, in fact, totally absent. Thus, by Popper's "black swan" falsification criterion, these examples serve to invalidate hypothesis II. Here's another argument that points in the same direction.

The essence of the scientific method is to provide a systematic procedure for testing alternative hypotheses about how to best explain a given set of observations. An essential element in this procedure is Occam's Razor, which asserts that when faced with several hypotheses that account equally well for a given set of observations, preference should be given to the simplest of the candidate hypotheses. Oddly enough, the conventional-wisdom hypothesis II above, which is the one almost everyone believes, is actually the most complicated of the four candidates, not the simplest! So for this reason, to accept hypothesis II it must do a better job of accounting for the observations. Not just equally well, but better, in order to be the hypothesis of choice. In this book, we present the argument that hypothesis IV explains the observations at least as well as hypothesis II and is simpler.

As a short aside, its interesting to ponder why hypothesis II is so universally accepted. Our feeling is that this universal belief in a very dicey proposition stems from a completely unjustified generalization from individual beliefs and feelings to the beliefs of a group. In other words, if I feel this way and everyone I know feels this way, then the group consisting of me and my friends must necessarily feel that way, too. As noted above, this is a totally false generalization. A group can and often does feel and behave very differently than any of its constituent members, viz., a group of rabid football fans. The root cause of this discrepancy between individual and group behavior is the network of interactions linking members of a group. This network gives rise to the emergent properties of group psychology and behavior, properties that cannot be seen by examining any individual making up the group.

At this point you might ask: what's the harm in adopting hypothesis II? After all, we've just conceded that feedback from events to mood does sometimes exist. So why not take the more complex hypothesis and cover all bases? The answer is that there is no harm in doing that other than you then move the question out of the realm of logical implication into the domain of likelihood and probabilities. In other words, you're now asking whether the feedback loop is present "most of the time" or "some of the time" or "almost never." Without an analysis of the issue from an exhaustive database of examples, it's difficult to give an unambiguous answer to this question. On the basis of the investigations seen to date, the feedback is almost always absent. The only exceptions are the sort of knee-jerk reactions that financial markets show in the immediate aftershock of a dramatic event like 9/11 or the London Underground bombing in 2005. But studies of these and similar events show that the impact on the social mood (i.e., the market averages) dissipates very quickly, sometimes in just a couple of hours or less. Basically, these events are governed by the transitory feelings of the moment, not beliefs at all. So for now, we stand by the argument that hypothesis IV is the best choice among the four candidate hypotheses.

In order to test any of the foregoing hypotheses, we need to have some way of measuring the social mood at any given instant and on all time scales so that we can correlate changes in mood with different types of events. So let's now turn our attention to this issue of measurement.

1.2.5
EXERCISES: IS SHANNON ENTROPY RIGHT?

Information is not knowledge.

Albert Einstein

- The Shannon Entropy H of a stream of information is the minimum number of bits of information needed to encode the stream.

The complexity mismatch between two systems, 1 and 2, is the difference in Shannon entropy between the two systems.

$$\Delta H = H_1 - H_2.$$

- The Shannon entropy is nearly identical to the thermodynamic entropy, S, in physics. We can think of the thermodynamic entropy as a measure of the complexity of a physical system. In particular, for an ideal gas, the difference in entropy between two gasses at different temperatures, T_1 and T_2 but the same density is

$$\Delta S = S_1 - S_2 \propto \ln\left(\frac{T_1}{T_2}\right).$$

We see that if system 1 has a higher temperature than system 2, then system 1 has the higher entropy and complexity.

What is the entropy difference between a uniform-density ideal gas at a constant temperature T separated by two infinite plates and a uniform-density ideal gas that has a linear temperature profile that goes from $T + \Delta T$ to T between the two plates? Which of the two systems has the higher entropy (complexity)?

- The Shannon entropy forms the basis for many measures of complexity that measure complexity by the amount of information needed to describe the system. But what if the questions that we wish to answer about the system are simpler than a complete description of the system? Shannon entropy measure yields high complexity for random systems. Shannon entropy is really a measure of randomness of the system. But very random systems can be simple if the questions we ask of the system are of an aggregate nature. If we are interested in statistical quantities, then our queries may be answered by simple statistical measures such as mean, median, standard deviation, skewness, etc., which are simply moments of the distribution. Probability distributions tend to be normal. In this situation, highly random systems are simple rather than complex. Complexity is maximized somewhere between highly random systems and very orderly systems. Again, the observer is involved in the complexity definition. If the observer is asking simple questions that can be answered by taking moments of the distribution, then Shannon entropy is not the proper measure of complexity when the system is very random.

1.2.6
MEASURING SOCIAL MOOD

In the Enron case discussed above, we have tacitly assumed that the social mood was measured by a stock market index, the S&P 500. This is not by accident. While there are many other possibilities for a "sociometer" to measure a group's mood, such as public-opinion surveys and questionnaires, the analysis presented in the volume *Mood Matters*, cited in the section Notes and References, concludes that no candidate measure of mood possesses all the desirable qualities of a stock index. Basically, the argument supporting a market index as a measure of social mood is that when an investor or speculator takes out a position in a stock, they are making a bet about the future on a particular timescale. The market collects all these bets and synthesizes them into a single number: a change of price. If there are more negative bets about the future of the stock, the price declines, more positive bets it rises.

At first hearing, many people argue that a stock index cannot reflect the mood of a population since only a minuscule fraction of a population is actively engaged in the actions of buying and selling stock that give rise to price movements in an index like the S&P 500 or the Dow Jones Industrial Average (DJIA). Therefore, a stock index cannot possibly account for the mood of an entire population. Shifted into the realm of physics, this line of argument is like saying that the thermometer on the wall of your office cannot possibly measure the overall temperature in the room because it doesn't take into account the behavior of every single air molecule. Of course, we know from the theory of statistical thermodynamics that knowledge of the behavior of a small fraction of the molecules is sufficient to extrapolate the behavior of the entire group since "all molecules are created equal" and they all obey the same rules of particle motion.

In the case of human populations, the objects in interaction (people) are not homogeneous; they are heterogeneous. Moreover, they do not all use the same rules to form their beliefs and actions. But rather than making the argument against using a stock index to measure social mood, these facts actually make the case easier.

First of all, stock traders do not exist in isolation from the rest of society. Traders read newspapers, watch TV, talk with their friends and families and, in general, exist as part of a rich social network. Their actions are influenced by the signals they receive from that network. So it is not the case that the thoughts and feelings of a broad part of the population is not reflected in a stock index.

Moreover, unlike the molecules of air in your office, not everyone in the population is created equal. Some people just have a greater ability to influence others by their words and actions. And such people tend to be those who are engaged in stock markets, either directly as traders or as investors and speculators. So again the market index reflects the beliefs about the future of a disproportionate fraction of the influential members of a population.

Of course, what we would really like is to be able to measure the collective mood of the population directly, not via a surrogate like a market index or a questionnaire. Recent work in this direction involved investigators that analyzed a large database of Twitter feeds. The analysis focused on categorizing the messages into positive and negative bins according to the psychological tone of the message as indicated by emotionally charged words. Words like "friendly" and "active" went into the positive category, while messages containing words like "on edge" and "panicky" were placed in the negative. The overall mood was then measured along six dimensions: calmness, alertness, sureness, vitality, kindness, and happiness. It turned out that one emotion, calmness, served very well as a leading indicator for what stocks would be doing three or four days in advance.

This study lends support to the notion that a stock market index reflects overall social mood, since the Twitter analysis is similar to a "survey" of the mood of the population, which the study shows is strongly correlated with what the stock market will be doing a few days in the future. So for the remainder of this book, we will employ a stock market index as our measure of social mood. Before proceeding to a discussion of the overall role we see for socionomics (a termed coined by financial analyst and social theorist Robert Prechter) as a driver of context, let's look at an example from the political arena to get into the spirit of things.

1.2.7
US PRESIDENTIAL ELECTIONS
AND SOCIAL MOOD

Conventional wisdom has it that political trends are a key determinant of the stock market's gyrations. As an election approaches, commentators endlessly debate the effect the outcome of the election will have on stock prices. Investors weigh up which candidates will influence the market to move up or down. Statements like, "If Jones is elected, it will be good for the market, but Smith's election will cause stocks to tank" are common.

If this causal relationship were even approximately correct, there would be evidence that a transfer of power from one party's leader to another affects the social mood, hence, the stock market, in some very specific ways. There would also be evidence that certain political parties or policies reliably produce bull or bear markets. There is no study showing any such connections or correlations. On the other hand, it's not hard to see just the opposite at work.

A strong and persistent trend in the stock market dramatically biases whether an incumbent president or the incumbent's party will be re-elected in a landslide or defeated. In all cases where an incumbent remained in office in a landslide, the stock market's trend was up at the time of the election. In all cases where an incumbent lost in a landslide, the stock market's trend was down—as it was prior to the 2008 and 2012 elections that swept Mr. Obama into the White House.

Again using the stock market index as a surrogate for how the American citizenry rates the future, we find that there is not a single case in which an incumbent was re-elected despite a deeply falling stock market or was defeated in a landslide despite a strongly rising market. Figure 1.2 shows the overall situation through the 1998 election. Here we see that if the mood of the populace is positive just prior to the election, the incumbent or his party are always returned to the White House; if not, they are thrown out.

With the ideas of context, drivers of context (complexity gaps and social mood), random triggers, and the like in hand, there is just one last item to deal with before embarking on a much more ambitious discussion of all of these elements. That is the issue of not only how to survive an X-event, but how to actually be a beneficiary of it. For that, we need some background ideas involving the resilience and the processes of social change.

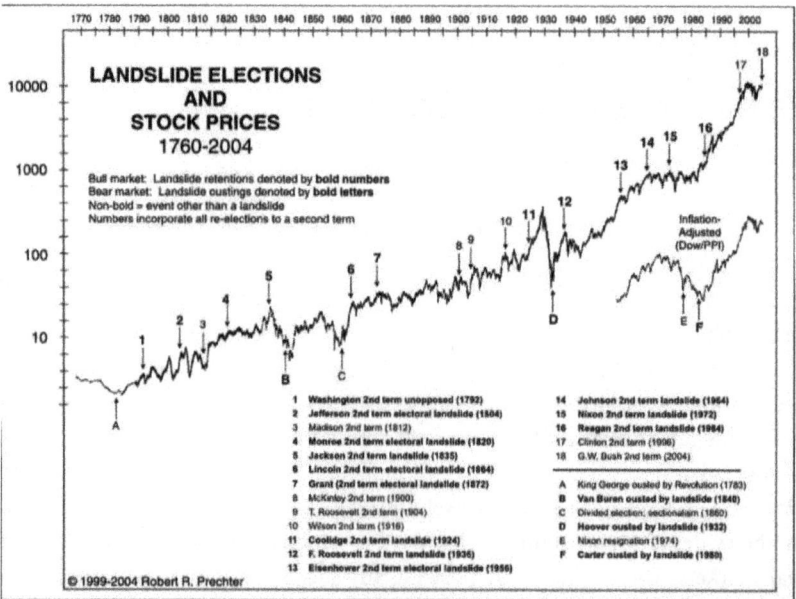

Figure 1.2 US Presidentail Election vs. the DJIA, 1760–1998

1.2.8
EXERCISES: SYSTEMS

Knowing reality means constructing systems of transformations that correspond, more or less adequately, to reality.

Jean Piaget

The purpose of this exercise is to introduce a simple heuristic network-based picture of a system—a conceptual model of constituents and their interactions.

- We describe a system as a network composed of nodes and directed edges. This is illustrated in Figure 1.3. The nodes represent individuals, departments, cities, atoms, street corners, equations, or anything we might describe by a noun. The edges represent interactions between the nodes. This could be anything we describe by verbs or flows. The edge may, for instance, represent information flow or product flow.

  We define two types of edges, strong and weak. A strong edge, for instance, may represent large information flow, while a small edge may represent small information flow. A *system* is defined as a group of nodes connected by strong edges. The interaction of the system with its environment is through weak edges. Outgoing edges from a system are outputs. Incoming edges are inputs. The totality of inputs to a system is the system's *context*. A network with no input or output edges is a *closed system*. The only truly closed system is the entire universe, which has no context.

  Identify several examples of systems in both the social and natural sciences. What are the main nodes? What do the edges represent? What are the inputs to the system? What are the outputs? With what other systems does each system interact? What would the graph that includes a regulatory agency and a regulated industry look like?
- Can a system become unstable and split into two systems—or two systems fuse into one? Would this result because of a change of values of the inputs? Would the system become unstable if inputs were added or subtracted? Can you think of examples of instability of real systems?
- A system can be composed of subsystems. For instance, a business may be composed of a sales department, a production facility, and a finance department. A sales department may be decomposed into regional sales divisions, which can be decomposed into districts.

What are examples of nested systems in natural and social sciences?

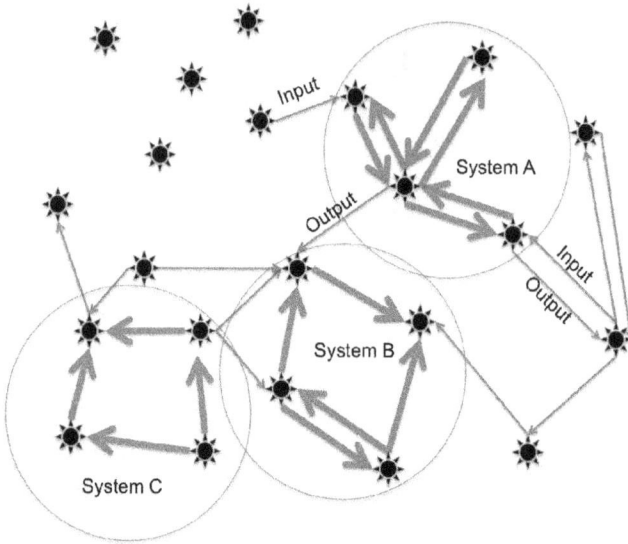

Figure 1.3 Systems. Nodes are portrayed by stars. Directed edges are portrayed by arrows. Strong edges are represented by heavy arrows. Weak are represented by light arrows. There are three systems, A, B, and C in the figure.

1.3
RESILIENCE: THE GOOD, THE BAD, AND THE ABSOLUTELY ESSENTIAL

In 1974, one of the authors of this book (JC) found himself working at the International Institute for Applied Systems Analysis (IIASA) just outside Vienna. Among the several applications-focused groups in residence at the Institute at that time was a team of systems ecologists from the University of British Columbia in Vancouver. A hot topic for that group was to pin down a working definition of what it would mean for an ecosystem to be "resilient." The group's leader, C. S. "Buzz" Holling, had introduced this idea in a seminar article a couple of years earlier, but in a rather informal way. The team at IIASA was struggling with how to formalize the resilience concept so that it could be both measured and included in mathematical and computational models of real-world ecosystems.

Given JC's background in mathematical control theory, where the idea of stability had already been well-established, he naturally gravitated to a working relationship with the UBC group's efforts to distinguish the way a resilient system differs from the kind of stable systems he was familiar with from the control theory world. As is almost always the case with new concepts introduced in one domain and interpreted by another, confusion reigned supreme as each group was convinced that its definition hit the sweet spot as the "right" definition to use for ecosystem modeling. These fumblings and gropings about were finally brought to a head in 1975 at a one-week conference held at IIASA bringing together not only mathematical modelers, but practitioners from ecology, economics, climate forecasting, and other domains concerned with whether their particular types of systems were or were not resilient.

Thumbing through the proceedings of that resilience workshop today, nearly forty years later, does not suggest that any knockdown definition of resilience emerged from the meeting. Most likely, the various participants returned to their usual haunts after the workshop and continued doing what they had been doing using the same working definition they brought with them to Vienna. But in the period since that get-together, many people have tackled the question of what constitutes a resilient system. And something that looks like a set of properties that the majority of researchers can agree upon is beginning to emerge. In this section we will describe those properties, as well as give a few applications illustrating how they can be applied in different situations. But first, a pair of warnings.

Upon first hearing the term "resilience," many people think it's just another word for "stability." And in the non-scientific vernacular, perhaps it is. But in the world of science, stability has a very specific meaning. A system is stable if after being perturbed from its current state by any type of disturbance, internal or external, after a sufficiently long period of time, the system returns to its state prior to the disturbance. In other words, the perturbation eventually "washes out" and the system behaves as if it had never taken place.

This is a very restricted notion of stability, since it tacitly assumes that the world outside the system remains unchanged while that washing out process unfolds. It also assumes that the shock to the system state has no impact whatsoever on the actual inner workings of the system itself; that is, the shock affects only the system state, not its rule of motion. In the 1970s, researchers in stability theory patched-up this latter problem by introducing the concept of "structural stability," in which the disturbance changes not only the system state but also its dynamics. But this is like putting a Band-Aid on a hole in your chest from a shotgun, and in no way captures the idea of resilience as seen by workers in ecology or the social sciences.

The second caution is to recognize that there is no such thing as a system being "resilient" in an absolute sense. There is only the relative notion of being resilient with respect to a particular type of shock. So a system might be resilient to a breakdown of the internet but totally vulnerable to, say, a major hurricane or a power failure. So when we speak about resilience in this book, it is always tacitly assumed that there is a particular type of shock in the background. The reader should keep both these points in mind: resilience is not a synonym for stability and it is a relative concept, not an absolute one.

The overriding point about resilience that Buzz Holling and others have continually emphasized over the past forty years is that a resilient system is one that can not only absorb a shock and continue to function, but can actually benefit from that shock. By this we mean that the system can reconfigure itself to take advantage of the new environment that the shock creates, in order to function even better than before the shock occurred. We'll see a few examples of this from the corporate world in a moment. For now, let's list the principal properties that a resilient system displays. We call these the "Four As":

Awareness The system monitors early warning signals for the types of shocks that could threaten it, and is able to take action to "batten down the hatches" if any of those shocks seems imminent.

Assimilation The system is able to survive the shock, perhaps by resisting it, maybe by absorbing the shock into its operation (assimilation) or through some other means. But survival of the shock is a necessary condition for a system to be resilient.

Agility The system is able to survey the changed landscape that the shock creates, and is capable of deploying its resources to filling one or another of the "niches" the shock opens up.

Adaptativity The system is ready to change its way of doing business if it finds a new niche that offers greater potential for growth and development than from its pre-shock activity.

So how to do we measure resilience? A crude, but reasonably effective, way is to simply assign a number between 0 and 10 to each of these four categories. Of course, this would be rather subjective. Nevertheless, experts on the operation of the system should be able to do this.

Now *define* the resilience of the system to be the *minimum* of these four numbers. We suggest the minimum because that would prevent trading-off one of the four properties for another in arriving at the overall resilience. The system's resilience is only as strong as its weakest link. Using the "minimum" operation ensures this will be the case.

Finally, we carry out this same exercise for each shock of concern and then take the minimum of all those minima as the overall resilience of the system. This "minimum of minima" process is quite workable and leads to a useful measure of how resilient any particular system actually is.

In addition to the theme of "unfriending the trend" by anticipating its onset, another thread running through this book is to note that X-events are generally as much of an opportunity as they are a problem. In short, there is almost always a "silver lining" to the cloud of death and destruction brought on by an X-event. The history of several corporate icons serves to admirably illustrate the adage that survival of a near-death experience, coupled with the ability to adapt to changing circumstances, is the secret sauce for success. And this does not apply just in the corporate world, but serves equally well in the world at-large. So to introduce the positive flip side of X-events, here is a very brief summary of three rags-to-very-great-riches stories from the American corporate world.

- **Microsoft:** While high-school classmates in the early 1970s, Bill Gates and Paul Allen started Traf-O-Data, a computer business that automatically read tapes for local governments from road traffic counters. Initially, their business moved onward and upward at a steady, but slow, pace—until the state of Washington threw a spanner in the works by offering to tabulate the tapes for the cities for free. Not to be deterred, Gates and Allen saw the potential of the personal computer that was just then emerging, and applied what they'd learned from their failed business about how to write software for a computer they didn't even yet have, creating a new start-up they called "Micro-Soft." The rest, as they say, is history. And to this day, Gates remains the world's wealthiest person on the annual *Forbes* magazine list of the ultra leisure class.
- **Apple:** Following his forced resignation from Apple in 1985, Steve Jobs formed the company *NeXT* to develop a computer work station for educators. But with a high price tag and a lot of bugs, the machine never really took off and Jobs' firm burned through hundreds of millions of investor dollars before finally being bought up by Apple in 1996. That acquisition also involved Jobs returning to Apple as interim CEO, a position he eventually leveraged to make Apple into what is today the single most valuable company in the world. But this phenomenal success wasn't accomplished by building computers. Rather, it emerged from Jobs' vision of what amounts to media devices for the masses, the iPod, iPad, iPhone, and Apple Watch. So as with Microsoft, Apple had to overcome a major shock to its business model and product line, adapting to fill a market niche that no one else saw at the time.
- **Kentucky Fried Chicken:** Since the time of the Great Depression, "Colonel" Harland Sanders had been serving his secret blend of herbs-and-spices fried chicken to guests at his restaurant and motel in Corbin, Kentucky. But in 1955, a newly built interstate highway bypassed Corbin, siphoning off most of his customer base. After selling the location and settling his debts, Sanders was broke. Prior to the collapse of his "empire," though, Sanders had already been exploring the idea of franchising his chicken restaurant. So he took to the road full-time to sell the franchises and had nearly 200 buyers and over 400 Kentucky Fried Chicken restaurants in place within five years.

What do these stories have in common?

First, there is a trend. In the case of Gates and Allen, the trend was their tape-reading company Traf-O-Data, which was chugging along in a more-or-less predictable fashion until the state of Washington threw a spanner in the works. Similarly, the Colonel was minding his motel and restaurant business in a pretty predictable, marginally profitable way for over twenty years until the US government stepped in and his customer base stepped out. The case of Apple is a bit different. There Steve Jobs stepped out or, more precisely, was shoved out as the firm continued to pursue its computer business. But eventually the computer business failed to really develop, at which point Jobs returned and redirected the company's product line to make the firm what it is today.

In each of these cases, an X-event blasted the firm out of an existing orbit and forced its management to reevaluate its entire line of business. The principal(s) had to open their eyes and look around to see what they might be able to profitably exploit using the new opportunities in the current business landscape. This level of adaptability was crucial, since to continue to pursue their previous line of business would have been tantamount to commercial suicide. This is the stage, incidentally, when most organizations do precisely that, leading to their ultimate or even immediate demise. This phase of a firm's evolution is what famed economist Joseph Schumpeter called "creative destruction." The X-event destroys the old landscape, while opening up new niches for an adaptive organization to explore.

Finally, there is the innovation and reconfiguration stage during which the organization launches a new initiative to replace their now-defunct original line of business. For Microsoft, it was the Disk Operation System (DOS) for personal computers; for Apple, it was personal media products like the iPhone and iPad, while for the Colonel it was the notion of franchising instead of actually producing and selling the end product himself. All of them worked. And all led to companies that ended up at or near the top of the global pyramid of successful and profitable organizations.

The key element in each of these success stories is the shock, the X-event, that forced the organization to reexamine its goals and possibilities and take appropriate action. As this book will continually emphasize, major change never, ever happens during the trending phase. You need an X-event to change the game. It is a necessary—but far from sufficient—ingredient. Most individuals, firms, and/or countries fail to recover from the shock and make their exit freeing-up space for the survivors and innovators to exploit a new social landscape.

The overall flow from existing trend through X-event to reconfiguration and on to rebirth and a new trend can be described pictorially in the "Fundamental Diagram of Human Social Processes" shown above. In the chapters to follow, we will offer a detailed account of each box and arrow in this diagram within the context of not only corporations and economies, but for individual human lives and even entire countries.

The observant reader will have already noted that the stories outlined above for corporations are very reminiscent of the story told by biologists for

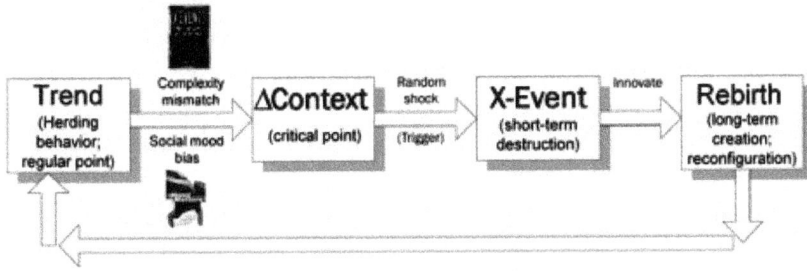

Figure 1.4

the process of evolution in general. Evolutionary biologists Stephen Jay Gould and Nils Eldredge termed this process of smooth trends followed by dramatic shocks, "punctuated equilibrium." Their argument was that evolution proceeds in fits and spurts. For long periods, nothing much is happening and species evolve new traits in a slow, fairly boring fashion (the trending phase). But every now and then a period of activity that we might term "revolutionary," as opposed to evolutionary, occurs during which old species disappear and new ones pop up like mushrooms in the forest. The Cambrian explosion that took place around 530 million years ago was one such period. In a few million years, the blink of an eye on the evolutionary timescale, most of the major animals, phytoplankton, and other organisms constituting today's world appeared, and the diversity of life as we now know it began.

The takeaway here is that most of the time nothing of significance is happening. This is the trending period when only "ordinary" events occur. Then an evolutionary X-event takes place, after which a very large number of new econiches are opened up for exploitation by organisms that survived the "shock." This gives the evolutionary process a huge, discontinuous boost. Afterwards, the system settles down and a new period of stasis begins. The asteroid that blew away the dinosaurs 65 million years ago is a good example of such an evolutionary X-event, opening up niches that our distant ancestors jumped in to fill. And, in fact, we wouldn't be writing this book and you wouldn't be reading it if that X-event had not taken place.

The "Fundamental Diagram" shown above encapsulates this basic argument, but for human social processes rather than biological ones. As human evolutionary processes unfold on a vastly shorter timescale than biological ones, we will be able to show the steps within the lifetime of a single individual or organization instead of how those same steps take place over the millions of years needed in the biological realm.

The final element in the story that we will tell here is probably the one of greatest interest for everyone alive today. We have seen that X-events are not only the drivers of major, discontinuous change, but are also unavoidable. Trends always change; surprises always occur. So the issue is not what we can do to prevent them, but rather what we can do to both anticipate and prepare for them. Instead of waiting until the shock occurs and then scurrying around trying to formulate a plan in real-time for dealing with the event, how can we get ready for tomorrow today? In the pages to follow, we will discuss this question from the standpoint of each level of social organization—individual, corporate, national, and environmental.

1.4
HURRICANES AS COMPLEXITY METAPHORS

Full fathom five thy father lies.
Of his bones are coral made.
Those are pearls that were his eyes.
Nothing of him that doth fade,
But doth suffer a sea-change
Into something rich and strange.
Sea-nymphs hourly ring his knell

William Shakespeare, The *Tempest*, Act 1, Scene 2

Hurricanes are extreme natural events. The purpose of this section is to use hurricane formation to illustrate the fundamental principles we have discussed so far. As we see from the quote from The *Tempest*, we are not the first to use hurricanes as a metaphor for change. We will use hurricanes to illustrate

- the fundamental concepts of complexity mismatch/gaps,
- extreme discontinuous shifts in the state of the system,
- localization in time and space with increasing complexity,
- and random triggers.

The goal is not so much to understand hurricanes, as it is to use the complexity of hurricanes as a metaphor for complex systems in general.

As we will see, hurricanes are created and driven by complexity mismatches (1) between the degree and gradients of heating of the Earth's surface and (2) the thermal transport mechanisms that move heat to bring the surface to a single temperature. For small mismatches, the atmosphere is calm and wind-free. As the mismatch increases, the atmosphere suddenly develops into global long-term weather patterns. As the mismatch increases further, violent hurricanes are suddenly and randomly triggered from locations of low pressure. In the case of weather, complexity mismatch is determined by temperature gradients. The higher the temperature gradient, the higher the complexity mismatch in the systems. The random trigger for hurricane formation is the random location of high-pressure sites near the equator. The main *action* of a hurricane is to transport heat from the bottom of the atmosphere to the top and from the equator to the poles.

1.4.1
SCIENTIFICALLY ACCURATE POETRY

Extreme events, whether natural or social, are awe-inspiring. It is easy to lose the wonder, mystery, and poetry of these massive events in scientific description. Before we jump into the science, let's take a brief interlude to emotionally motivate our discussion of hurricanes. In pre-scientific times, the origins and behavior of such awesome events would be described in mythical poetic language. The mythology would be used to inform the behavior of the population. This is similar to the role of science in modern life. What would a hurricane creation myth look like that is scientifically accurate? Is it possible to capture the poetry of a hurricane and still be scientifically correct? If we can, then we have illustrated an important principle: disparate descriptions of phenomena can all be consistent with each other. This is a common observation in the natural sciences, particularly in physics. In poetic language the hurricane myth might look something like the following:

In the beginning was the calm.
The air sat upon the sea and land and did not move.
The temperature here was the same as the temperature there.
And the sunlight penetrated the air as if it were invisible.

The sunlight struck the sea and heated it.
The temperature was no longer the same here as there.
And the sunlight struck the sea, and sea became hotter.
And great rolling boiling winds were formed from out of the calm.

The winds captured the heat from the sea and carried it high into the air.
And the Earth began to spin dividing the wind into three parts.
And the sea continued to heat.
And near the equator there was a dip in pressure.
And the wind rushed in,
But the spin kept the wind at bay.

And the wind pressed harder until a great cyclone was formed.
And the cyclone carried heat from the sea to the sky.
And the wind blew the cyclone from the east to the west.

And two gyres came as the heat was released.
And the rains came harder.
And there were thunder and lightning.
And the land filled with water
That slowly drained into the sandy soil
And met with the great underground river
That flowed to the sea.

And the sunlight struck the sea and heated it.

1.4.2
SPIRAL OF COMPLEXITY

Now that we have had a poetic interlude, let's take a look at the description of a hurricane in scientific language. Hurricanes are a consequence of increased system complexity resulting from temperature gradients. The increased complexity of external temperature gradients leads to increased complexity of the atmosphere. The atmospheric complexity does not increase gradually with increasing temperature complexity, it increases in sudden jumps. The spiral of complexity is displayed in Figure 1.5. We will illustrate the process with a set of increasingly complex thought experiments starting with the example of a simple static atmosphere in a temperature gradient.

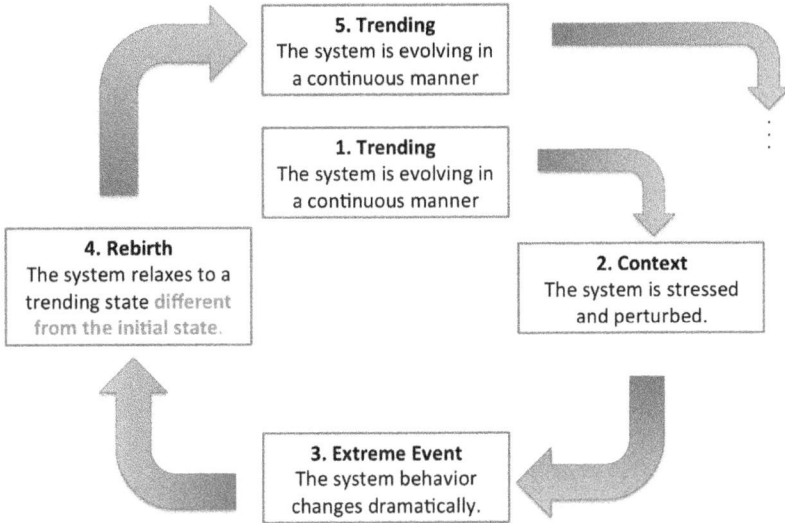

5. Trending
The system is evolving in a continuous manner

1. Trending
The system is evolving in a continuous manner

4. Rebirth
The system relaxes to a trending state different from the initial state.

2. Context
The system is stressed and perturbed.

3. Extreme Event
The system behavior changes dramatically.

Figure 1.5 Spiral of Complexity. The system starts off in a trending state, a reasonably well defined state. External pressure is applied to the system. In the case of hurricanes, the pressure results from increased temperature gradients. As the external pressure on the system increases, the system suddenly changes to a new configuration. The change is usually seeded by a small random perturbation. The system then relaxes to a new trending state. The process repeats as the external pressure continues to increase. Each successive trending state builds on the complexity of the previous trending state. This will become more important when we discuss social systems.

1.4.3
THERMAL CONDUCTION

Let's first consider the simplest atmosphere possible. Consider an atmosphere of height h. This is an approximation. Real atmospheres decrease their density gradually with altitude so that a well defined height is not possible. We, however, can define h as the altitude that encompasses most of the atmosphere. We imagine that the atmosphere is still; there are no winds. There are no temperature gradients. A thermometer anywhere in the atmosphere will have the same temperature reading T. We say that the atmosphere is in thermal and mechanical equilibrium. It has a defined temperature and nothing is moving. For our purposes, we can think of the atmosphere as a fluid with fluid properties of viscosity, thermal diffusivity, etc.

Now, let's imagine that we heat the Earth's surface a small amount with sunlight. We bring the temperature of the Earth up to $T + \Delta T$. We maintain the temperature at the top of the atmosphere at its original value T. Energy, in the form of heat, now flows from the Earth through the atmosphere to the top of the atmosphere, where it is dissipated into free space. Heat energy is the energy in random motion of molecules. The molecules of the Earth are moving faster than the molecules at the top of the atmosphere, therefore the surface of the Earth is hotter—it has more heat—than the top of the atmosphere. The molecules collide at a rate of about a billion collisions per second. The energetic molecules on the surface transfer their energy to the top of the atmosphere through the random collisions of the molecules. This is called *thermal conductivity* or *diffusion*.

1.4.4
EMERGENCE OF ORDER: RAYLEIGH-BÉNARD INSTABILITY

As we raise the temperature further, something remarkable happens. Thermal diffusion is no longer able to effectively transfer heat from the surface to the top of the atmosphere. We see the formation of convection, or winds. Vertical winds carry air from the surface to the top of the atmosphere. There the air cools off and its heat is deposited in the upper atmosphere. The air moves along the top of the atmosphere continuing to release its heat until the air increases its density because of the cooling and starts to fall back to the ground. Once again at ground level the air moves along the surface of the Earth picking up heat until it once again is light enough from reduced density to rise again as vertical wind. These winds form circular cells that move air in one direction in the upper atmosphere and in the opposite direction in the lower atmosphere. This is called Rayleigh-Bénard convection. Heat is transported not only upwards but also sideways in a direction from hotter surface temperatures to lower surface temperatures. The cells are nature's way of driving the atmosphere back into thermal equilibrium. Beautiful pictures of the phenomena in liquids can be seen on the Rayleigh-Bénard Wikipedia site.

The threshold for the sudden onset of Rayleigh-Bénard convection in a gas is determined by the Rayleigh number R_a

$$R_a = \frac{g}{\nu \alpha}\left(\frac{\Delta T}{T}\right)h^3$$

where ν and α are physical properties of the fluid. Here, $\alpha = 1.9 \times 10^{-5}$ m^2/s is the thermal diffusivity of air, and $\nu = 1.48 \times 10^{-5}$ m^2/s is the kinematic viscosity of air. Onset of the instability occurs when R $\approx$ 1700.

1.4.5
SUDDEN COMPLEXITY SHIFTS

This paragraph is so important that we bold it for emphasis. This is our first example in the natural sciences of a concept that is central to this book. **We can think of our motionless, thermally constant atmosphere as the simplest possible atmosphere. The atmosphere, under these conditions, is in thermal and mechanical equilibrium. The temperature gradient is a measure of the distance the atmosphere is from equilibrium. We can think of the temperature gradient as a crude measure of the complexity of the external drivers. The greater the externally imposed temperature difference, the greater is the complexity of the external drivers in contact with our atmosphere. As the complexity of the external drivers of the system increases, the complexity of our system, the atmosphere, also increases to match the external complexity. The complexity is not adjusted continuously, but rather in discrete discontinuous jumps. This is a constant theme in this book—for both natural and social systems. Systems in contact can experience a complexity mismatch that leads to sudden shifts in the systems that bring the complexity of the systems and drivers more in line with each other.**

1.4.6
HADLEY, FERREL, AND POLAR CELLS

Rayleigh-Bénard convection accounts for the transport of heat from the surface of the Earth to the upper atmosphere, but how is heat transported from the hot equator to the colder poles? Rayleigh–Bénard convection can also account for much of the heat transported from the equator to the poles. The convection cells are large enough so that the upward flow of warm air near the equator is balanced by a downward flow of air at much higher latitudes. Heat is not only convected upward, but also toward the poles by the cells. There are two types of cells on Earth that account for this heat transport. The cells that transport heat from the equator to the mid–latitudes are called Hadley cells. Cells that transport heat from the mid–latitudes to the poles are called Polar cells. There is a less defined set of cells that exist between the Hadley cells and the Polar cells known as Ferrel cells. The largest portion of the heat transport is performed by Hadley cells.

Figure 1.6 displays a simplified schematic of the three types of cells. The Hadley cells and the Polar cells transport heat from the warmer latitudes toward the colder poles. In contrast, the Ferrel cells transport heat in the opposite direction, from cold to warm. The Second Law of Thermodynamics requires that closed systems move toward thermal equilibrium—toward a uniform temperature distribution in which order in the system is destroyed. Another way of stating the second law is that closed systems become more disorderly with time. Ferrel cells resist the movement of the system to thermal equilibrium. They are islands of order in the atmosphere. This can happen because our atmosphere is not a closed system. Sunlight, through heating, is driving the system away from equilibrium. As the atmosphere attempts to relax to thermal equilibrium the system generates islands of order like the Ferrel cells. The disorder of the closed atmosphere/sun system overall, however, increases, thus preserving the second law.

Another way to think about Ferrel cells is that they are a type of refrigerator. They operate in a manner that attempts to cool the polar regions further, although not enough to overcome the heating of the polar cells. The Hadley cells and Polar cells provide the free energy to power this refrigerator, much like burning coal provides the free energy to power your kitchen refrigerator. Ferrel cells are much like ball bearings between the Hadley cells and Polar cells. Ferrel cells are less stable than the other two types of cells. This causes the variability of the weather in temperate climates.

1.4.7
EFFECT OF EARTH'S ROTATION

Why are there multiple cells transporting heat from the equator to the poles? Wouldn't just one cell be simpler? Wouldn't one cell eliminate the extra complexity generated by the Ferrel cells? There must be some type of extra external complexity that is creating the extra complexity in our atmosphere. In fact, the extra external complexity driving our atmosphere is the rotation of the Earth. Earth's rotation introduces a virtual force on the moving atmosphere—the Coriolis force.

The Coriolis force is easy to visualize. Imagine you are standing on the North Pole, and you throw a baseball directly south, which is any direction if you are standing on the North Pole. The ball experiences only the gravitational force so it will travel in a parabolic trajectory in the original direction it was thrown. While the ball is in the air, however, the Earth has rotated a small amount. The ball will actually land a little to the right of where you expected it to. It will seem to you, standing on the North Pole and rotating with the Earth, that a force has pushed the ball to the right. In general the ball appears to be forced to the right in the Northern Hemisphere and to the left in the Southern. This causes large-scale wind patterns to rotate counterclockwise in the Northern Hemisphere and clockwise in the Southern.

There is a number, like the Rayleigh number for the Rayleigh-Bénard instability, that informs us if the Coriolis force is important in our situation. This number is called the Rossby number and is given by

$$R_o = \frac{v}{2\omega \sin\varphi L}$$

where v is the speed of an object, ω is the rotational speed of the Earth in radians per second, φ is the latitude, and L is the length scale. If R_o is less than one then the Coriolis effect is important.

Suppose we are interested in length scales of the order of the distance between the equator and the pole. Below what speed will the Coriolis force become important? Call this speed the *Coriolis threshold*.

At speeds below the Coriolis threshold, the force is large, and we might expect the wind to be redirected to the right (left) before it is able to reach the north (South) Pole. This will prevent the formation of a cell that stretches from the equator to the pole. For wind speeds higher than the Coriolis threshold, the Coriolis effect should be negligible, and we would expect a single large cell to form. In fact, Hadley cells extend from the equator only to about 30° latitude before they are directed sideways by the Coriolis force. The sideways redirection is responsible for the jet streams at high altitudes and trade winds at lower altitudes. Since the Hadley cell cannot make it the entire distance to the pole, the heat must be transported to the pole by multiple cells. This is the mechanism behind the multiple cells in Figure 1.6.

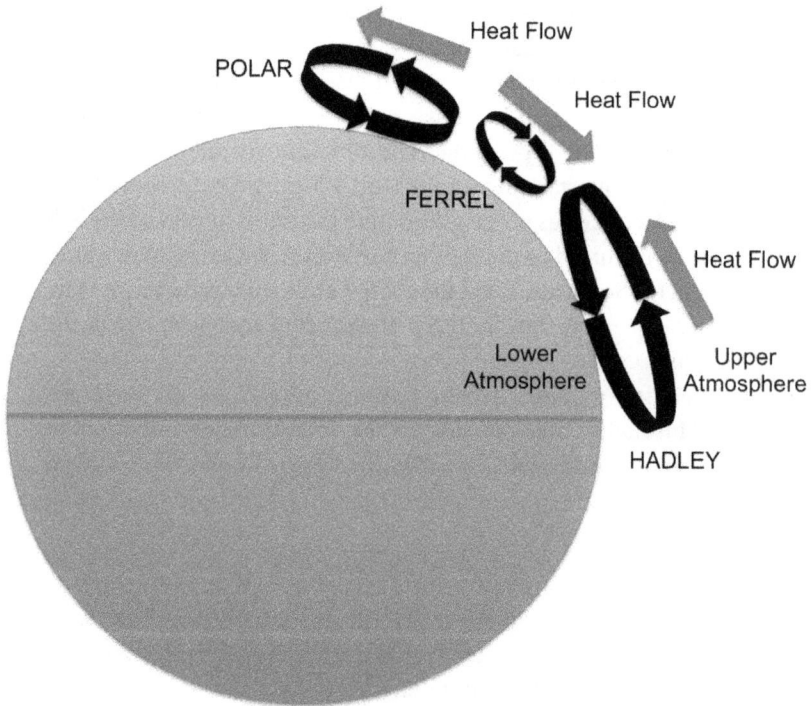

Figure 1.6 Hadley, Polar, and Ferrel cells. Note that the Ferrel cells transport heat from the colder poles toward the warmer equator.

1.4.8
SUDDEN CREATION OF HURRICANES

What happens when the surface heating increases further? One might imagine that the wind speed in the Hadley cell will increase to a point in which it is above the Coriolis threshold, and a single cell would extend from equator to pole that efficiently transports heat. Something else happens before that, however—hurricanes form.

Hurricane formation illustrates the next important concept in the book—the random trigger. The large cells that transport heat from equator to poles are not very surprising. They have been in existence as long as people have been paying attention to such matters. Jet streams, trade winds, and prevailing westerlies are reasonably dependable and have been integrated into human social and economic systems such as shipping and air transport. **Hurricanes, on the other hand, are surprising. One cannot say with accuracy where or when they form or where they will go. The predictability of the cells is a consequence of their large size. They are constrained by the size of the Earth, which tames their unpredictability. Hurricanes, on the other hand, are smaller and are formed in the vastness of the equatorial seas. Their exact location of formation is determined by very local wind, water, and temperature conditions—a random trigger. This is the so-called butterfly effect in which the flapping of a butterfly wing in one part of the planet significantly affects the weather in another part.**

Like the Rayleigh-Bénard instability, hurricane formation occurs rapidly once a threshold is exceeded. The first threshold condition is that the water should be above 26° C (78° F) to a depth of about a meter. There must be a significant temperature gradient in the atmosphere. The Coriolis effect must be significant. The Coriolis effect is zero at the equator, so this requires hurricane formation to occur some distance from the equator. Hurricanes form at greater than 5° latitude. Finally, a low-pressure perturbation is necessary to initiate the formation. Small pressure fluctuations occur randomly over the surface of the Earth. When conditions are right at the location of one of these random perturbations, a hurricane forms at that location. The pressure fluctuation acts as a random trigger for the formation of the hurricane. The onset of the hurricane is rapid; the low pressure at the center of the hurricane is enhanced; the hurricane becomes a stable atmospheric swirling structure.

1.4.9
BUT . . . HURRICANES ROTATE IN
THE WRONG DIRECTION

There is a problem, however. Hurricanes rotate in the *wrong direction*. At sea level they rotate to the left (counterclockwise) in the Northern Hemisphere and to the right (clockwise) in the Southern. We have seen that the Coriolis force drives wind to the right in the Northern Hemisphere and to the left in the Southern, which is just the opposite of hurricane rotation. At higher altitudes, however, hurricane rotation switches polarity and moves in agreement with the Coriolis force. There is clearly another layer of complex interactions that is occurring. In fact, the extra complexity is due to the interaction of the Coriolis force with pressure gradients. This is illustrated in Figure 1.7 where it can be seen that the counterclockwise circulation is due to a balancing of the pressure force and the Coriolis force in the radial direction. The circulation pattern officially becomes a hurricane when the sustained winds exceed 33 m/s (74 mph).

1.4.10
HEAT TRANSFER TO THE POLES

We see how a hurricane transfers heat from the Earth's surface to the upper atmosphere. How does it transfer heat from the equator toward the poles? The hurricane must move. The wind from the Hadley cells blow the hurricanes. We saw that the wind in the Hadley cells traveled southward near the surface. The Coriolis force turned the winds to the right so that by the time the air was near the equator the Coriolis force had turned the wind so that it was moving toward the west. This is the source of the trade winds. Hurricanes simply move along with this wind current in a westerly direction. **This is very interesting from a complexity perspective. We have a situation in which a structure, the hurricane, at one level of complexity is directed by a structure, the Hadley cell, at one lower level of complexity. We will see this again in social structures.**

The hurricane moves westward, in the Northern Hemisphere, as a consequence of the Hadley cell, but the poles are north of the

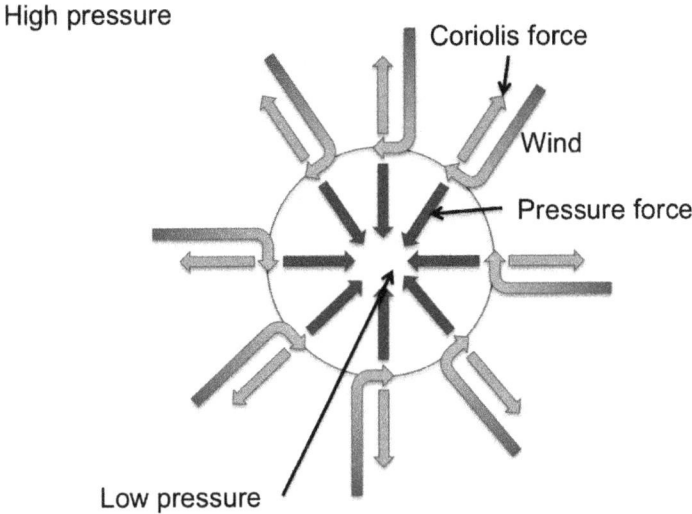

Figure 1.7 Counterclockwise circulation at the bottom of the atmosphere in the Northern Hemisphere. The wind in hurricanes moves counterclockwise near the Earth's surface in the Northern Hemisphere. This is opposite to the Coriolis force. What is the mechanism for this "backwards" air flow? Air is drawn to the low-pressure perturbation. The Coriolis force turns the wind toward the right in a clockwise manner. The inward pressure force and the outward Coriolis force balance each other in the radial direction leading to flow directing to the left (counterclockwise) rather than the right (clockwise). Wind is directed upward, and there is outward flow at the top of the atmosphere. The Coriolis force dominates at the top of the hurricane and the flow is directed to the right (clockwise) at the top of the atmosphere.

equator, not west. How does a hurricane move northward so that it can deposit its heat near the poles? It turns out that two subsidiary vortices are formed by the hurricane called *beta gyres*. These two vortices create a secondary background wind that moves the hurricane in a northwest direction in the Northern Hemisphere. This motion is called *beta drift*. The hurricane interacts with the wind from the Hadley cell to create a secondary drift northward.

As we have seen, the atmosphere becomes increasingly complex as the strength of the external driver, in this case the temperature gradient, becomes more intense. We could continue this exercise and discuss how, upon even greater temperature gradients, hurricanes spawn water spouts, but the point is probably already made. With increasing driver intensity the system makes discrete jumps to ever more complex structures. The structures become more localized as the complexity increases. As the structures become more localized, the triggers for the creation of the structures become more random, thus decreasing the predictability of the creation and behavior of the structures. Structures at a lower level of complexity can guide the more complex structures as we saw with Hadley cells directing the motion of hurricanes. In anticipation of problems in social systems, we can think of the background winds generated by Hadley cells that direct the movement of hurricanes as the *mood* of the atmosphere around the hurricane. These few points will be illustrated many times in this book.

EXERCISES: COMPLEXITY OF HURRICANES

Hurricane season brings a humbling reminder that, despite our technologies, most of nature remains unpredictable.

Diane Ackerman

1. Calculate the percent temperature difference between the surface and the height of the atmosphere, which we take to be 10 km, that is required to initiate the Rayleigh-Bénard instability. Assume the temperature is 300 K. What is the temperature difference required to initiate the instability? What is the likelihood that the Earth's atmosphere is currently in the convection regime rather than the conduction regime? Remember

$$R_a = \frac{g}{\nu\alpha}\left(\frac{\Delta T}{T}\right)h^3$$

2. Suppose the wind moves at 10 m/s. At approximately what scale length will the Coriolis force become important?
3. From the Euler equations that describe fluid motion, identify the two forcing terms that balance the inward and outward motion. Assume that fluid is moving in a circle. What are the conditions for balancing the two force terms?
4. Energy is released as heat when water condenses from vapor. A typical hurricane releases about 8.6 megatons of energy in

one minute through the release of energy from water condensation. How many bumps per minute is that? (See Exercise 1.1.2.) How does this compare with world power usage? Compare the energy flux from a hurricane with energy flux of the world power usage. How does this compare with the amount of kinetic energy in the wind?

5. Describe the hierarchy of atmospheric heat transport in terms of a network described in Figures 1.8 through 1.10. Is more than one description possible? Are there subsystems and subsystems of subsystems? Is the connection between the Hadley cell and the hurricane weak or strong? If it is weak, does this mean that the hurricane is a subsystem? What is the context of a hurricane? Describe the transition of heat transport from global to local scales. Is there a random trigger that initiates a Hadley cell? Explain. How is a random trigger different from a threshold? At what scales do random triggers become important in atmospheric heat transport? Why?

6. Describe the changing structure of the system as the temperature gradient increases. Is the change in structure continuous or discrete?

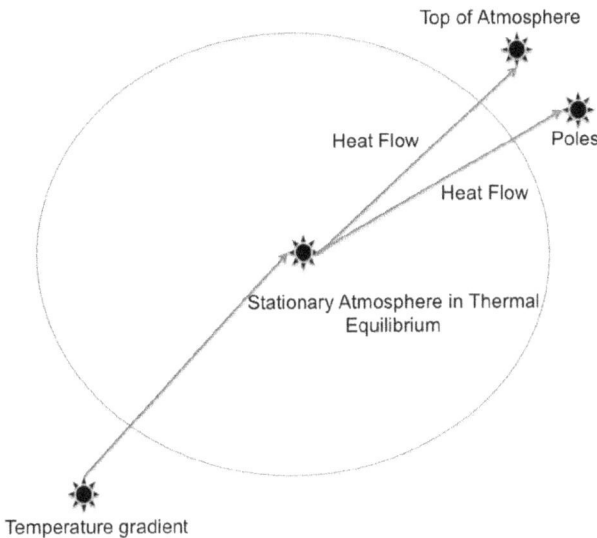

Figure 1.8 Conceptual picture of the causal chain that transports heat from the Earth's surface near the equator to the top of the atmosphere and to the poles. The atmosphere as a system for a very small temperature gradient. The heat flow is conductive. There is no wind. The temperature gradient drives thermal conduction of heat through the stationary atmosphere to the top of the atmosphere and to the poles.

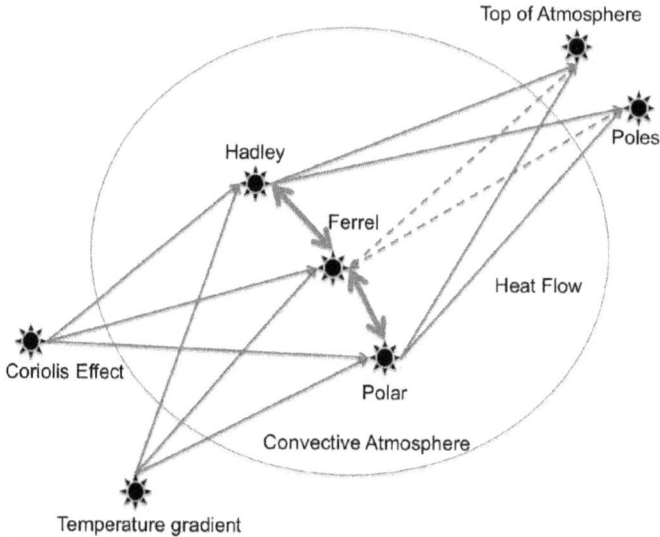

Figure 1.9 The atmosphere as a system for a larger temperature gradient. The heat flow is convective. Convective wind cells develop. Note that the Ferrel cell convects heat opposite to the temperature gradient. This is indicated by dashed arrows. The number of inputs has increased by one. The number of internal nodes has also increased. Therefore the complexity of the atmosphere has increased to match the increased complexity of the external heating.

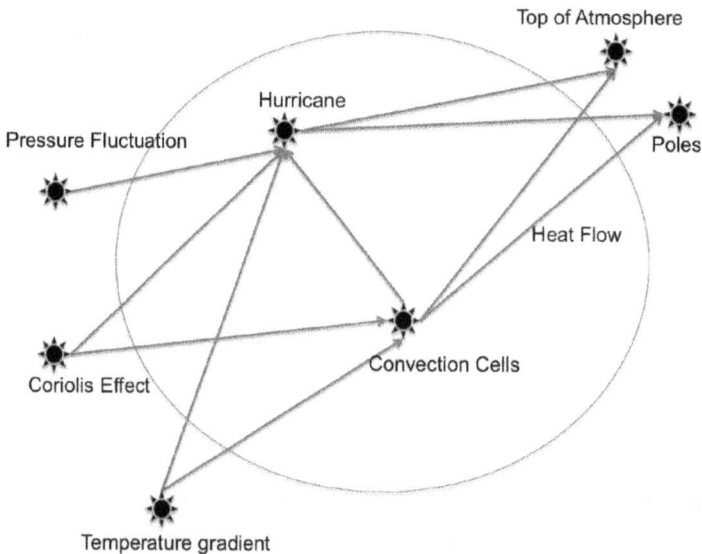

Figure 1.10 Atmospheric system with hurricanes. The convection cells have been condensed to a subsystem. The subsystem, whose internal cells are connected by strong edges, is illustrated in Figure 1.9.

1.5
DISCUSSION AND RESEARCH QUESTIONS

And the day came when the risk to remain tight in a bud was more painful than the risk it took to blossom.

Anais Nin

1.5.1
EXTREME VALUE THEORY

In extreme situations, the entire universe becomes our foe; at such critical times, unity of mind and technique is essential—do not let your heart waver!
Morihei Ueshiba

Risk is often defined in terms of the probability and consequence of an adverse or otherwise event. As such, risk is essentially a two-dimensional quantity that is typically captured via a probability distribution. Once one has a probability distribution for an adverse event, any number of approaches can be used to assist decision-makers in choosing the most preferred approach to addressing the risk. The challenge, of course, is determining the probability distribution. Of particular concern are low-probability, high-consequence events such as catastrophic floods, earthquakes, and the like. Since these events are relatively rare, it may seem to be an impossible task to generate a reasonable probability distribution for such an event.

It turns out that there is an approach called the extreme value theory that can be used to estimate the "tail" of the probability distribution where the extreme events occur. The maximum of a set of independent and identically distributed random variables can be shown to converge at one of three distribution types following normalization. Thus, by identifying the maximum values from a series of observations (e.g., annual maximum water level), one can estimate the probability of events that are more extreme than have yet been observed.

The key idea is that the theory depends on the events being independent of each other. This is a strong assumption.

1. Given the existence of such analysis techniques, why is it necessary to study X-events?
2. Why might traditional extreme event analysis not properly capture the probability of an X-event?
3. How might the processes that lead to X-events violate the assumptions of extreme value theory?

1.5.2
FEEDBACK

Other times, you're doing some piece of work and suddenly you get feedback that tells you that you have touched something that is very alive in the cosmos.

Leonard Nimoy

Two potential sources of complexity in a given system are feedback loops and their close relative, adaptive behavior. Positive feedback can amplify behavior, while negative feedback tends to extinguish behavior. Feedback and adaptation are particularly prominent in biological systems as organisms can learn from past events and change their behavior accordingly. This is especially true of more complex organisms such as humans who can learn, predict, and pass lessons on to others. While quite useful for survival, this can be problematic when we want to model the behavior of a biological system. Because organisms can learn, interact, and adapt we cannot always model their behavior with independent and identically distributed random variables. For example, let us suppose we are the CEO of a company and we need to make a major investment decision regarding a new product line. However, the profitability of this product line depends in part on what our competitor plans to do. Imagine that we want to assign a probability distribution to the amount our competitor will invest in developing a similar product.

1. Do you think that your competitor is making that decision independently of what you are doing? Or do you think that he or she is trying to anticipate what you might be doing?
2. If you had a past record of investment decisions made by your competitor, would you be comfortable building a probability distribution from that record?
3. Might you be concerned that your competitor would change his or her behavior in response to outcomes?

Now scale this idea up to an entire social system filled with many individuals that are learning, and adapting, and communicating with each other.

1. Would you feel comfortable modeling their behavior using a series of independent and identically distributed random variables?
2. Might there be some circumstances where this is an acceptable approximation?
3. What factors might differentiate these situations from those where you find the approximation unacceptable?

1.5.3
EXTREME VALUE THEORY REDUX

> As human beings, we have the blessing and the curse that we're able to adapt to almost anything. No matter how extreme the circumstances you're in, they become normal.

Kevin Powers

Now let us revisit the concept of extreme value theory. When we consider an extreme natural event such as an asteroid colliding with the Earth, we expect that asteroid impacts are independent events. Unlike people, asteroids don't communicate or actively change their behavior. Facetiously, we would not expect one asteroid to tell his friends that, "Earth looks like a great planet to impact, let's all go together!" Thus, one might be reasonably comfortable using the geologic record of past asteroid impacts to infer a probability distribution for future asteroid impacts provided we had a reasonable number of such events in the record. This is not to suggest that there are not factors that may cause the probability to shift over time, but rather we don't expect any major feedback effects that would wildly shift aster-oid behavior.

1. For human-caused X-events such as market crashes, wars, and rebellions, would you feel comfortable using extreme value theory based on the historical record to develop a probability distribution for such events in the future?
2. If you do, would you be willing to invest in mitigating such risks based on the resulting probability distributions?

Another way to think about the risk of extreme events is to think about a landscape of hills and valleys. Let's say you have a marble. If the marble is sitting in the bottom of a valley, then it would take a fairly strong push to knock the marble out of the valley. If, on the other hand, the marble is balanced on the top of a hill, the slight-est nudge could send it rolling down the hill. Generally speaking, when we engineer a system, we engineer it to be a valley. For exam-ple, small earthquakes occur all of the time. Consequently, when we design a building we make sure it dampens the earthquakes rather than amplifying them. Thus, we barely notice the countless small earthquakes, and most modern structures can even handle moder-ately sized quakes. Thus, figuratively our building design is a valley with respect to an earthquake. It would take a pretty big earthquake to knock us out of our metaphorical valley and have the building fail. Consequently, when we worry about an extreme event such as an earthquake, we can focus on developing a probability distribution of the random trigger, the earthquake itself. We can do this because we do not expect buildings to spontaneously reconfigure themselves into an unstable configuration that amplifies earthquakes. Our metaphor-ical landscape is stable. Here extreme event theory may be applicable.

Unfortunately, this is not necessarily the case when we consider social systems. Social systems are constantly adapting and chang-ing—in other words, spontaneously reconfiguring themselves. Thus, in our metaphor, the landscape itself is constantly changing. One day we could be in a valley, and the next we could be on a peak. If we are on a peak, a small nudge that might have been previously negligible all of sudden triggers radical changes as we go rolling down a hill. Thus, a high-probability, low-consequence event can suddenly become a high-consequence event due to feedback loops. This is where extreme value theory breaks down. We can no longer focus only on the proba-bility of the trigger event, we also need to consider the structure of the system in question and how it evolves over time.

1. What are some historical examples of extreme, human-caused events that seemed to be triggered by a minor, perhaps even seemingly inconsequential event?
2. How would you characterize the stability of the social system prior to the extreme event?
3. What do you think led to the change in the stability of the social system?
4. Can you think of examples in which a social system was in a stable state so that it successfully survived a very extreme trigger event?

1.5.4
UNDULATING LANDSCAPE

> *Life is like a landscape. You live in the midst of it but can describe it only from the vantage point of distance.*

Charles Lindbergh

Let us consider the case where we have an existing building, but we have run out of available space. Rather than building a whole new building, we decide to let each new tenant simply add another floor to the top of the building. As each new floor is added, the risk of the building collapsing increases. Nothing in the environment has changed. Rather we have changed the building. If we keep adding floors, the building will become so unstable that it will suddenly and catastrophically collapse—probably due to an insignificant trigger event that we could never determine.

While this scenario may seem far-fetched, it happens in social systems on a regular basis. The most prominent, recent example is the world-wide financial crisis resulting from the housing bubble. In short, the demand for mortgage-backed securities outstripped supply. As a result, investment banks developed securities that effectively resold the same mortgages over and over again. Consequently, the market was more leveraged than most realized. This created an unstable situation in which the slightest perturbation could cause the system to collapse—which is ultimately what happened. The building came tumbling down.

1. If modeling the probability of the trigger event is not sufficient, we need to look for changes in the landscape. While this might be straightforward for a physical system such as a building, it is not so obvious for a social system. How would we even define the structure of a social system? What aspects would be relevant?
2. What might we look for in a social system that would serve as a warning sign of a dangerous shift in structure?
3. Do you think that there are any general metrics that we could use to measure that stability of any social system or are they necessarily context specific?

1.5.5
FEEDBACK AND SOCIAL MOOD

If you have twenty guys in the room and you just bring in one girl, you change the entire mood and everyone plays different.

Jack White

One way to characterize the landscape for a social system is the "mood" of the population. That is the collective effect of everyone's beliefs about the future. When the social mood is positive, people generally have positive expectations for the future and act accordingly (e.g., expand businesses, hire workers, have children, buy houses, etc.) In contrast, when the social mood is negative, they make the opposite choices. Thus, social mood biases the social system's response to a random event. This would suggest that the social mood forms at least part of the social system's landscape.

The interesting aspect of social mood is its seeming potential for feedback loops. For example, positive expectations about the future state of the economy may lead to decisions that improve the state of the economy. Which, of course, reinforces the belief that the economy is improving, and leads to further decisions that improve the economy. For negative social mood, the reverse happens. So for a social system, one way to monitor shifts in the landscape would be to monitor social mood.

1. If you had a reliable means to measure social mood, what would you be looking for? How would you know if you were on a peak or in a valley?

2. Why is it incorrect to assume that positive social mood means you are on a peak and negative social mood means that you are in a valley?
3. Do you think that social mood is sufficient to characterize the landscape for a social system or do you think that other factors are involved? If so, what do you think those factors are?

1.5.6
RESILIENCE OF SOCIAL SYSTEMS

Resilience is all about being able to overcome the unexpected. Sustainability is about survival. The goal of resilience is to thrive.

Jamais Cascio

Resilience refers to the ability of a system to recover and even benefit from a disruption. Up to now we have discussed the stability or robustness of a system against a disruption. That is the ability of the system to absorb the disruption without significant consequence. Stable systems return to their original state after a disruption. Resilience, on the other hand, relates to recovery after a significant event has occurred. Resilient systems do not necessarily return to their original state after a disruption. They may move to a different state, but the system keeps functioning. For example, the robustness of the financial system refers to its ability to absorb problems and keep operating. The resilience of the financial system refers to its ability to resume normal operations—perhaps with a different structure—after it has collapsed and failed. As with robustness, it is more intuitive to define resilience for a physical system than a social system. Yet, X-events can and do happen in social systems fairly often. Thus, we are very much concerned with how to recover from them, or be resilient.

1. How might one characterize the resilience of a social system? What features might one look for?
2. Do you think there is a way to measure the resilience of a social system?
3. How do you think social mood might affect the resilience of a social system?
4. Are there other factors besides social mood that influence social resilience?

BIBLIOGRAPHY

Boisot, Max and Bill McKelvey. "Complexity and organization–environment relations: Revisiting Ashby's law of requisite variety." In *Complexity and Management*, edited by Bill McElvey Peter Allen, Steve Maguire, 279–298. Los Angeles: Sage, 2011.

Boulter, M. *Extinction: Evolution and the End of Man*. London: Fourth Estate, 2002. Mass extinction due to comets, meteorites, asteroids and the like.

Cap, Ferdinand. *Tsunamis and Hurricanes*. New York: Springer Wien, 2006.

Casti, John. *X-Events: The Collapse of Everything*. New York: HarperCollins, 2012.

Darling, David. "Chicxulub crater." *Internet Encyclopedia of Science*, 2007. www.daviddarling.info/encyclopedia/C./Cicx.html.

David, L. "Scientists simulate asteroid Armageddon." www.space.com.

Emanuel, Kerry. *Divine Wind*. New York: Oxford University Press, 2005.

Fountain, H. "Armageddon Can Wait: Stopping Killer Asteroids." *New York Times*, November 2002.

Goldsmith, D. *Nemesis*. New York: Walker Publishing Co., 2007.

Gumbel, E. J. *Statistics of Extremes*. Mineola: Dover Publications, 2004.

Haimes, Y. Y. *Risk Modeling, Assessment, and Management*. Hoboken: John Wiley and Sons, 2011.

Hallam, A. *Great Geological Controversies*. Oxford University Press, 1989. For a recent account of the entire question of Near-Earth Objects, their origin, detection, and mitigation, the best available account is given in the volume.

Hsu, K. *The Great Dying*. New York: Harcourt, Brace, Jovanovich, 1986.

Lloyd, Seth. "Measures of complexity: a non-exhaustive list," 2014. http://web.mit.edu/esd.83/www/notebook/Complexity.PDF.

Li, Xiaofan and Bin Wang. "Barotropic dynamics of the beta-gyres and beta-drift." *Journal of Atmospheric Science* 51 (1994): 746–756. http://www.soest.hawaii.edu/MET/Faculty/bwang/bw/pubs/28.html.

Mariotti, J. *The Complexity Crisis*. Avon, Mass: Platinum Press, 2008.

North Carolina State Climate Office of North Carolina hurricanes—development, 2014. http://www.ncclimate.ncsu.edu/climate/hurricanes/development.php.

Prechter, R. "Ask not what your candidate can do for the stock market; ask what the stock market can do for your candidate." *Market Technician* 61 (June 2008).

Raup, D. *Extinction: Bad Genes or Bad Luck?* New York: W.W. Norton, 1991. Bookshelves sag under the weight of volumes outlining theories of mass extinction due to comets, meteorites, asteroids and the like. This is one of the better ones.

Reif, F. *Fundamentals of Statistical and Thermal Physics*. New York: McGraw-Hill, 1965.

Remo, J., editor. *Near-Earth Objects: The United Nations International Conference*, volume 822, 1997.

Shannon, Claude E. *The Mathematical Theory of Communication*. Universtity of Illinois Press, 1949.

Tainter, J. *The Collapse of Complex Societies*. Cambridge, United Kingdom: Cambridge University Press, 1988.

"Waiter, there's a mountain in my soup," 2007. www.exitmundi.nl/comets.htm.

Warshofsky, F. *Doomsday*. New York: Readers Digest Press, 1977. Geological controversies involving close encounters with planetary bodies, tectonic shifts in the earth's crust, the age of the Earth, the coming and going of ice ages and the like have always been a puzzle for scientists, as well as a source of huge controversy. Along with *Great Geological Controversies*, this volume outlines some of these debates.

2
DRIVERS OF CHANGE

2.1
TRENDS AND TRANSITIONS

At a random moment in time, the generic behavior of any social system is to be in a trending pattern. In other words, if you ask how will "things" (e.g., the GDP of an economy, the financial market averages, the political climate) look tomorrow, the answer is that they will be just a bit better or a bit worse than today, depending on whether the trend at the moment is moving up or down. This is a large part of what makes trend-following so appealing: it's easy and it's almost always right—except when it isn't! Those moments when it isn't are rare (infinitesimally small in the set of all time points, actually) and the event is usually surprising within the context of the situation in which the question about the future arises. These special moments when the current trend is rolling over from one trend to another are the critical points of the process. And if that rolling over involves great social damage in terms of lives lost, dollars spent, and/or existential angst, we call the transition from the current trend to the new one an X-event. In the natural sciences, especially physics, such a transition is often associated with a "flip" from one qualitatively different type of structure or form of behavior to another, as with the phase transition from water to ice or to steam.

A central question arising from the above scenario is whether we can we predict where the critical points will occur. In situations where you have a large database of past observations about the process and/or a dynamical model that you believe in for the system's behavior, then you can sometimes use tools of probability and statistics and/or dynamical system theory to identify these points with a modicum of precision. This is often the case in the natural sciences, but it's almost never the case in the social domain. In the human sphere, we generally have too little data and/or no believable model, at least no data or model for the kinds of "shocks" that can send humankind back to a preindustrial way of life. In short, we are generally dealing with "unknown unknowns."

In this X-events regime, it's unlikely that we'll ever be able to predict the location of the critical points with the same sort of accuracy and reliability that we're accustomed to in the natural sciences. As we noted in the last chapter, this is due to the fact that events, X- or otherwise, are always a combination of context, which determines the space of possible events, and a random trigger that picks a particular event out of that spectrum of possibilities as the one that's actually realized. In other words, at any given time the context, which is always dynamically shifting, admits a variety of possible events that might be realized. The one event that is in fact actually observed/experienced at the next time moment is determined by a random "shove" that sends the system into one "attractor" from the set of all possible events the context admits. Since by its very nature a random trigger has no pattern, it cannot be forecast. Hence, the specific event that turns up cannot be forecast either. Note that this does not mean that every possibility is equally likely. It simply means that while some possible events are more likely to be seen than others, the random factor can step in to give rise to a realized event that is a priori unlikely, thus surprising.

The problem with speaking here about "likelihoods" is that this terminology has built into it the assumption that there is some probability distribution available for evaluating the relative likelihood of the occurrence of the possible events. But when it comes to the X-events regime, where there are neither data nor models, this assumption simply falls apart. There may indeed exist such a probability distribution. But if so, it resides in some platonic universe beyond space and time, not in the universe we actually inhabit. So what to do? How do we characterize and measure risk in an environment in which probability theory, statistics, and dynamical system theory cannot be effectively employed?

We have shown earlier that a way out of this no-data quandary is to focus on the drivers of context change—the change in landscape. The argument presented earlier is that the two principal drivers are the social mood, which drives the spectrum of possible events that might ensue from the current situation, and the complexity gap between interacting systems (plus the random trigger) that picks out the event that is actually realized from the possibilities. A quantum theorist would recognize this set up immediately: the social mood is analogous to the Schrödinger wave function, while the complexity gap plays the role of the agent/observer that collapses the wave function into a single point, the event actually measured/observed.

The social mood and complexity gap are what we might term "context-free" drivers of context and change, since they are not dependent on the particular type of event we're considering or even the specific time and place where the current trend is unfolding. They exist independent of these factors. On the other hand, we have "context-dependent" factors that also act to impact what events actually occur. Some authors term such factors "drivers" as well, although for our purposes they play a role as second-level drivers that serve more as drivers of the context-free drivers that we are focusing on. A very good example of this phenomenon was presented by noted Harvard historian Niall Ferguson in an article on turning points in history published in the *New York Times* at the end of 2012. It's worth briefly summarizing Ferguson's argument in order to show the distinction between the two types of drivers, context-free social mood/complexity gap, and context-dependent drivers of those drivers.

2.1.1
FERGUSON'S DRIVERS OF HISTORICAL CHANGE

Ferguson begins with the metaphor that history is like an oil tanker: it doesn't turn on a dime. He then says that what does change suddenly on an oil tanker is the emotions of the crew (cf. social mood!). "Nine hundred ninety-nine days out of a thousand the crew obeys their orders and does their work. But very occasionally there is a drama. The men mutiny and the captain is clapped into irons. Or pirates board the ship. Such events are what historians love to study and call 'revolutions.' Still the ship plows onward." So a system theorist's critical point is an historian's revolution.

In his account, Ferguson goes on to note what he calls six slow-acting drivers of historical change. They are:

1. Technological innovation;
2. The spread of ideas and institutions;
3. The tendency of even good political systems to degenerate;
4. Demographics;
5. Supplies of essential commodities;
6. Climate change.

What almost jumps off the page when reading this list is that every single item on the list is actually an event, or more generally, a constellation of events taking place over an extended period of time. So unlike the drivers of social mood and complexity gaps, which are rather abstract and do not pertain to any specific event or cluster of events, Ferguson's list of drivers is more like a list of slowly-unfolding events. Under that interpretation, we could think of them as events driven by mood and complexity. In other words, a consequence of the deeper drivers, not the cause. Of course, in Ferguson's story, his drivers are indeed the cause of historical change; in our setting, they are the effect of drivers at a deeper level, not causes at all.

The point of this observation is that social mood and complexity gaps are always present and do not depend on context, at all. On the other hand, the type of drivers Ferguson lists come and go, and his list would almost surely be different if it had been prepared, say, a hundred or five hundred years ago. It's in this sense that we call them context-dependent drivers, not context-free. The take-home lesson from this observation is that time scales matter. A slowly-unfolding event can be seen as an event at one timescale, but as a driver of an event taking place on a shorter timescale.

To return to Ferguson's list, all the events on that list are ultimately driven by social mood and complexity gaps simply because those two drivers are always present. On the other hand, a long-timescale event like technological innovation can indeed serve as a driver of the shorter-timescale phenomenon of, say, the emergence—and the end—of globalization.

More worrying is the third item on the list, the tendency of political systems to degenerate. Almost all studies of institutional quality show that in the majority of Western countries there has been a serious decline in the rule of law. And not just the rule of law, but in trust in institutions in general. According to Ferguson, this slow flow of events is driving much of the slowdown in economic growth and productivity in Western countries since the turn of the millennium.

We'll return to this theme of drivers of historical change, both context-free and contextdependent, in a later section, where examples will be given in more detail of both types. But beforehand, let's first have a look at the five stages of the collapse of human systems identified by Russian emigre, engineer, and social analyst Yuri Orlov. In particular, we want to explore how a combination of social mood and complexity overload give rise to these stages.

2.2
FIVE STAGES OF COLLAPSE

In her 1969 book *On Death and Dying*, psychiatrist Elisabeth Kubler-Ross identified five stages of grief that constitute the process of coming to terms with death for terminally ill patients and their family. These five stages begin with denial, where the patient imagines a false reality in which the impending death is absent. Once the patient recognizes that denial will not make the situation disappear, the second stage of anger appears, in which people either get angry with themselves or with those close to them. They strike out with angry statements, such as "It's not fair," "Why is this happening to me?" and so forth. After venting their anger, the patients enter a bargaining stage, where the individual hopes to make a deal for a bit longer life with some higher power. For instance, the patient may say I'll reform my life, reconcile with my family, give my worldly belongings for a few more years of life. When this stage runs its course, depression sets in. Here the patient shifts into a mode of thinking that involves things losing any meaning. Basically, they say, "I'm going to die soon, so why care about anything?" Finally, the individual comes to acceptance of their impending death, and begins thinking how to use the time remaining to them to prepare themselves and their loved ones for their mortality.

In around 2008, Yuri Orlov noted that many commentators were using the Kubler-Ross stages of grief as a way of structuring the process of humanity's "death" through global ecological mismanagement. Orlov noted that the collapse of societies also seemed to take place in five collapse states, each of which involves a loss of faith in some taken-for-granted social structure that humans rely upon for the functioning of everyday life. James Quinn described Orlov's five stages in the following way:

Stage 1: Financial Collapse Faith in "business as usual" is lost. The future is no longer assumed to resemble the past in any way that *allows risk to be assessed* and financial assets to be guaranteed. Financial institutions become insolvent; savings are wiped out and access to capital is lost.

Stage 2: Commercial Collapse Faith that "the market shall provide" is lost. Money is devalued and/or becomes scarce, commodities are *hoarded*, import and retail *chains break down* and widespread shortages of survival necessities become the norm.

Stage 3: Political Collapse Faith that "the government will take care of you" is lost. As official attempts to mitigate widespread loss of access to commercial sources of survival necessities fail to make a difference, the political establishment *loses legitimacy* and relevance.

Stage 4: Social Collapse Faith that "your people will take care of you" is lost, as social institutions, be they charities or other groups that rush to fill the power vacuum, run out of resources or fail through *internal conflict*.

Stage 5: Cultural Collapse Faith in the goodness of humanity is lost. People lose their capacity for "kindness, generosity, consideration, affection, honesty, hospitality, compassion, charity." *Families disband and compete* as individuals struggle for scarce resources. The new motto becomes, "May you die today so that I can die tomorrow."

As Quinn further notes, these stages do not follow in lock-step, one immediately after the other. They are overlapping, so that elements of one stage are still unfolding as the next stage begins. For instance, the first three stages are already apparent in the United States today. The initial stage exploded on to the world stage in fall 2008 and is still unfolding as the global financial system continues to melt down. Once the financial collapse gets into full swing, commercial collapse will soon follow since ready and reliable credit is an essential element in keeping the supply chain of goods flowing from the manufacturing regions in Asia to the shelves of Wal-Mart and The Gap. We are also now seeing bits and pieces of the stage of political collapse making itself felt, as the legitimacy of government and its leaders is increasingly discredited by the voting public as each day goes by.

We draw attention to the italicized passages in the descriptions of the five stages above. Everyday words like "risk assessment," "hoarding," "breakdown," "legitimacy," "internal conflicts," "disbanding," and "competition" are precisely the descriptors that one would associate with the types of events we can expect to see when the overall social mood is strongly negative and/or the complexity gaps in social infrastructures are stretched to their breaking point. So for a critical observer of today's social, political, financial, and cultural structures, these words come easily off the tongue. Negative social mood, essentially fear of the future, is rampant worldwide. And the concomitant stretching of the infrastructures of everyday life beyond sustainable levels is equally evident.

So the general relationship between Orlov's five stages of collapse and the context-free drivers of social mood and complexity overload is rather clear. But what about the context-dependent drivers outlined by Ferguson? For example, which of the five stages of collapse are driven by the spread of ideas and institutions? Which are most impacted by changing demographics? And which can be laid at the doorstep of climate change?

As we described them above, each of Orlov's five stages of collapse involves a loss of faith in something. But the only item on Ferguson's list that relates to a loss of faith is the second one, the degeneration of even good political systems. This is essentially the same as Orlov's third-stage collapse of the political system. But if we regard this as a driver, the cause of something, not a consequence, then we can ask what a political collapse causes. Basically, it drives the stage 4 social collapse.

One might argue that from a Western perspective an external driver like technological innovation is analogous to a "collapse" of certain parts of the Western commercial sector, perhaps computing or even more directly high-tech manufacturing. The same argument might be used to link Ferguson's spread of ideas and institutions to a collapse of Western domination in math and science by young people. But this analogy is a weak one, at best. So if our concern rests with understanding the reasons societies collapse, the context-free drivers are clear, while the context-dependent drivers give insight into the particular collapse of the Western world as we're experiencing it today. When the Eastern world that's now reemerging as the dominant global social structure begins its own collapse a century or two from now, it remains to be seen whether the particular context-dependent drivers identified by Ferguson will still be the relevant drivers for that upcoming collapse. In his book *Collapse*, Jared Diamond argues that some of those same elements play a role in almost every societal collapse. A driver like climate change appears on both Diamond's and Ferguson's lists. But, then, a context-free driver like complexity overload also appears on both our list and Diamond's—but not on Ferguson's. On balance, it appears that we can say that both types of drivers enter into the collapse of every civilization. But the context-dependent list will likely be different in each case, while the context-free drivers are universal across both space and time.

Our goal in this chapter is to underscore the way social mood and complexity overload/mismatch enter into the dynamics of not only civilizations, but other long-term social processes in the economic and geopolitical arenas. We now do that by way of several mini-chapters focusing on the processes of globalization, finance, global population change, and the degeneration of political systems.

2.3
MOOD AND COMPLEXITY AS LEADING DRIVERS

Globalization: Examining the way in which people, money, goods, and everything else makes its way around the world, we see the specter of complexity hanging like a shroud over every step of the process. The process of globalization has given corporations a vast array of procedures (degrees of freedom) for the development of new products, for the manufacture of existing products, for the marketing of wares by picking and choosing where and when these functions are carried out. Thus, in a world with no national boundaries or constraints, trans-national corporations command a huge level of complexity. On the other hand, the system composed of the global population, at-large as represented by national governments, has given up most of whatever freedom it had to regulate what can and cannot cross borders without having to pay. In short, nations have voluntarily reduced their complexity in the business realm to a minimal level. As always, as that complexity gap between business and government widened so did the social stress of growing unemployment in Western countries, as all but the high-skill jobs moved to Asia. We are seeing the end result of this mismatch in these very days, as the US tries desperately to address the problems of a jobless recovery from the financial crash of 2007, while Europe struggles to deal with an even more seri-ous financial crisis, not to mention the social disruption emerging from its own dangerously high levels of unemployment, particularly in the southern countries of the European Union like Greece, Italy, Spain, and Portugal.

As the ongoing tension between the United States and China dramati-cally illustrates, net exporters like China must accept an appreciation in the value of their currencies. On the other hand, net importers like the US have to devalue. Of course, the exporting countries strenuously resist taking this step, as the revaluation process will bring the flow of goods and money into balance—precisely what the exporters do not want. Initially, this obvious fact gets played out in diplomatic circles. But if the diplomats don't get the job done within some acceptable period of time, financial markets will step in to do it for them. The result of that leveling of the playing field will not be pretty. In fact, this is another good example of a complexity mismatch that is very likely to be resolved by an X-event, namely, a massive devaluation of the US dollar, protectionist legislation, and a host of other actions that will only accelerate the process of the world economy falling into a deep deflationary depression. Here's an example illustrating this basic problem of globalization.

The formation of the EU can certainly be seen as a "joining, globalizing, coming together" type of event. And indeed that event, the 1957 Treaty of Rome, took place at a time of increasingly strong feelings on the part of Euro-pean governments that the time had come to unite into a single political body. Despite some setbacks in getting the EU Constitution approved in 2005–2008, the history of the EU has been pretty much onward and upward—until now. In recent years, forces of "separation" and "localization" have begun to dominate, showing up in events ranging from the unwillingness of prosperous states in the EU to prop-up the finances of the weaker members on to talk of the re-imposition of border controls by some countries so as to stem the flow of unwanted economic refugees from the Balkans, Turkey, and elsewhere.

When organizations, especially states or an empire, encounter problems, the time-honored way to solve them is to add another layer of complexity onto the organization. Basically, this solution is the well-known process of "bureaucratic creep," as we outlined in the opening chapter. As problems accumulate, the bloat of bureaucracy increases to the point where the entire resources of the organization are consumed in just maintaining its existing structure. When the next problem comes along, the organization falls off the "complexity cliff" and simply collapses. Many times this complexity cliff shows up when two (or more) systems are in interaction. The gap in complexity between them becomes too big to sustain and an X-event emerges to close it. We saw this process earlier in the collapse of the repressive regimes in Tunisia and Egypt, both of which were facilitated by a rapid upgrading of the complexity of the lower-complexity system, the citizenry of each country, via social networking and modern communication channels. The governments could neither suppress this complexity buildup, nor keep up with it themselves. The end result was, of course, the X-event of rapid, violent regime change.

To illustrate this principle in the context of the EU, think of the Eurozone countries as a system in interaction with the rest of the global economy. If the countries were not in the Eurozone, they would have many options at their disposal to address changing economic times. They could, for instance, manage the supply of their own currencies, raise or lower interest rates, impose trade tariffs, and the like. In short, they would have a high level of complexity arising from the many different types of actions available to be taken.

Instead, though, the Eurozone members are severely constrained since no country can act unilaterally but must act in unison as per the dictates of the European Central Bank (ECB). So a complexity gap arises between a high-complexity system (the non-EU world) and a low-complexity one (the Eurozone states). Loans from the wealthier Eurozone countries to the indebted ones, along with other efforts by the ECB to bridge this complexity gap will almost surely end up falling into the category of "throwing good money after bad." Ultimately, this will lead to human nature's default solution for such problems, which in this case will be the extreme event of a collapse of the Euro, and very possibly the EU itself. Here it is no pun to call it a "default" solution.

It's clear from the foregoing discussion how the notion of a complexity gap continues to drive the world economic system from one of globalization to that of localization. As for our second primary driver, social mood, the chart in Figure 2.1 below shows the Dow Jones Industrial Average from 1974–2002. Marked on the chart are prominent events in the unfolding globalization process as it took off during this period. Note how events contributing to the overall process of expansion and globalizing tended to occur during periods of especially positive social mood, while just the opposite types of events took place when the mood turned negative. The entire process seemed to have flattened out around the year 2000, as seen in the chart. Figure 2.2 shows how the DJIA continued from 2000 to 2014.

So here we see how the question marks in Figure 2.1 were filled in. As an exercise, the reader might like to identify important events in this time interval and place them onto the chart.

Now let's turn our eye from global economic changes to the long-term phenomenon of the dynamics of global population growth and decline. Here we will also see how our two main drivers, complexity overload and social mood, impact this process.

World Population Dynamics: Driven by the fact that global population increased by nearly 140 percent during the second-half of the twentieth century, trend-following seers of the future envision population levels soaring onward and upward for the next 50–100 years at a similar, although not necessarily identical, rate. Conventional wisdom has it that this population growth will be concentrated in Africa and Asia, as shown in Figure 2.3 from the UN Population Division. Here we see the population (measured in millions) at three points in time. The picture that emerges from this projection is one of population decline in Europe, along with fairly moderate growth in Latin America and North America. The action, though, resides in Asia and especially Africa where growth rate exceeds 100 percent in Africa and over 40 percent in Asia. The overall picture here is clear: a global population increase of about 2 billion people, almost all of it concentrated in Africa and Asia.

The implications of this conventional wisdom has it that extrapolation of the above population picture suggests a world of 2050 having a dramatically increased focus on financial services for pensions and healthcare services and facilities for the aged world, accompanied by major shifts in biotechnology and pharmaceuticals in the developed world.

These sorts of projections of differential population changes in the East and the West have been well-chronicled (see Notes and References), so don't bear repeating here.

Instead, let's look at an X-event whose occurrence would cast serious doubt upon parts of the standard upward, if not onward, picture.

To begin this, consider Figure 2.4 showing the fifty-year percentage change in total global population. This chart should be read as follows: Pick a year, say 2000, and read the percentage change from the chart, which for the year 2000 is 140 percent. This means that in the half century preceding the chosen year, global population increased by 140 percent, which happens to be the largest half-century change on the entire chart. What's immensely revealing about this figure is that in the year 2050 global population will increase only about 20 percent from its level in 2000 (a nominal increase of around 1.4 billion), and should actually begin to decline in about 2070 from its level in 2020. So the enormous increase seen in the second half of the twentieth century was not the beginning of a trend, but rather an anomaly, and in the second part of this century population will actually start falling dramatically.

Figure 2.1 The Dow Jones Industrial Average, 1974–2002 with Globalization Events

It's well worth asking the question: why can we expect a worldwide population decline in the second part of this century, a decline at a rate even faster than the rise during the last century? The answer is multifold, of course. But the primary driving factor is decreased fertility rates. This phenomenon has already been on offer in most of the developed world for at least the past couple of decades or more, most prominently in the countries of Western Europe. Prime examples include Italy and Germany at 1.4 children per woman, Holland's rate of 1.8 and a rate of 1.9 in the UK, all well below the replacement level of 2.1. Figure 2.5 shows the global situation, along with the fact that the rapid decline of fertility is not something confined to developed countries, but is now being seen in many Muslim countries around the world as well, with the fertility decline in Iran, Turkey, and Pakistan even exceeding the global rate. Many reasons have been advanced for this fertility decline, ranging from family planning policies in China and India to the widespread availability of contraceptives and even to partnership

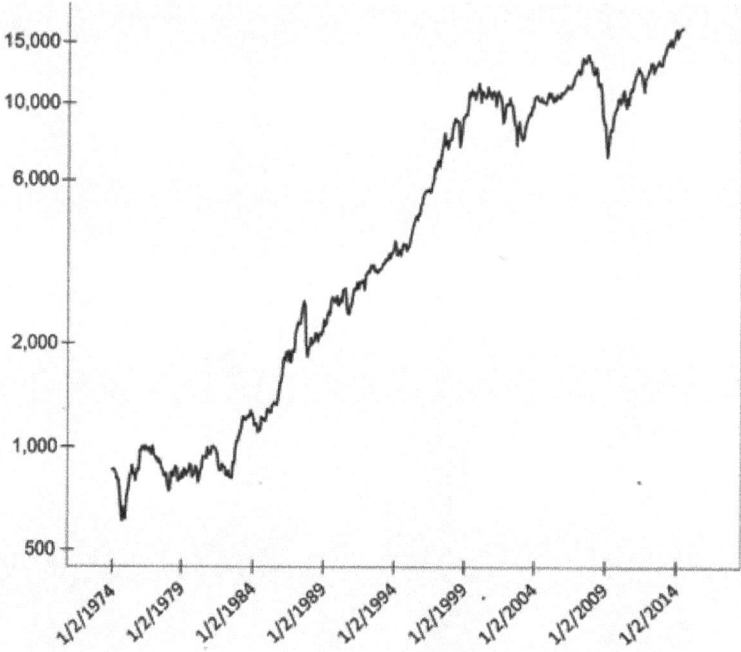

Figure 2.2 The Dow Jones Industrial Average, 1974–2014

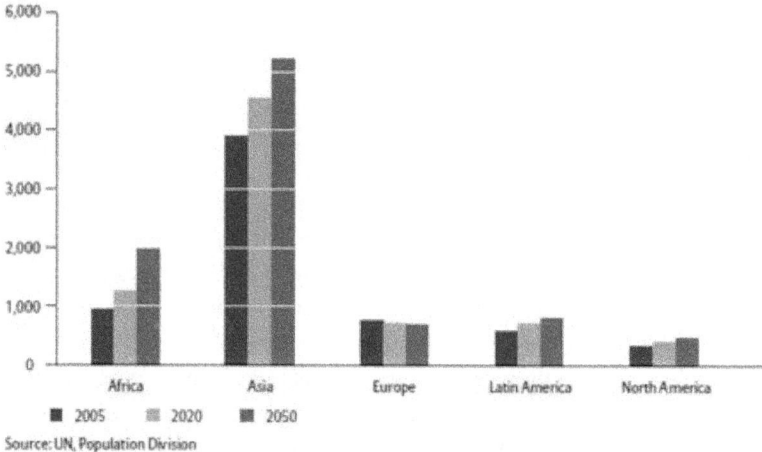

Figure 2.3 Population in millions by continent for three times.

instability. No doubt all these things make their contribution. But by far the most convincing explanation is the dramatic increase in literacy around the world.

On the surface, one would think that it's totally uncontroversial that literacy is a good thing. Knowing how to read and write is an essential step in moving upward in an increasingly knowledge-based world. But as is often the case

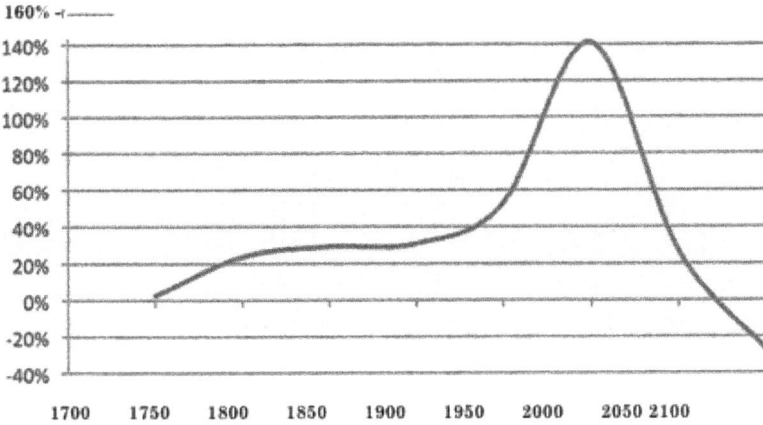

Figure 2.4

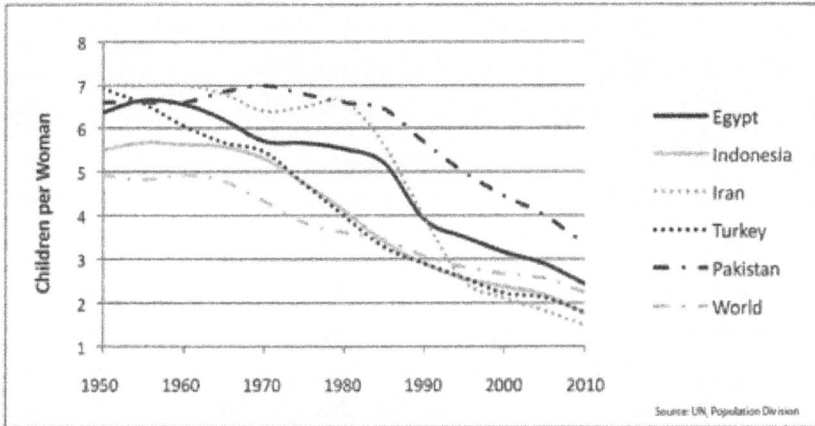

Figure 2.5

in life, you have to be careful about what you ask for since you might actually get it! And in this case seeking an educated, literate population has much more profound consequences than one might initially imagine, consequences that are not always for the better.

It's often argued that another driver of reduced fertility is urbanization, the massive shift of population from the countryside to urban megalopolises like Tokyo, Mexico City, Seoul, and Sao Paulo. Equally likely, if not more so, is that increased literacy is a principal driver of not only reduced fertility but also of urbanization. The line of reasoning is as follows: literacy in agrarian communities widens the horizons of those who are educated, not to mention widening the gap between the educated and those who are not. The newly opened lifestyle possibilities opened up by education, in particular, through reading, can and does motivate the newly literate to create a future for themselves different from their parents and grandparents, one residing outside the scope of farming and a traditional rural life. To realize this vision, a move to an urban area with its broad spectrum of alternative lives and lifestyles is the obvious next step. This urge for a change in lifestyle is especially true for women, who once they can read and write begin to envision a life that does not involve having half a dozen children (or more!), while at the same time managing a household in the countryside.

Here we see a textbook example of a complexity gap driving the landscape of events to position the global population dynamic on a sharp mountain peak, ripe for being pushed over the edge by an X-event. On the one side, we have the traditional role of women in low-income, undeveloped societies, a role involving very few degrees of freedom for women who essentially followed the pattern of their mothers, grandmothers, and great-grandmothers. That role was to tend to their husband, the house, and family and forget about any other kind of life. That low-complexity system has come into conflict with the modern world, especially the communication infrastructure, which allows women everywhere to envision previously unheard of possibilities for their lives. This fact, coupled with dramatically increased educational opportunities for women in Third World countries, has created a complexity gap that is reaching the breaking point. In a few countries, like Iran, this gap has been recognized by political leaders. But mostly the politicians have tried to preserve the status quo, which as we now know is a futile effort and will assuredly lead to the undoing of the old way of doing things. This fact has also contributed mightily to the mass migration from the countryside to cities where opportunities for women are manifold.

Compelling evidence for the strong negative correlation between fertility rates and literacy is shown in Figure 2.6, which shows these two quantities for almost all the countries in the world, together with the correlation line displaying a strongly negative slope. This picture opens up the issue of the implications of the huge decline in global fertility as mass education takes hold in high-population regions in Africa and Asia.

The demographic story emerging from these pictures is not pretty. Especially grim are the figures for the population of currently large nations that are due to get smaller, a lot smaller, before the end of the current century. Assuming that fertility rates do not change from their current levels, by the end of this century the economically active segment of the population (those between 15 and 59 years of age) will shrink by 40 percent in Western Europe and by about two-thirds in Eastern Europe and East Asia. At the same time, the working-age population in the United States will grow by about 25 percent. To give some perspective to these figures, the total population of the low-fertility countries like Germany and Italy will fall by 40–60 percent. Thus, today's 80-million strong Germany will shrink to a country of fewer than 40 million people by

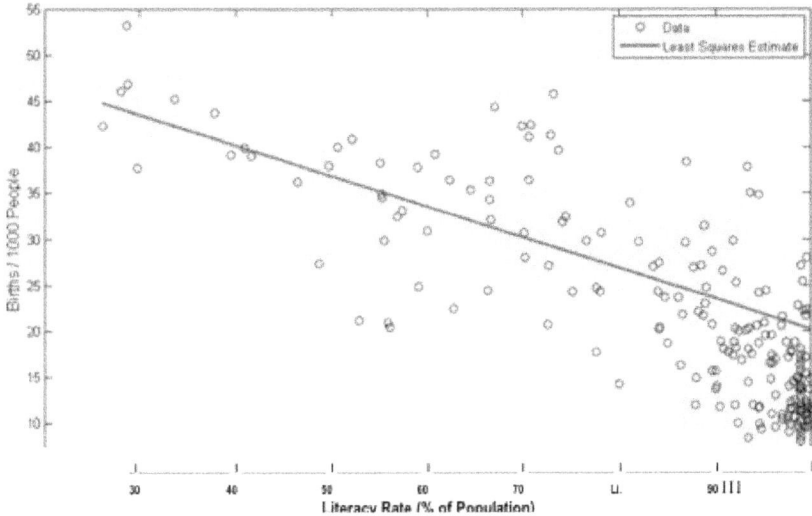

Figure 2.6

the year 2100. In Japan the situation is even worse. There we can expect to see half the total population being 65 or older by the middle of this century, not the end.

The ongoing population collapse across virtually all the industrialized world described by these facts and figures will disrupt the entire global economy and threaten political stability everywhere. Currently, countries like Russia are in a demographic death spiral, and as aging and population decline becomes progressively more pronounced, economies and tax revenues will implode across Europe and East Asia. At the same time, we will have the problems of pensions and healthcare described earlier in the conventional scenario. Only the United States seems in a position to weather this particular storm, as it will still have enough workers to support the elderly.

Even more remarkable than what's happening demographically in the developed countries of Europe and East Asia is the rapid rate at which the Muslim countries are nipping at their demographic heels. In the last 50 years, fertility in the Muslim world has dropped at a rate more than double that of the world at large. Muslims in the Arab world, Iran, Turkey, Malaysia, and South Asia are all experiencing this decline, with Iran's fertility having fallen by almost six children per woman as seen in the chart shown above.

It's also a point worthy of note that for the most part the Muslim world has no public pension or healthcare programs. The elderly rely upon their children to take care of them instead. Today, most Muslims have several working-age children who serve this role. By 2050, most aged Muslims will have only one or two children, echoing a situation already pressing upon Europe. Over the next half century, the average age in Europe will increase only from 40 years to about 46; in the Muslim world, the average age today is in the early 20s.

But it will increase to 40 or more by 2050, and by 2070 these countries will have a higher fraction of aged dependents than Western Europe. So the relative economic burden will be far heavier in the aging Muslim countries than almost anywhere else in the world. This fact leads to a very dark aspect of the aging problem that may eclipse the serious, but rather modest, stress induced in Western societies as outlined in the conventional wisdom scenario stated at the beginning of this story.

On September 10, 2010, Iranian president Ahmadinejad declared in a meeting in Alborz province, "Two children is a formula for the extinction of a nation, not the survival of a nation . . . Negative population growth will cause the extinction of our identity and culture . . . To want to consume more than having children is an act of genocide." These sentiments echoed remarks made in May 2010 by Turkish Prime Minister Tayyip Erdogan, who stated, "If we continue the existing trend, 2038 will mark disaster for us." And the "disaster" he envisioned was nothing less than the destruction of Turkey and the death of Turkish culture.

In his eye-opening book *How Civilizations Die*, political commentator and scholar David P. Goldman describes a not unlikely outcome of the demographic scenario just chronicled for Iran and Turkey. There Goldman states

> Mahmoud Ahmadinejad vocalizes a desperate sense of urgency: Iran was the first country to throw out a Western-oriented, secular government and replace it with an Islamist theocracy. On its own terms, Iran's Islamist experiment has failed. The treatment is killing the patient. That makes Iran dangerous. Iran is a mortally wounded beast, but a beast still at the peak of its destructive power.
>
> Declining populations do not necessarily portend a peaceful outcome. On the contrary, in the short term they may well motivate aggressive behavior, provoked by a belief that the opportunity to fight may never return.

In other words, what do such societies have to lose by taking enormous risks and engaging in ultra-aggressive behavior, even up to and including unleashing a nuclear holocaust? After all, such an action would be simply one last desperate roll of the dice prior to total extinction. This is what the world of the future should fear about the demographic time bombs ticking in the world today, not merely an excess of aged dependents requiring pensions and health care. Such issues may well be seen as inconsequential side shows to what is already brewing in the Islamist world.

On this unhappy note we leave consideration of population decline as an X-event driven by complexity mismatches and the implications of that decline for reshaping the world and consider our final long-timescale X-event, one that underlies a large number of the social ills facing societies today. This is the problem of growing distrust in institutions—governments, corporations, and even our neighbors.

Loss of Trust in Institutions: Earlier, we saw that historian Niall Ferguson lists six external drivers of historical change. The one Ferguson claims that is almost always overlooked by political scientists is what he describes as "the tendency of even good political systems to degenerate." The argument is that as a successful political system ages, it acquires an ever-increasing number of special interests lobbying for a bigger share of the society's resources. This is an example of the process of "complexity overload." The unrelenting pursuit of these special interests leads to an erosion of civic virtue and the ultimate demise of the once-successful but now eroded political system. Ferguson discusses this process at great lengths in his volume *The Great Degeneration*, so there is no need to repeat those arguments here, other than to note Ferguson's claim that the degeneration of the political order helps explain the slowdown in growth and productivity we have witnessed in the Western world over the past decade.

Another observer of this phenomenon of political degeneration is Richard Edelman, president of the world's largest independent public relations firm. He notes, "From the sovereign debt crisis in Europe, to the government's response to the earthquake in Japan, from the high-speed rail crash in China, to the debt ceiling fight in Washington, people around the world are losing faith in their governments." Figure 2.7 taken from the 2012 report by Edelman's firm on trust in governments and institutions makes this point graphically clear. A question that immediately arises from the growing public mistrust of governments in particular and institutions in general is how will angry citizens translate their anger into action?

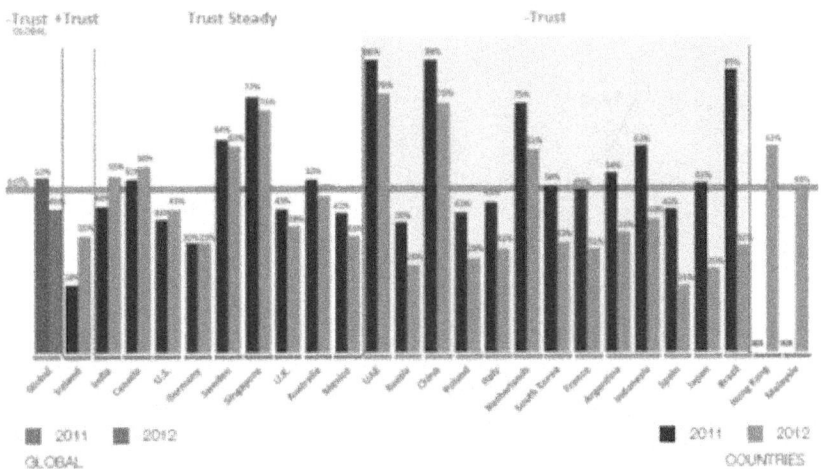

Figure 2.7

One answer to this question was offered by the late economist Albert O. Hirschman. While at Harvard in 1970, Hirschman wrote about how people respond to the erosion of institutions ranging from firms to states. His analysis showed that people choose one of two options: exit or complain. In other words, either abandon the institution or try to change it. Put another way, quit your job or speak to your boss.

In his seminal paper on this dichotomy, Hirschman argued that in earlier times in the US people voted with their feet and exited, since there was always more room to leave the existing disorder behind. This general sentiment was expressed by Horace Greeley in 1865 with the famous statement, "Go West, young man, go West and grow up with the country." But in today's world, there is no "West." So the exit option is no longer available, especially if you believe you already live in the best country on earth.

If you believe in the exit option, the alternative is not to reform government, but to get rid of it. On both sides of the Atlantic this has taken the form of the creation of competing, private-sector alternatives to services previously the prerogative of government. Witness the emergence of private schools, private prisons, and private health coverage, as a reaction to disenchantment with the socialist state, especially in Western Europe.

An even more ominous picture of the growing mistrust of government is given by a survey done by the Pew Research Center in the US, Figure 2.8, that aims to document public attitudes toward the US government from 1958 to the present. The survey accounts for people who say they trust the government in Washington, DC either "just about always" or "most of the time."

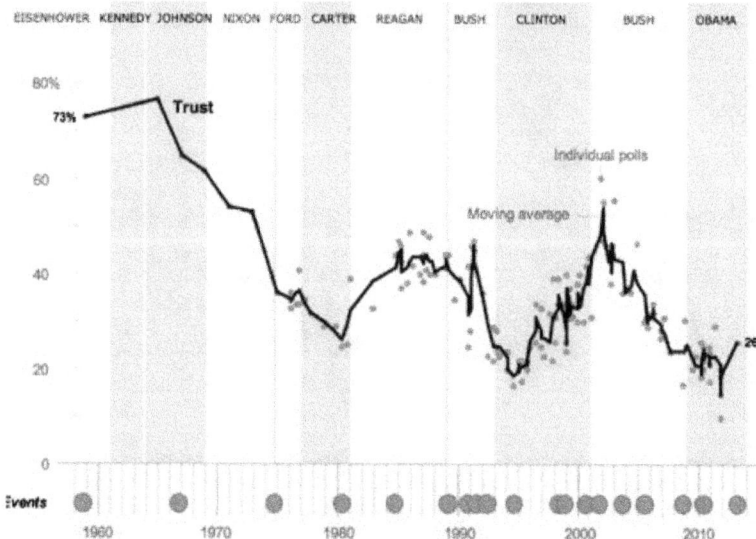

Figure 2.8

Historically, the survey shows that public mistrust in government was associated with specific events: the Watergate investigation in the 1970s and the House Banking scandal in the early 1990s both being good illustrations of this phenomena. But today's disenchantment with the government is difficult to trace to any specific event. Rather, what seems to be happening is a steady and growing belief that politicians in Washington simply cannot be trusted.

If this is really a political death of a thousand cuts with no specific events to blame, then one must conclude that there is no clear-cut cure for the malady that ails the government. It may well be that we are simply in an age when trust in institutions will never again approach the levels it reached in the past.

But this conventional wisdom of a creeping dissatisfaction of the body politic regarding trust in government and institutions is a rather benign implication. Let's look at others that may well turn out to be much worse.

The general collapse of trust noted above for government is even worse when it comes to other institutions. For example, Edelman's 2013 survey shows that 50 percent of the respondents trusted business firms to generally do what is right. But only 18 percent trusted business leaders to tell the truth—a gap of 32 percent between the institution itself and those leading the institution. As Edelman expressed it, leaders' truthfulness was "pretty pathetic." So what does this "truth gap" between institutions and their leaders imply? It should come as no surprise to see that people are now placing their trust in nongovernment, non-business institutions. Trust now moves to experts, such as academics or a peer like a friend on Facebook. So the leadership crisis at the institutional level gives rise to people developing a very different view than in the past about who they take seriously and turn to for facts rather than platitudes.

To illustrate this shift, Edelman's survey showed that among the informed public of university-educated, higher income people, 69 percent saw an academic or an acknowledged expert as being a credible source of information. Similarly, 61 percent viewed "someone like themselves" as a reliable source. By way of

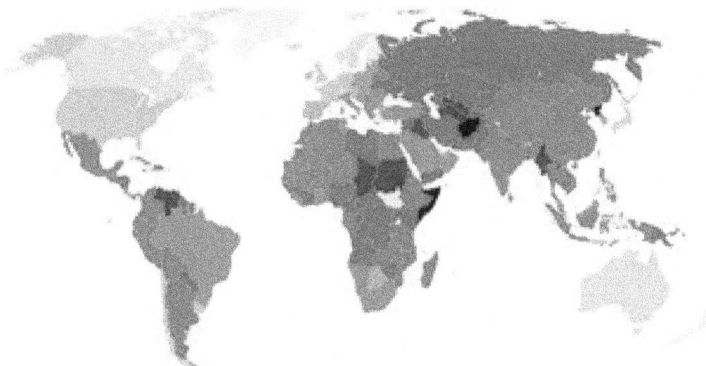

Figure 2.9 World Corruption. The darker shades represent high corruption. The lighter shades represent lower levels of corruption."

contrast, only 43 percent of those in the informed public regarded a corporate CEO as credible. More ominously, this shift in confidence from traditional leaders in government and industry has also given rise to a worldwide belief of growing corruption on the part of business and government leaders. Figure 2.9 shows a global map of corruption from the organization Transparency International.

The picture emerging from these stories and graphics suggests an ever-increasing slide into the kind of stress (complexity gaps) between citizens and their leaders in government and industry that often portends major social disruptions (think of the so-called Arab Spring uprisings as an example). The world-wide declining social mood also enters into this story. In general, the increasingly negative mood suggests collective events that are for the most part characterized by labels such as "separating," "localizing," and "rejecting." Of course, public distrust of institutions in general fits right into this picture. People are indeed rejecting politicians, creating protest groups targeting corporations (separating), and turning away from the overall globalization phenomenon as we described earlier. The consequences of a growing lack of trust in society would make the conventional picture of slowdowns in growth and productivity look positively attractive by way of comparison.

2.4
DISCUSSION QUESTIONS: COMPLEXITY MISMATCH AND MOOD

Observe constantly that all things take place by change, and accustom thyself to consider that the nature of the Universe loves nothing so much as to change the things which are, and to make new things like them.

Marcus Aurelius, *Meditations*

2.4.1
WHY IS THE TREND "NORMAL" BEHAVIOR?

- At any given point in time, why are you more likely to be right if you forecast the continuation of a trend than a change?

- Social behavior is typically stochastic (i.e., exhibiting seemingly random fluctuations). How do we know when a change is large enough to say that trend has shifted?
- A common, first order model of stock prices is something called geometric Brownian motion. (Think of it loosely as exponential growth plus noise.) Brownian motion has the interesting property that it is infinitely jagged. Thus, in a sense, every point is a turning point. A typical price chart for a stock certainly looks jagged everywhere. Given that stock prices seem to jump around, how does one know how large a change indicates a fundamental shift in the market versus a temporary jump?

2.4.2
WHY IS IT DIFFICULT TO ASSIGN A PROBABILITY TO AN X-EVENT?

- Probability theory is a model of uncertainty. It is tempting to ask the question: what is a probability? But that really isn't a meaningful question. A better question is what kind of real phenomena can we model using probability? If we have no historical data regarding the past occurrence of an event or conditions have changed since we collected historical data regarding past occurrences, what basis would we have for parameterizing any probability model describing the event?
- How would we estimate the probability of an event that has never happened before (or at least we have no record of it happening before)? Is that even possible?
- There is a view of probability called subjective or Bayesian probability. In this view, probability does not model the objective frequency of occurrence. Rather it represents a person's degree of confidence in the truth of a statement or occurrence of an event. As such, each person may have a different subjective probability for the occurrence of a particular event. When there is little historical data to estimate the probability of an event, some risk analysts elicit subjective probability assessments from domain experts. What characteristics do you think an expert should have in order to provide reliable subjective probability estimates? If you were to elicit a subjective probability of a particular X-event, do you think an expert would perform any better than a non-expert?

2.4.3

IS SOCIAL MOOD AN AGGREGATION OF EVERYONE'S SUBJECTIVE PROBABILITY OF THE FUTURE?

- It has been noted in some situations that aggregations of collective assessments are more accurate than any individual assessment (the wisdom of crowds). For example, averaging the economic forecasts of multiple economists may be more accurate than relying on any single economist. Some have even argued for establishing futures markets to estimate probability of extreme events such as terrorist attacks. (When someone makes a bet on the occurrence of a future event, they are revealing their subjective probability that event will occur.) Do you think that using a futures market would result in better predictions of X-events than consulting with an expert?
- If we define the social mood as society's collective beliefs about the future, then is the social mood just a weighted aggregation of everyone's subjective probabilities about the future? Is everyone's assessment of probability weighted equally in the social mood or do some have a greater influence than others?
- Unequal influence is an argument in favor of using market indices as a metric for social mood. Those who have more to invest have a greater influence on the market index; consequently, they receive more weight in our aggregate metric for mood. Do you think that those with more resources to invest in the market have a greater influence on social mood? Do you think that those that have more resources to invest have a better understanding of the current social mood (i.e., other people's beliefs about the future)? Based on your answers to the previous questions, do you think that a market index is a good proxy metric for social mood?

2.4.4

HOW DOES HERDING AFFECT SOCIAL MOOD?

- In neoclassical economics, the economy is governed by the rational expectations hypothesis. In essence, people may make random errors in predicting the future, but their errors are not systematic.

Thus, we would expect an aggregate measure such as stock price to reflect the best possible estimate of the future earnings of a company. Do you think that the rational expectations hypothesis holds in the real market?

- A common theoretical model for a stock price movement is the lognormal probability distribution. A lognormal distribution is a thin-tailed distribution in that extreme price movements are relatively rare. The lognormal distribution is a member of the Gaussian or normal distribution family that are based on the central limit theorem. In short, the central limit theorem states that under a particular set of conditions, the sum of independent random variables converges to a normal distribution. In the case of stock prices, if we assume that the rational expectations hypothesis holds, we would expect the aggregation of everyone's independent investment decisions to converge to a member of the normal family of distributions (i.e., lognormal). However, the distribution of real stock prices are thick-tailed. In other words, extreme price movements are much more common than a lognormal distribution would suggest. This suggests that individual investment decisions are not independent of each other. How does this affect your assessment of the rational expectations hypothesis?

- Palmer and his colleagues at the Santa Fe Institute in Santa Fe, New Mexico developed a virtual stock market populated by virtual agents. Each of the agents could change its investment rules over time. They found that when agents could only update their investment rules slowly, then the market converged to the rational expectations hypothesis because the bad rules were weeded out over time. However, if the agents could update their investment rules quickly, then the virtual stock market exhibited bubbles and crashes just like the real stock market because bad rules could feed off each other. Do you see any parallels between this example and the behavior of social mood? What are the implications for the volatility of social mood as modern communications technology and social media increase interconnectivity and the rate at which people can share ideas, opinions, and data?

- When individuals make investment decisions based on the ideas and actions of others, independence is lost, and extreme price movements should be expected. In other words, bubbles and crashes are common and can be independent of a company's fundamentals. If peoples beliefs about the future are not independent (i.e., they are influenced by the beliefs and actions of others), then we should expect herding behavior. Bubbles and crashes in mood are normal. If we use the stock market as an analogy, we might expect these bubbles and crashes in mood to be independent of events in the real world. Do you believe that social mood can shift independently of a major, external trigger event?

- Psychologists have found that people assess subjective probabilities using heuristics (i.e., rules of thumb). One such heuristic is the availability heuristic, which assumes that the easier it is to bring an instance of the event to mind, the more likely it is. The availability heuristic works on the principle that events that occur frequently are more easily recalled than events that occur infrequently. The problem is that other factors besides frequency can affect the ease of recall. When the availability heuristic misfires on a large scale, an availability cascade can result. The media reports on a minor event that catches the attention of a portion of the public. This portion of the public becomes worried about the event. This of course creates even more concern on the part of the public. The feedback loop continues as the media exaggerates the story in the competition for ratings. Eventually, the public grows so concerned that they demand political action to address the issue. Thus, the feedback loop increases the perceived probability of the event far beyond what is justified. What role does the modern media play in the creation of mood bubbles and crashes? How does the heuristic basis of human estimation of probabilities affect fluctuations in social mood?

2.4.5
WHY ARE SHIFTS IN THE TREND A SURPRISE?

- If we view the social mood as the collective aggregation of society's beliefs about the future, then the most positive beliefs about the future occur at the point that the trend changes. This is true by definition. Thus, the change in trend must always be a surprise. Once again, we can use the stock market as analogy. If everyone thought that the stock market were about to rise, they would pay sky high prices for stock . . . causing the market to crash. Conversely, the crash must be a surprise, otherwise people would not have paid the prices they just paid. Thus, we would expect shifts in social mood to be a surprise to most. Given the previous discussions that bubbles and crashes can happen without significant external events to trigger them, does this reinforce the notion that shifts in social mood are a surprise?

- Even in a bubble market, the fact that the market is in a bubble may be widely recognized. Yet this does not cause an immediate crash. Why? Timescale is important. Just because someone thinks the bubble will pop eventually doesn't mean that he or she thinks it will pop today. If we return to the idea of using a stock market as a measure of peoples expectations of future performance, and extract a probability of future stock performance just prior to the crash, the prediction would be that the stock will continue to go up in the short term. How does this affect your opinion about using subjective probability to assess the probability of an X-event? What if we used a future market instead of a stock market so that people could make explicit bets on different time scales? Does this improve the situation or is there still an implicit bias? What does this mean about the predictability of X-event? Is it ever possible to assess a probability of an X-event or is it always truly a surprise?

2.4.6
SHIFTS IN SOCIAL MOOD ARE DIFFERENT IN GOING FROM OPTIMISTIC TO PESSIMISTIC THAN PESSIMISTIC TO OPTIMISTIC

- The logic of Discussion Question 2.4.5 is just as valid if the shift in social mood is from pessimistic to optimistic as it is if the mood shift is optimistic to pessimistic. Observations, however, indicate that there is usually asymmetry between optimism and pessimism. Optimism builds slowly, while pessimism occurs after an extreme event.
- Why is there a discrepancy?

2.5
DEMOGRAPHIC TRANSITION

Since all models are wrong the scientist cannot obtain a "correct" one by excessive elaboration. On the contrary following William of Occam he should seek an economical description of natural phenomena. Just as the ability to devise simple but evocative models is the signature of the great scientist so overelaboration and overparameterization is often the mark of mediocrity.

George E. P. Box

Death: You're an interesting young man. We'll meet again.
Young Boris: Don't bother.
Death: It's no bother.

Woody Allen, *Love and Death*

The purpose of this section is to illustrate an extreme event that involves the entire population of the planet and that is occurring as you read this. It will also illustrate how beliefs and mood may affect this event. This extreme event is known as the *demographic transition*. The demographic transition is a population trend from high birth and death rates to low birth and death rates with a simultaneous increase in population. Birth rates during the transition drop more slowly than death rates, which is the cause of the increased population size. The transition starts with a decline in mortality, which has been attributed to improved health and living conditions. While the earlier transitions of Western European countries took more than 100 years to complete, the transitions that are currently occurring seem to be proceeding at the much faster pace of a few decades. When compared with historical timescales of a few thousand years, this transition is almost instantaneous.

The characteristic time series of the demographic transition is illustrated in Figure 2.10. The event is triggered by a sudden drop in childhood death rates, which lowers the total death rate for the population. The surviving children grow and procreate leading to an increase in birth rate and population. The total fertility rate, in this case the number of children per woman, then starts to drop. Since the drop in birth rate lags the drop in death rate, the population size increases to a new stable plateau.

2.5.1

WHAT DO WE MEAN BY A MODEL?

We will make many models in this book. The purpose of a model is to organize a set of assumptions and the implications that arise from the assumptions, and to make testable predictions. In essence, a model is an organized way to generate testable hypotheses. A model may be 1) a verbal description of a process as in Darwin's theory of evolution by natural selection, 2) a statistical fit to data as in least-squares regression, or 3) a hypothetical set of rules or mathematical equations that define key properties and causal relationships in the system such as Einstein's theory of Special Relativity.

Models are not reality. The model assumptions need not be realistic. Typically, model assumptions are gross simplifications of well-known reality. Model assumptions often come from the artistic intuitive side of the modeler's brain. The main requirement of any model is that it must make at least one prediction that is not obvious from a straightforward observation of the data under study. For example, Einstein postulated that the speed of light c was constant in all frames of reference. One of several implications of this hypothesis was that mass m could be converted into energy E according to Einstein's famous formula $E = mc^2$. This non-obvious prediction was verified experimentally, thus lending credence to the speed-of-light hypothesis and the consequences of the supposition.

Our model for the demographic transition is given by definition 3) a rule-based set of hypothetical equations describing population dynamics associated with the demographic transition. We will describe the model and will identify non-obvious predictions suggested by the model. The postulated rules are designed to capture the essence of population dynamics on timescales longer than an expected lifetime. No attempt will be made to accurately model data on timescales shorter than a lifetime. While not unknown in demography, the model-based approach adopted in this paper is more common in the natural sciences.

We will be modeling a system, the demographics of populations. It is important to define what is included in the system, what is outside the system, and what is a driver of the behavior of the system. The trigger for the transition is assumed to be the sudden drop in childhood deaths. This is caused by events external to demographics, namely improvements in healthcare, education, economic wellbeing, and a host of other causes not directly associated with demography.

It is important to note that this does not mean that there was not also a drop in death rates for older people. It is just that the death of an older person has less effect on the birth rate than the death of a person who has not yet procreated.

The model will quantify the nearness of populations to each other based on behavior of demographic variables. Also, it will quantify and measure the progress of the populations through the demographic transition. It will relate population aging to the effects on fertility of exogenous economic and cultural variables. The model will also place constraints on demographic variables. In other words, some combinations of demographic variables are very unlikely in this model. The model will also make some forecasts on the trajectories of the demographic variables through the transition. These are all testable predictions of the model.

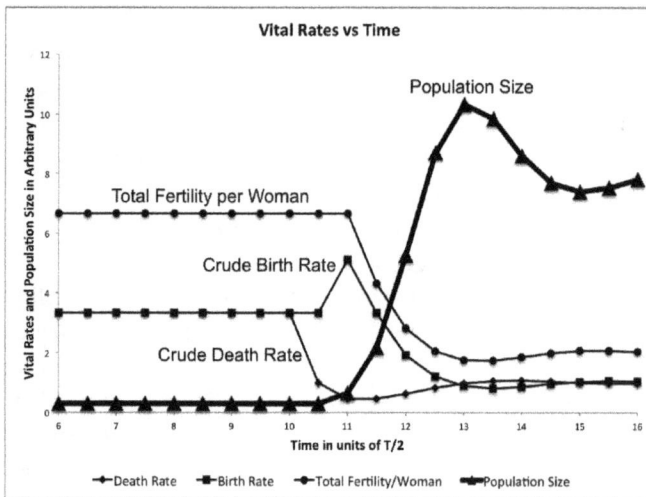

Figure 2.10 Time-Series of Vital Rates. T/2 is the time for one generation. The event is triggered by a sudden drop in childhood death rates, which lowers the total death rate for the population. The surviving children grow and procreate leading to an increase in birth rate and population. The total fertility rate, in this case the number of children per woman, then starts to drop. Since the drop in birth rate lags the drop in death rate, the population size increases to a new stable plateau. The curves in this plot are actually output from Core Model. The parameters are defined in the text. Here, $\alpha = 1$, and Y is taken initially to be 70 percent of B. The units of time are one generation. The birth, death, and fertility are in arbitrary units, although they are in proper proportion to each other. The population size is in arbitrary units.

2.5.2
IRRIGATION SYSTEM: FLOWS

Yes. A garden needs a lot of care and a lot of love. And if you give your garden a lot of love, things grow. But first, some things must wither. Some trees die.

Chauncey Gardiner in *Being There*

It is the mark of an educated mind to be able to entertain a thought without accepting it.

Aristotle

Before we dive into the model for the demographic transition let's do a *Gedanken*, or thought, experiment. A *gedanken* experiment is one that exists only in people's imaginations. It is the creation of a *what-if* world in which the rules may be a little different than those to which we are accustomed, and the objects that occupy the world are very simple. They provide the inquirer with a simple imaginary laboratory for testing ideas.

Einstein was the master of *gedanken* experiments. At the time of his discovery of special relativity actual laboratory experiments indicated that the speed of light waves was the same no matter which frame of reference the observer of the light was in. This is much different than waves that occur in water or air. In the "normal" world an observer can travel at the same speed as a water wave. When he or she does this, the wave appears to be not moving. This is not true for light. Einstein created worlds of imaginary clocks and fast-moving trains, and then asked questions such as, "If I traveled at the same speed of light, what would the light look like?" and, "If a clock were on a moving train, what time would it be on the train, and what time would it be for a person reading the clock from the ground?" Einstein answered these simple questions based on the rules of the world he set up and came up with conclusions that were verified in the real world with real experiments.

The model for the demographic transition, the *Core Model*, we present in this book is a *gedanken* experiment. Unfortunately, when we interacted with sociologists and demographers, our *gedanken* experiment turned out to be not very intuitive for them. Sociologists are scientists who have thought deeply about the complications of human inter-action. The simplicity of the thought experiment ran counter to the human complexity they dealt with every day. So we decided to present in this book first a *gedanken* experiment that was even simpler than Core Model and did not involve human beings at all. The parameters are defined in the text. Here, $\alpha = 1$, and Y is taken initially to b. This makes it easier for humans to jettison hard-learned information they know about human beings. This makes it easier to ask and answer questions in the imaginary world of the thought experiment. We call this simpler experiment the *Irrigation Model* because it is a model for watering gardens. We then present the Core Model. Core Model is a slight generalization of the Irrigation Model that substitutes water in pipes with the flow of humanity through their life spans. The models are validated if the explanations and predictions they make coincide with observations of real populations in the real world.

The Irrigation Model is illustrated in Figure 2.11. Suppose we have two gardens we would like to irrigate, but we have only one water pump. We can water the two gardens simultaneously if we pump the water into a single pipe and then split that pipe into two separate pipes, one for each garden. Now suppose we divert some water to the first garden very close to the pump. The water to the first garden is sent almost as soon as the pump pumps it. The remaining water flows to the second garden. The physics of water flowing through a pipe is very complex. We ignore this complexity and assume the water flows through the pipes at a constant speed.

Now suppose halfway down the pipe to the second garden there is a flow sensor. The sensor instructs the pump on how much water the pump should generate until the sensor senses a different flow rate. The signal to the pump is to pump water at a new rate propor-tional to the flow rate detected by the sensor. After passing through the flow sensor, the water in the pipe then flows the remainder of the distance down the pipe to the second garden. This is all we need to derive our first key result. We use symbols in the next paragraph to describe the various flow rates through various pipes at various times. Do not let the symbols confuse you. We are only talking about water pumped through a pipe with a sensor that tells the pump how much water to pump.

For convenience, let's choose our unit of distance such that the pipe to the second garden is two units long, and let's choose our unit of time such that it takes two units of time for a drop of water to travel the length of the pipe to the second garden. To start things off, let's assume the pump is turned off and there is no water in the pipes. At time $t = 0$ the pump is turned on and immediately starts pumping water at a rate $B(0)$. Some of the water $Y(0)$ is immediately diverted to the first garden. The remainder of the water $B(0) - Y(0)$ travels down the pipe to the second garden and reaches the halfway point at time $t = 1$. The flow sensor measures the flow of water to be $C(1) = B(0) - Y(0)$. The sensor sends a signal to the pump to start pumping water at a rate of $B(1) = f C(1) = f[B(0) - Y(0)]$. Here, f is just a proportionality constant. The water at the halfway point then travels down the pipe until it reaches the second garden at time $t = 2$. The flow to the second garden starts at that time and the flow rate is $D(2) = C(1) = B(0) - Y(0)$. At time $t = 2$ the water that was pumped at time $t = 1$ has just reached the halfway point of the pipe to the second garden. This process continues for subsequent timesteps. This means that the pump generates at a rate of $B(2) = f C(2) = f[B(1) - Y(1)]$, with similar relationships for all the flows.

Suppose we compare the flow of water that is generated at a given time $t = 2$ with the amount of water that flows to the second garden at the same time. From the relationships in the previous paragraph this means that the ratio of flow rate pumped to flow rate reaching the second garden is

$$\frac{B(2)}{D(2)} = \frac{f[B(1) - Y(1)]}{B(0) - Y(0)} \qquad (2.1)$$

and in general

$$\frac{B(t+2)}{fD(t+2)} = \frac{B(t+1) - Y(t+1)}{B(t) - Y(t)} \qquad (2.2)$$

where we have divided both sides of the equation by f.

Equation 2.2 relates the flow rates at the pump and at the second garden at a given time to flow rates in the pipe to the second garden at earlier times. It is probably not clear why this is important at this stage. Very shortly we will relate Equation 2.2 to how water is distributed in the pipes. We will then have a relationship between the creation/loss of water in the pipes and the manner in which water is distributed in the pipes. This result can be applied to any problem with feedback in which objects are created and then destroyed at one of two later times—like for instance, human beings who are born and then can die either before they procreate or after they procreate, if they decide to procreate at all.

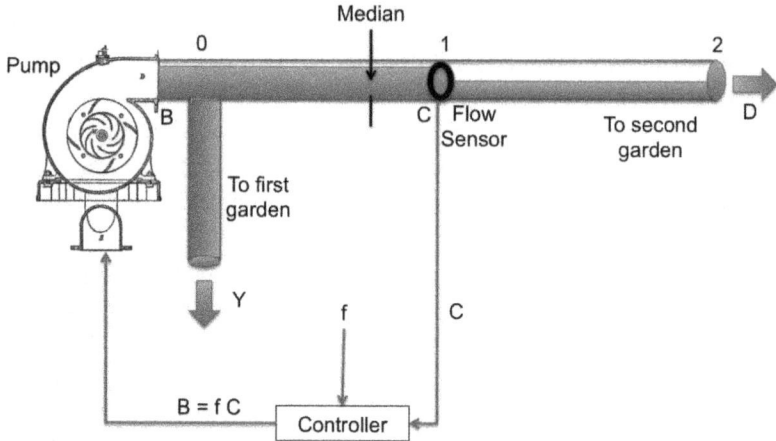

Figure 2.11 Irrigation System. A pump pumps water into a pipe at a rate B. Some of the water Y is directed to one garden. The rest D is directed to a second garden. The pipe to the first garden is at the same location as the pump. The pipe to the second garden is 2 length units long, and it takes 2 time units for the water to travel the length of the pipe. Halfway along the pipe is a flow sensor that detects how much water C is flowing through the middle of the pipe at any given time. The controller signals the pump to pump at a rate f C, where f is an externally determined constant. The median is the point along the horizontal pipe at which half of the water in the horizontal pipe is to the left and half is to the right. At time t = 0 a certain flow of water at rate B(0) is pumped into the pipe. At time t = 1 the water has reached the halfway point and is detected by the flow sensor. The sensor then sends the pump instructions to immediately change its water flow to B(1) = f C(1) = f [B(0) − Y (0)]. The initial bolus of water reaches the end of the pipe at time 2 and is equal to the amount of water that passed through the sensor at time 1, which is D(2) = C(1) = B(0) − Y (0). The process continues with new plug of water created at every time step. The median measures how the water is distributed in the pipe. If the left half of the horizontal pipe has more water, the median is in the left half of the pipe. If the right half of the horizontal pipe has more water, the median is on the right. If we measure the age of a drop of water as the time elapsed since it left the pump, then a median on the left indicates a younger population of water than if the median were on the right.

2.5.3
IRRIGATION SYSTEM: DISTRIBUTION OF WATER

A vegetable garden in the beginning looks so promising and then after all little by little it grows nothing but vegetables, nothing, nothing but vegetables.

Gertrude Stein

Once when lecturing to a class he [the physicist Lord Kelvin] used the word 'mathematician' and then interrupting himself asked his class: 'Do you know what a mathematician is?' Stepping to his blackboard he wrote upon it: $\int_{-\infty}^{\infty} e^{-x^2} dx = \sqrt{\pi}$. Then putting his finger on what he had written, he turned to his class and said, 'A mathematician is one to whom that is as obvious as that twice two makes four is to you.'

From S. P. Thompson, *Life and Work of Lord Kelvin*, Macmillan, London, 1910.

The mathematician Littlewood wrote, "Many things are not accessible to intuition at all, the value of $\int_0^\infty e^{-x^2} dx$ for instance."

From J. E. Littlewood, Newton and the Attraction of the Sphere, *Mathematical Gazette*, vol. 63, 1948. These two stories about mathematicians were conveyed to us by Thomas Burch.

We continue the story of the irrigation system by considering how water is distributed in the pipes, in particular the pipe to the second garden. The median location of the water in the pipe to the second garden is that point in which half the water in the pipe is to the left of the point and half is to the right. We are not considering the water in the pipe to the first garden. If the median lies in the left half of the pipe, there is more water in the left half of the pipe; if the median is on the right then most of the water is on the right. If the median is located to the left as illustrated in Figure 2.11 then the amount of water to the left of the median at time t is the rate at which water enters the pipe to the second garden times the time it takes to get to the median point l.

$$[B(t-1)-Y(t-1)]l(t) \tag{2.3}$$

This quantity must be equal to the amount of water to the right of the median, which is the amount of water to the halfway point of the pipe plus the amount of water in the right side of the pipe.

$$[B(t-1)-Y(t-1)][1-l(t)]+[B(t-2)-Y(t-2)] \tag{2.4}$$

Setting Equations 2.3 and 2.4 and performing some simple algebraic manipulations yields

$$\frac{B(t-1)-Y(t-1)}{B(t-2)-Y(t-2)}=\frac{1}{2l(t)-1} \tag{2.5}$$

This is true for any time t. This means that Equation 2.5 can be written

$$\frac{B(t+1)-Y(t+1)}{B(t)-Y(t)}=\frac{1}{2l(t+2)-1} \tag{2.6}$$

Comparing Equation 2.6 with Equation 2.2 yields

$$\frac{B(t+2)}{fD(t+2)}=\frac{1}{2l(t+2)-1} \tag{2.7}$$

And since we can choose any time we want Equation 2.7 simplifies to

$$\frac{B(t)}{fD(t)}=\frac{1}{2l(t)-1} \tag{2.8}$$

for $l < 1$. Similarly we have

$$\frac{B(t)}{fD(t)}=3-2l(t) \tag{2.9}$$

for $l > 1$. When $l = 1$ then

$$\frac{B(t)}{fD(t)}=1 \tag{2.10}$$

This is a most remarkable result. Equation 2.8 through 2.10 relate the flows, which are represented on the left-hand side of the equation with the distribution of water within the pipe to the second garden. Another way of stating this is that if one knows the distribution of water within the pipe, one can make a statement about the comparative flows into and out of the pipe.

Okay, I know what you are thinking. This seems like a great deal of mental effort to go through to water a garden. However, if one thinks of the flows as birth rates and death rates in a population with Y representing childhood deaths, then Equation 2.8 through 2.10 state that one can make a statement about those birth and death rates *at a given time* if one knows the fertility rate and the median age of the population *at the same time*. The inverse can also be said. If one knows the birth and death rates at some time, then one can make a statement on the age distribution and fertility of the population at the same time.

2.5.4
IRRIGATION SYSTEM: SYSTEM BEHAVIOR

. . .and we've got to get ourselves back to the garden.

Joni Mitchell

Up to this point we have regarded f as an externally given constant. Let's see how the irrigation system behaves for different values of f. Consider the case in which $f = 0$. Then, no matter what is the flow in the center of the pipe, the controller sends out a signal $B = fC = 0$ and the pump turns off. If f is very, very large, then for any amount of water in the center of the pipe, the signal the controller sends the pump is $B = fC \to \infty$ and the pump tries to pump more and more water until the system breaks—either the pipes burst or the pump falls apart. If $f = 1$, then $B(t) = C(t) = B(t - 1) - Y(t - 1)$ is the signal the controller sends to the pump. If there is any water at all going to the first garden, then $B(t) < B(t - 1)$ and the pump eventually turns off.

There is a value of f in which the flow is steady. In steady flow, B, C, and Y are independent of time. The signal the controller sends the pump is

$$B = fC = f(B - Y) \tag{2.11}$$

or equivalently we have

$$f = \frac{B}{B - Y}. \tag{2.12}$$

We see that, except for very special values of f that the irrigation system is unstable; it either turns itself off or pumps so much water it destroys itself. This is true even if the value of f is only slightly different from the stable value in Equation 2.12.

If we think of water as humans, then the case of the pump turning itself off corresponds to extinction. The case of the system pumping so much water that the system destroys itself is the population explosion. And f plays the role of fertility, the number of children per person in a lifetime.

If we go back to the garden example, we would like to be able to adjust f in such a manner that the flow of water through the pipes is smooth. We need to be able to change f as the system is operating so that the system automatically achieves a stable state of constant flow.

2.5.5

IRRIGATION SYSTEM: CONTROLLING THE FLOW OF WATER

> *Agriculture looks different today—our farmers are using GPS and you can monitor your irrigation systems over the Internet.*

Debbie Stabenow

The challenge in controlling the irrigation system is to find a mechanism to automatically adjust f such that the flows become laminar. We would like the water to be evenly distributed through each pipe, but particularly in the pipe to the second garden—the first garden is very close to the pump so its pipe is so short that the flow is unimportant. We also want the system to be stable to small perturbations away from its smooth flow.

As we pointed out, the median can be used as a measure of the distribution of water in the pipe. If the median is in the middle of the pipe, the water is evenly distributed. If the median is to the left of center, there is more water in the left side of the pipe. Conversely if the median is on the right side. In our example, if l is less than one, then we want to decrease the pump output because the water on the left is too low. If

$$f(t) = l(t)f(t-1).$$

(2.13)

This is described pictorially in Figure 2.12.

2.5.6
IRRIGATION SYSTEM: DYNAMICS OF THE IRRIGATION SYSTEM

Someone told me that each equation I included in the book would halve the sales.

Stephen Hawking

We can collect the complete dynamics of the system into a single collection of equations

$$B(t) = f(t)[B(t-1)-Y(t-1)] \tag{2.14}$$

$$D(t) = B(t-2)-Y(t-2) \tag{2.15}$$

$$l(t) = \frac{1}{2}\left[1+\frac{f(t)D(t)}{B(t)}\right] \quad \text{for} \quad l(t) \le 1 \tag{2.16}$$

$$l(t) = \frac{1}{2}\left[3-\frac{B(t)}{f(t)D(t)}\right] \quad \text{for} \quad l(t) > 1 \tag{2.17}$$

$$f(t+1) = l(t)f(t) \tag{2.18}$$

If we assume that $Y(t)$ is given, then Equations 2.14 through 2.18 form a closed system of equations that can be integrated in time. One integration is illustrated in Figure 2.13 which displays the dynamics of the system that is initially in equilibrium. At time $t = 10$ the valve to the pipe to the first garden is suddenly closed. The system finds a new equilibrium after a brief period of oscillation.

In the demographic system, the sudden drop in flow to the first garden represents a sudden drop in childhood deaths. The flow to the second garden represents people who live a full life past the age of procreation. The control parameter f represents fertility. The overshoot of the new equilibrium by the median is significant for the understanding of aging populations in developed countries. When the childhood death rate drops suddenly, there is an initial drop in the median age of the population as birth rates exceed death rates. However, as fertility drops and birth rates drop the population ages before settling down to a uniform distribution of ages.

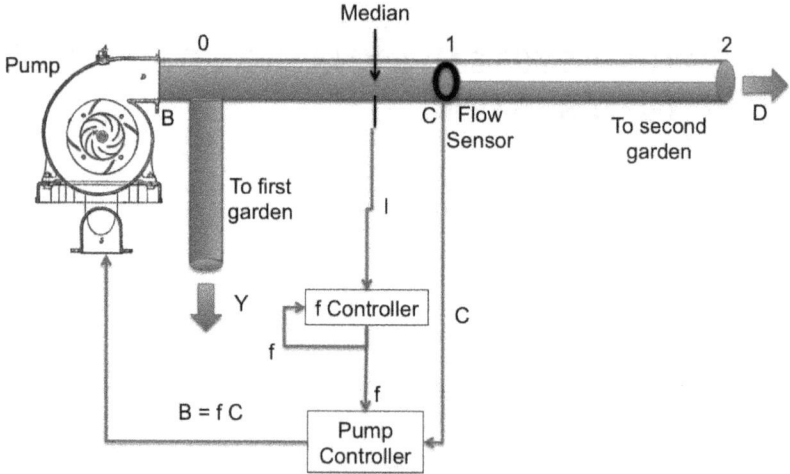

Figure 2.12 Control of the Irrigation System.

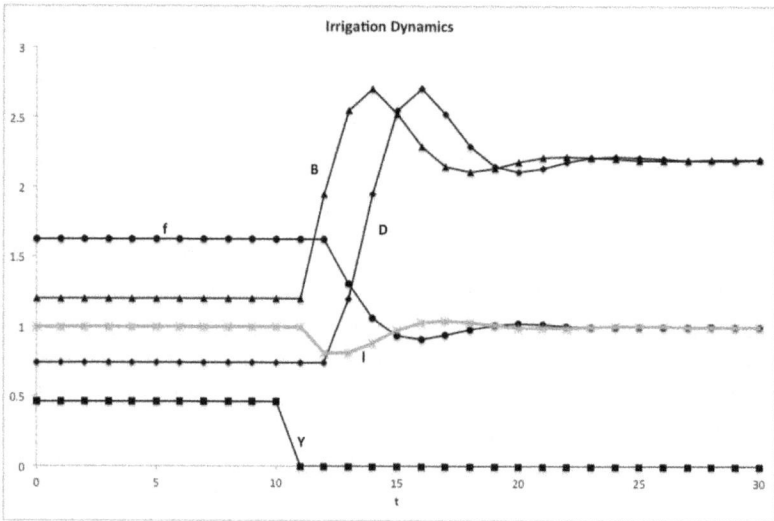

Figure 2.13 Dynamics of the Irrigation System. B is the flow of water injected into the system by the pump. Y is the flow to the first garden. D is the flow to the second garden. l is the median location of water in the pipe to the second garden. And f is the control parameter. The initial value of f was $f = B/(B - Y)$. At time $t = 10$ the flow to the first garden was suddenly shut off. The system is resilient and finds a new equilibrium. The analogy to the demographic transition is that B is the birth rate. Y is the death rate of people who have not survived to procreate. The sudden drop in Y represents a sudden drop in childhood deaths. D is the death rate of those people who have lived a full life. l is the median age of the population. And f is the fertility, the number of children created per person.

2.5.7
EXERCISES: DYNAMICS OF THE IRRIGATION SYSTEM

A lot of the interesting issues and dynamics within a city occur over things such as socio-economic issues or ethnic issues. But they require a much more elaborate model of human behavior.

Will Wright

1. Verify Equations 2.14 through 2.18
2. Hold Y at a constant value. In an Excel spreadsheet, integrate Equations 2.14 through 2.18 in time. Demonstrate that the Irrigation Model is now stable and the system is driven to a steady flow.
3. Start the system in steady state. Hold Y at a constant value, and then drop it to a lower value while integrating the equations. Are the dynamics qualitatively similar to the dynamics in Figures 2.10 and 2.13?

2.5.8
HEY! . . . WHAT ABOUT WOMEN'S EDUCATION AND ECONOMIC DRIVERS OF FERTILITY?

There is considerable evidence that women's education and literacy tend to reduce the mortality rates of children.

Amartya Sen, *Development as Freedom*, 2000, p. 195

World fertility surveys indicate that anywhere from one third to one half of the babies born in the Third World would not be if their mothers had access to cheap, reliable family planning, had enough personal empowerment to stand up to their husbands and relatives, and could choose their own family size.

Donella Meadows

The flows in the Irrigation Model became laminar when we adjusted the control parameter f to even out the water in the pipe to the second garden. The parameter f is the analog for fertility in the case of demography. In demography it is widely observed/believed that women's education, availability of contraceptives, culture, religion, urbanization, and other economic factors play roles in changing fertility. It would be rare for a demographer to claim that changes in fertility are directly affected by imbalance between the numbers of old and young people. It would be more likely that the demographer would note that age imbalance is causing an economic imbalance that is impeding modernization including better healthcare and education of women, and that this is then affecting fertility rates. In the language of the Irrigation Model, this would mean that the f Controller does not get a signal directly from the median l sensor. Rather, the f Controller is receiving signals from other types of sensors in the garden that depend on the steady flow of water—on the median lying halfway down the pipe to the second garden. The f sensor would then "measure" the value of the median l through the intermediaries of the garden sensors. This would add some time delays into the system, and the water flows would become somewhat less responsive to control.

We could expand the Irrigation Model so that the f Controller received signals from various sensors in the garden that depended on steady flow. This would be equivalent to expanding the demographics to include affects on fertility outside of demographics in the worlds of education, culture, and economics. But that significantly complicates the model, and if our goal is understanding the processes, that level of complication is a hindrance. Rather than complicate our models a great deal, let's make them only slightly more complicated by sweeping all the interesting science outside the measurement of water flows and distributions into a single free parameter that controls the level of response of the f Controller to the median distribution. Let's call this parameter α and modify the f Controller, Equation 2.18, to

$$f(t+1) = f^{\alpha}(t)f(t). \qquad (2.19)$$

2.5.9

EFFECTS OF CONTROLLER RESPONSIVENESS

The root cause of the looming energy problem—and the key to easing environmental, economic and religious tensions while improving public health is to address the unending, and unequal, growth of the human population. And the one proven way to reduce fertility rates is to empower young women by educating them.

Lawrence M. Krauss

One cannot be deeply responsive to the world without being saddened very often.

Erich Fromm

We can dial α to match any level of responsiveness to the water distribution. If $\alpha = 0$, then the f parameter remains unchanged,

$$f(t+1) = f(t). \qquad (2.20)$$

The system is completely unresponsive to the water distribution.

As α increases so does the responsiveness of the f Controller. When $\alpha = 1$, we recover our original f Controller, Equation 2.18. This is the most responsive. It does not make sense to allow α to be greater than one. In that case, the controller becomes unresponsive to $l < 1$ and very responsive to $l > 1$.

The response of the median l to three levels of $\triangleleft$ is displayed in Figure 2.14. The conditions are the same as in Figure 2.13. For $\alpha = 1$, we recover our original behavior displayed in Figure 2.13. If we reduce the responsiveness α to $\alpha = 1/2$, then the water flow finds a new equilibrium very much greater than the original flow. This is displayed in Figure 2.15. If we reduce the responsiveness to zero, then the system is completely unstable. This is displayed in Figure 2.16.

It is instructive to examine the response of the median displayed in Figure 2.14. The response of the median when $\alpha = 1/2$ is sluggish compared with the oscillatory response of the median when $\alpha = 1$. In the demographic transition, this means that a rapid response to changes in the population age distribution leads to oscillatory behavior of the age distribution. In other words, a young population overshoots its new final equilibrium after a perturbation and becomes an aging population before it settles down to its new equilibrium.

This completes our discussion of the Irrigation Model. We have alluded to demographic analogs several times in the discussion. We will build a proper model of simple demographics, the Core Model, in the next section. It is best to understand the Irrigation Model before moving on. In its essence, Core Model is basically the Irrigation Model with water variables replaced with demographic variables.

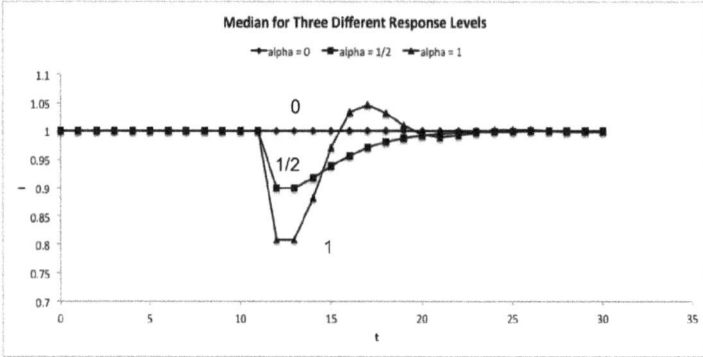

Figure 2.14 Medians for Three Values of α.

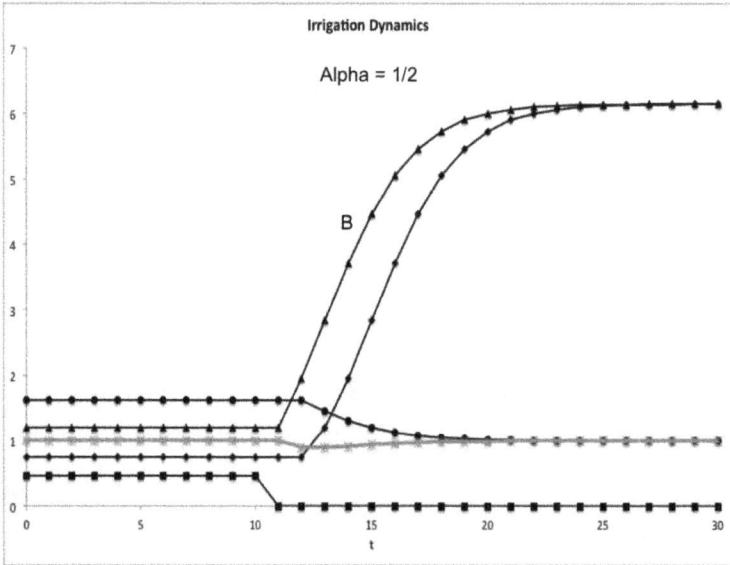

Figure 2.15 α = 1/2.

2.5.10
CORE MODEL

> *And there's a lot of that stuff with people bringing their kids, kids bringing their parents, people bringing their grandparents—I mean, it's gotten to be really stretched out now. It was never my intention to say, this is the demographics of our audience.*
>
> Jerry Garcia

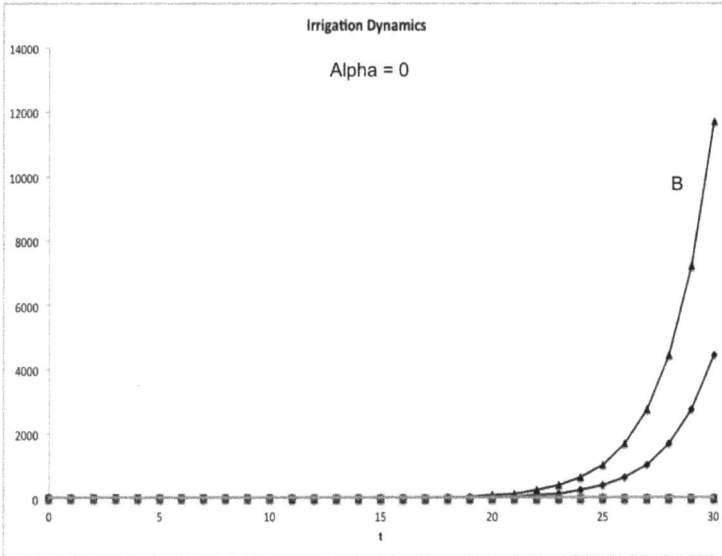

Figure 2.16 α = 0.

We now have the background to create the *Core Model*, that captures the essence of the demographic transition. We will use many of the same symbols in the Core Model that we used for the Irrigation Model. This should not lead to confusion. The context should make the meaning clear. Moreover, using the same symbols makes the analogy between human rates in Core Model and water flow rates in the Irrigation Model.

The Core Model is based on three basic observations:

1. *People are born.*
2. *People die.* Some die in childhood, the rest at a later age.
3. *People give birth.* If there are so many children in a family that the family is in economic and social distress, the number of children women have tends to decrease. If there are very few children in the family, then biological, social, and economic pressures tend to increase the number of children in the family.

There are other minor assumptions, but these three observations are the foundation of the model.

As we will show, these three simple observations allow us to approximate the dynamics of the demographic transition. This type of approximation is unavailable in most X-events. The observations constrain the dynamics and the possible trajectories of the population size. This is a remarkable result.

The Core Model is based on the following measurable demographic variables that describe the demographic transition:

$T^\dagger$ Median age of the population
T_e Average life span of both males and females in the population
d Crude death rate per capita (crude rates exclude migration)
f Total fertility (births) per person (the replacement rate is $f = 1$)
b Crude birth rate per capita
N Number of people in the population
y Childhood death rate per capita (this is the per capita death rate for those people who die before they procreate)

The Core Model is illustrated in Figure 2.17. It is assumed that there is a maximum life span given by T. This is the expected lifetime of someone who has survived an early death. Time is divided into discrete units of $T/2$. Actual time t is given by

$$t = \frac{nT}{2} \qquad (2.21)$$

where n is an integer. Variation on timescales smaller than a time step are not considered.

In most of the treatment we will consider fertility as the number of children per person rather than per women. This means that the fertility replacement rate for the case of no childhood deaths is one. We also assume that the number of women in a population equals the number of men.

We, for simplicity, also do not consider migration at this stage. This can be addressed in the next generation of the model.

2.5.11
VITAL DEMOGRAPHIC VARIABLES

Politics is for the present, but an equation is for eternity.

Albert Einstein

Darwin's theory of evolution is a framework by which we under-
stand the diversity of life on Earth. But there is no equation sit-
ting there in Darwin's Origin of Species *that you apply and say,*
"What is this species going to look like in 100 years or 1,000 years?"
Biology isn't there yet with that kind of predictive precision.

Neil deGrasse Tyson

The number of births per year at time step n is $B(n) \doteq b(n)N$ (n). The number of early deaths is $Y(n) \doteq y(n)N(n)$. Early deaths are assumed to occur immediately after birth. Birth and early deaths per year remain constant for one time step, at which time the surviving people who were born at the beginning of the time step give birth themselves. The birth rate at time step $n + 1$ is then

$$B(n+1) = f(n+1)B'(n), \qquad (2.22)$$

where

$$B'(n) \doteq B(n) - Y(n), \qquad (2.23)$$

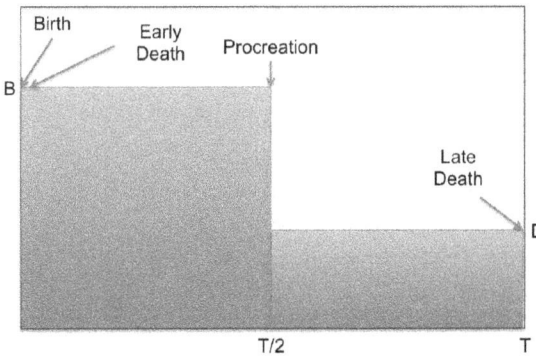

Figure 2.17 The Core Model. People have three roles: to be born, to procreate, and to die. Some die early. It is assumed that early deaths occur soon after birth. The remainder of the population live to their expected lifetime (after surviving early death) T at which time they die. At the halfway point in life T/2, people give birth to children. Here, T/2 is the time step, which is called, in this paper, a generation. Time is expressed as t = nT /2 where n is an integer. The number of children born per year during time step n is B(n). The number of people who die early during time step n is Y (n). The number who die late is $D(n) = B(n-2) - Y(n-2) \doteq B'(n-2)$. The number of children a person has at time step n is f (n). The replacement rate is f = 1. The total population at timestep n is $N(n) = B'(n-1)T / 2 + B'(n-2)T / 2$.

and $f(n)$ is the total fertility at time n. Fertility is defined such that $f = 1$ is the replacement rate, the amount of children born per person (male or female) to just replace the population. Equal numbers of males and females are assumed. The mathematical implications of these assumptions are straightforward and left for the reader to work out in Exercise 2.5.17.

In the case that the early death rate Y is zero, the life expectancy, T_e, is equal to the maximum life span, T, Equations 2.41 and 2.44 in Exercise 2.5.17 reduce to

$$\frac{b}{fd} = \frac{T_e}{4T^\dagger - T_e} \quad \text{for } 2T^\dagger < T_e \quad \text{younger population} \qquad (2.24)$$

$$= \frac{3T_e - 4T^\dagger}{T_e} \quad \text{for } 2T^\dagger \geq T_e \quad \text{older population.}$$

where the time is the same for all quantities. The top line is for younger populations and the lower link is for older populations.

We call Equation 2.24 the *Equation of State* (EOS). The model predicts that Equation 2.24 holds when childhood death rates are zero. The EOS simply states that the ratio b/fd is a function of the life expectancy T_e and the median age $T^\dagger$. When $2T^\dagger < T_e$, then the ratio is given by the upper equation. When the converse is true, the ratio is equal to the function of T_e and $T^\dagger$ on the lower line. When $T_e = T^\dagger$, both the upper functions and the lower functions as well as the ratio are equal to one.

The ratio b/fd is composed of the vital demographic variables. Therefore, here it is given the name *vital ratio* represented by the symbol v.

$$v = \frac{b}{fd} \qquad (2.25)$$

The vital ratio, which contains birth rates, death rates, and fertility rates, is one measure of the net increase or decrease in the population size.

Another important ratio is

$$a = \frac{T_e}{2T^\dagger}. \qquad (2.26)$$

Here, a is called the *age ratio*. It is a measure of the age distribution in the population. If half the expected lifetime is greater than the median age ($a > 1$), then the population has more young people than old people. It is a young population. If half the expected lifetime is less than the median age ($a \leq 1$), then there are more old people than young people in the population. The population is older. High (low) median age with respect to the expected lifetime implies an older (younger) population. High (low) median age with respect to the expected lifetime implies an older (younger) population.

The EOS can be written in terms of the ratios as

$$v = \frac{a}{2-a} \quad \text{for } a > 1 \quad \text{younger population}$$

$$= \frac{3a-2}{a} \quad \text{for } a \leq 1 \quad \text{older population.}$$

$$(2.27)$$

Equation 2.27 simply states that, *for populations with no childhood deaths*, the growth or decline in the population size as represented by the vital ratio, v, depends only on the age distribution of the population. This agrees with intuition. Mathematically, the EOS is a *manifold*, a surface in the space of demographic variables on which the variables lie.

It is important to note that the vital ratio and the age ratio are not constructed arbitrarily. They are quantities that emerge from the premises of the model. They are *derived* quantities. The main point is that the statics and dynamics of the demographic transition behave more simply when expressed in these variables.

2.5.12
STATICS OF THE DEMOGRAPHIC TRANSITION

The reality is that financial markets are self-destabilizing; occasionally they tend toward disequilibrium, not equilibrium.

George Soros

The second prediction of the Core Model addresses populations in stationary equilibrium, the state in which the rate of natural increase, $r = b - d$ is zero, and the population size is unchanged. Those countries in which the childhood death rate is not necessarily zero can be in a stationary equilibrium state that satisfies

$$b = d$$

for b and d constant in time. Core Model then predicts that the state of the system lies along the *stationary manifold*

$$v = a \tag{2.28}$$

$$\frac{b}{fd} = \frac{T_e}{2T^\dagger} \tag{2.29}$$

for countries in a stationary state. Stationary states must lie on the stationary manifold. Dynamical states in which the childhood death rate is zero lie on the EOS manifold. There is only one point E that lies on both the stationary manifold and the EOS manifold. This is the state that is stationary and has a childhood death rate of zero. This is the equilibrium point, or *stationary fixed point*, for a population with low childhood death rates. At the stationary fixed point

$$b = d$$
$$f = 1$$
$$T_e = 2T^\dagger. \tag{2.30}$$

The Stationary Manifold and the EOS are plotted in Figure 2.18 along with data from OECD countries, which tend to be developed, and all other countries. [CIA, 2014d,a,e,b,c, OEC, 2014b] When childhood deaths are sufficiently rare, the dynamical states of the model are constrained to lie on the EOS manifold of Equation 2.24. The OECD countries, which tend to have low childhood death rates, tend to follow the EOS manifold.

2.5.13
CLUSTERING OF WORLD POPULATIONS

If you spend time with crazy and dangerous people, remember their personalities are socially transmitted diseases; like water poured into a container, most of us eventually turn into or remain whoever we surround ourselves with. We can choose our tribe, but we cannot change that our tribe is our destiny.

Stefan Molyneux

World populations can be clustered based on their stage in the demographic transition. This is illustrated in Figure 2.18. There are three clusters that are late in the transition. These are the Aging countries that would seem to have overshot the relaxation to equilibrium, the origin, in Figure 2.18, the Uniform countries that lie near the stationary equilibrium, the origin, and the Young countries that appear to be approaching the stationary, the origin. These three clusters are characterized by their median age with respect to the expected lifetime. The populations in the Aging cluster have high median ages. The populations in the Young cluster have low median ages. The populations in the Uniform cluster have median ages that are half the expected lifetime.

There are two clusters that are earlier in the transition. These are characterized by their geography or economy. African populations tend to have low ratios of b/fd. Oil countries tend to have high ratios.

In the data set, 22 of the 36 OECD countries are in the Aging cluster. All the Aging OECD countries have such low fertility that the populations are not replacing themselves. According to Core Model, this means that most of the OECD countries are in an advanced state of the transition. Core Model predicts that the fertility in these countries will increase driving the population to an even age distribution. This has been noted in demographic observations.

There are 3 of 36 OECD populations that are within 1 percent of being completely uniform: the United Kingdom, France, and South Korea.

There are 11 OECD countries that have young populations. The most dramatic of these countries is Mexico with a high birth rate, a low death rate, high fertility, and a high ratio $b/fd = 3.35$.

There are no OECD countries in the Africa or Oil clusters. In the case of the Africa cluster, the median age is low and the ratio b/fd is also low. The Africa cluster is composed entirely of sub-Saharan African countries. Core Model indicates that these early-transition African countries have not yet experienced significant fertility decline. This is consistent with the observations (See Bongaarts and Casterline, 2013 for a thorough discussion).

The Oil cluster is composed mostly of countries involved with oil and natural gas production: United Arab Emirates, Qatar, Libya, Kuwait, Brunei, Bahrain, and Singapore. The remaining countries in the cluster tend to be isolated tourism-based islands.

All other countries not mentioned tend to lie in the Young cluster. Two important populations in this cluster are China and India.

China is located very near Korea, an OECD country with a uniform population. The dynamics of the Chinese population may be similar to Korea's. The closest OECD population to India is Brazil. According to Core Model, the countries in the Young cluster are in advanced stages of the demographic transition and are moving towards the stationary fixed point.

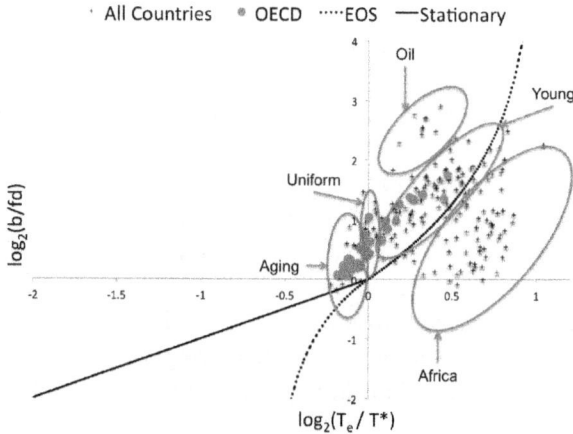

Figure 2.18 Countries of the world. $2T\dagger \doteq T^*$. The logarithms to the base 2 of the vital ratio and the age ratio are taken to compress the scale. The EOS manifold is the dotted curve. The stationary manifold is the solid line. Round dots are OECD countries. Small crosses are non-OECD countries. The origin is the equilibrium point for populations with no childhood deaths. No special clustering algorithms were used to group the countries. The clusters are based on a purely visual grouping of the clusters in this space. The world's populations can be classified into five structures based on dynamics: Aging, Uniform, Young, Africa, and Oil. Aging countries include most European countries such as Germany and Russia. The African cluster is composed of sub-Saharan countries. The Young cluster is composed of "spin-off" countries such as the United States, Australia, Brazil, and Mexico. Korea is a Uniform country. Saudi Arabia and Bahrain are in the Oil cluster.

2.5.14
DYNAMICS OF THE DEMOGRAPHIC TRANSITION

> *Some calamities—the 1929 stock market crash, Pearl Harbor, 9/11—have come like summer lightning, as bolts from the blue. The looming crisis of America's Ponzi entitlement structure is different. Driven by the demographics of an aging population, its causes, timing, and scope are known.*

George Will

Figure 2.18 is a snapshot of the demographic transition. We can turn the picture into a movie by making an assumption of how the fertility depends on the other demographic variables. Specification of the fertility closes the mathematical model—the number of equations equals the number of unknowns. The measure of the number of children per family, within the context of Core Model, is the median age. If the median age is low compared with life span, then there are many children per family. Conversely, if the median age is high, there are few children on average per family. The following relationship between fertility and median age is imposed.

$$f(n+1) = \left(\frac{T^*(n)}{T} \right)^{\alpha} f(n) \qquad (2.31)$$

Here, α is an adjustable parameter. For positive α, this relationship lowers the fertility when the median age is low and raises it for high median age. All the details of the economics that drive fertility rates are encapsulated in the exponent α. If α is large, then the population has the ability to respond quickly to economic forces. The sudden availability of cheap birth control, for instance, can increase the value of α thus increasing the ability of the population to respond to the stresses of large family size. Conversely, if α is small, the population does not have the ability to respond to the stresses of large or small families.

In Core Model α is a free parameter. This means that it depends on variables that are outside the model. There are a number of things that might affect fertility outside the boundaries of Core model: women's education, methods and availability of birth control, economic conditions, amount of time that women lactate, infanticide, cultural norms, political constraints, religious beliefs, and urbanization to name a few. We can therefore think of α as capturing the mood of the population in some general sense. It defines the coupling of the demographic system with other social systems.

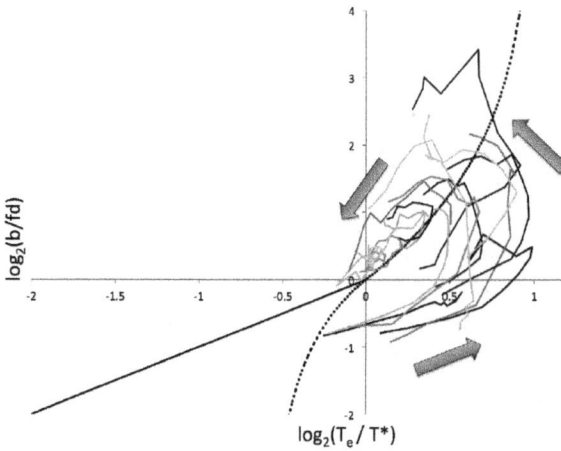

Figure 2.19 Trajectories for a representative sampling of countries. The time ranges from 1953 to 2013. Note the counterclockwise flow consistent with Core Model. The sequence of events start with a decrease in the death rate. This increases the ratio of births to deaths. The increase in births leads to the population becoming younger. The fertility responds to the increase of children by decreasing. This causes the population to age. This all happens on a relatively short timescale of a few generations. The state overshoots the equilibrium leading to an aged population. The state then relaxes to an equilibrium. The countries represented are Chad, Kenya, Kuwait, Saudi Arabia, Mexico, Brazil, United States, Australia, China, India, France, United Kingdom, Germany, Japan, Russia, Sweden, Singapore, and Qatar.

2.5.15
EXERCISES: POPULATION EXPLOSION

It's coming home to roost over the next 50 years or so. It's not just climate change; it's sheer space, places to grow food for this enormous horde. Either we limit our population growth or the natural world will do it for us, and the natural world is doing it for us right now.

David Attenborough

The rate of population growth in the absence of migration is given by

$$\frac{dN}{dt} = rN \qquad (2.32)$$

where N is the size of the population, t is time, and $r = b - d$ is the replacement rate. The crude birth rate b and crude death rate d have units of births/deaths per capita per year. If the replacement rate is positive and constant, then the population grows exponentially. If it is negative and constant, the population decays exponentially. Typical values for the birth and death rates are 30 per thousand people per year.

The solution to Equation 2.32 for constant r is

$$N = N_0 \exp(rt). \qquad (2.33)$$

The doubling time for the population is given by

$$t_2 = \frac{\ln(2)}{r} \qquad (2.34)$$

1. If there are no deaths, what is the doubling time of the population if the birth rate is 30 per thousand people per year?
2. Before about 1000 CE the doubling time of the population was 200 years or longer. If the birth rate is 30 per thousand people per year, how close must the death rate be to the birth rate to give a doubling time of 200 years?
3. What mechanisms could lead to the death rates and birth rates being so close together in an era before birth control?

2.5.16
DISCUSSION QUESTIONS:
POPULATION EXPLOSION

> *As a woman leader, I thought I brought a different kind of leadership. I was interested in women's issues, in bringing down the population growth rate . . . as a woman, I entered politics with an additional dimension—that of a mother.*

Benazir Bhutto

We saw in Exercise 2.5.15 that the birth and death rates before about 1000 CE were equal to each other on average to within about 10 percent. What is the mechanism that keeps the birth and death rates so close to each other in an era before birth control? Thomas Burch [2014] suggested that natural selection would be sufficient to maintain this equilibrium.

1. Any local population that has a death rate more than 10 percent greater than the birth rate would quickly become extinct. What would happen if the the birth rate were significantly *greater* than the death rate? Would the population become extinct as well?
2. Could this natural-selection mechanism alter the genetic makeup of the surviving populations? How might this be expressed in phenotypes? Could the surviving populations develop a drive to maintain the birth rate close to the death rate? If so, how would this be expressed? Are there hormonal mechanisms that drive a desire for a certain age distribution in the population?
3. If there is a drive to optimize the age distribution in a population, how would this drive be fulfilled in a pre-modern society in the absence of modern birth control? What are the candidate mechanisms: infanticide, varying social support for child rearing, adjusting marriage age, adjusting lactation time?

2.5.17

EXERCISES: DEMOGRAPHIC TRANSITION

Each day is a little life: every waking and rising a little birth, every fresh morning a little youth, every going to rest and sleep a little death.

Arthur Schopenhauer

- The number of people who were born in time step n and survived early death live until their maximum age T, at which time they die. Show the total number of deaths per year D at time step $n + 2$ is then

$$D(n+2) = B'(n) \qquad (2.35)$$

and the total population N at time step $n + 2$ is

$$N(n+2) = B'(n+1)\frac{T}{2} + B'(n)\frac{T}{2}. \qquad (2.36)$$

- Show that the birth b and death d rates per person per year at time n are

$$b(n) = \frac{B(n)}{B'(n-1)+B'(n-2)}\frac{2}{T} \qquad (2.37)$$

and

$$d(n) = \frac{B'(n-2)}{B'(n-1)+B'(n-2)}\frac{2}{T}. \qquad (2.38)$$

- Show that the ratio of birth to death rates at time n is

$$\frac{b(n)}{d(n)} = \frac{B(n)}{B'(n-2)} = \frac{f(n)B'(n-1)}{B'(n-2)}. \qquad (2.39)$$

- The median age of a population is the age at which half the population is younger and half is older.
  Show that if the number of younger people exceeds the number of older people, then the median age in our model is less than $T/2$. The condition for $T^\dagger$ to be the median age is then

$$B'(n-1)T^\dagger(n) = B'(n-1)\left(\frac{T}{2}-T^\dagger(n)\right) + B'(n-2)\frac{T}{2} \qquad (2.40)$$

which yields

$$\frac{B'(n-1)}{B'(n-2)} = \frac{T}{4T^\dagger(n)-T} \quad T^* = 2T^\dagger < T. \tag{2.41}$$

- Show that, in the limit of zero childhood deaths, Equation 2.41 becomes

$$\frac{b(n)}{f(n)d(n)} = \frac{T_e}{4T^\dagger(n)-T_e} \quad T^* = 2T^\dagger < T \quad y \to 0. \tag{2.42}$$

$T^\dagger \geq T/2$ yields

$$B'(n-1)\frac{T}{2} + B'(n-2)\left(T^*(n)-\frac{T}{2}\right) = B'(n-2)(T-T^*) \tag{2.43}$$

which yields

$$\frac{B'(n-1)}{B'(n-2)} = \frac{3T-4T^\dagger(n)}{T} \quad T^* = 2T^\dagger \geq T. \tag{2.44}$$

- Show that, in the limit of zero childhood deaths, Equation 2.44 becomes

$$\frac{b(n)}{f(n)d(n)} = \frac{3T_e - 4T^\dagger(n)}{T_e} \quad T^* = 2T^\dagger \geq T \quad y \to 0. \tag{2.45}$$

- The life expectancy at birth, T_e, for people born at time n for our model is proportional to the number of people born at time n who survive to age T over the total number of people who were born into that cohort including those that died shortly after birth. Show that this can be written

$$B(n)T_e(n) = [B(n)-Y(n)]T$$
$$\frac{T_e(n)}{T} = \frac{B'(n)}{B(n)} = \frac{B(n)-Y(n)}{B(n)}. \tag{2.46}$$

- Show that given a set of initial conditions and the early death rate as an external driver, Core Model can be evolved in time. The initial conditions are given when two consecutive values of the birth rate $B(0)$ and $B(1)$, the median age $T^*(1) = 2T^\dagger(1)$, and the fertility $f(1)$ are specified. The external driver of the model is the death rate for early death Y. The driver is specified when its values are given for all time. The evolution is then

$$\frac{T^*(n)}{T} = F(B') \tag{2.47}$$

where

$$F(B') = \frac{1}{2}\left[1 + \frac{B'(n-2)}{B'(n-1)}\right] \quad T^* < T \tag{2.48}$$

$$= \frac{1}{2}\left[3 - \frac{B'(n-1)}{B'(n-2)}\right] \quad T^* \geq T.$$

and the remaining finite difference equations are

$$f(n) = \left(\frac{T^*(n-1)}{T}\right)^a f(n-1) \tag{2.49}$$

$$B(n) = f(n)B'(n-1) \tag{2.50}$$

with the auxiliary relationships

$$T^\dagger = \frac{T^*}{2} \tag{2.51}$$

$$B'(n) = B(n) - Y(n) \tag{2.52}$$

$$y(n) \doteq \frac{Y(n)}{N(n)} \tag{2.53}$$

$$D(n) = B'(n-2) \tag{2.54}$$

$$N(n) = \left(\frac{B'(n-1) + B'(n-2)}{2}\right)T \tag{2.55}$$

$$b(n) = \frac{B(n)}{N(n)} \tag{2.56}$$

$$d(n) = \frac{B'(n-2)}{N(n)} \tag{2.57}$$

$$\frac{T_e(n)}{T} = \frac{B'(n)}{B(n)} = \frac{B(n) - Y(n)}{B(n)} = \frac{b(n) - y(n)}{b(n)} \tag{2.58}$$

and

$$F(B') = \frac{1}{2}\left[1 + \frac{f(n)d(n)}{b(n)}\right] \quad T^* < T, \ Y = 0 \tag{2.59}$$

$$= \frac{1}{2}\left[3 - \frac{b(n)}{f(n)d(n)}\right] \quad T^* \geq T, \ Y = 0.$$

Equations 2.47, 2.49, and 2.50 define the time evolution of the system. They comprise a set of nonlinear finite-difference equations. The equation of state Equation 2.24 follows from Equations 2.47 and 2.59.

- Code the evolution equations into a simple spreadsheet or into any other type of code and recover the curves of Figure 2.10. Show that if the childhood death rate does not go completely to zero that Core Model predicts the populations to move in a counterclockwise direction in Figure 2.18 qualitatively similar to the flow in Figure 2.19.

- The demographic transition as a system is displayed in Figure 2.20. Which nodes are internal to the system? Which nodes are external? Which nodes and edges represent the context of the system? The edges represent relationships—equations. Which equation is associated with each edge? Which node(s) are directly affected by variables such as women's education, available birth control, and infanticide? Which node(s) are affected by vaccines? Are these nodes internal or external to the system? Is there an internal feedback loop? Describe it. What if fertility were removed from the system by holding it constant? What can be said about the system? Does the internal feedback loop still exist? The answer is no. Why? Do the EOS and stationary manifolds still exist? The answer is yes. Why?

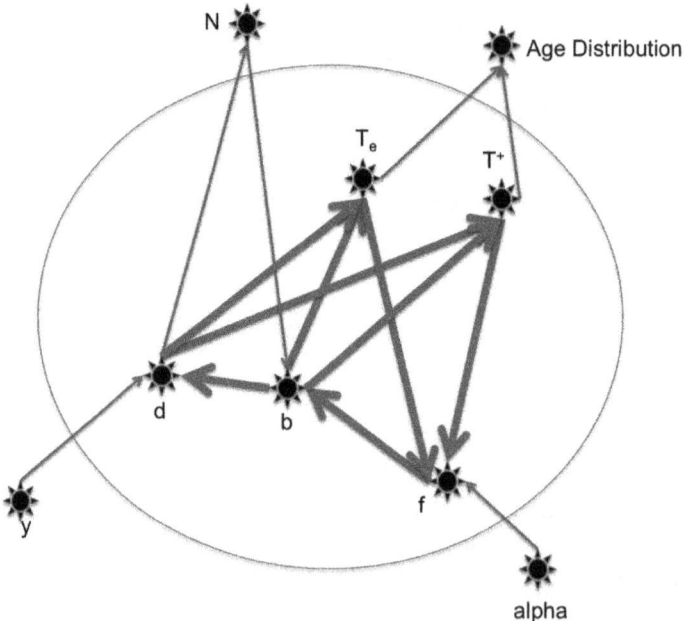

Figure 2.20 Demographic Transition as a System

2.5.18
DISCUSSION QUESTIONS: DEMOGRAPHIC TRANSITION

> *The fertility cycle is a cycle entirely of living creatures passing again and again through birth, growth, maturity, death, and decay.*

Wendell Berry

> *The management of fertility is one of the most important functions of adulthood.*

Germaine Greer

Comment on the following assertions.

- The driver for the demographic transition is the drop in childhood deaths. This is due to improved healthcare and living conditions. The reduction in childhood deaths is a consequence of changes in economics and other social systems, and therefore represents a complexity mismatch between economic systems and demographic systems.
- In the case of the demographic transition, a population starts in a near steady state in which the birth rate is approximately equal to the death rate. The death rate for people who have yet to procreate, the childhood death rate, is significant. The fertility, at this stage, is greater than the death rate in order to replace the children who died. The common observation is that a sudden drop in the childhood death rates triggers the extreme event, the demographic transition. The drop in childhood deaths starts a cascade of events that culminates in the system returning to a steady state different from the original steady state. This is a rebalancing of the population.
- Core Model is a simple accounting of births and deaths with an added assumption on how the fertility change is related to age distribution in the population. The key speculative causal relationship in the model is associated with fertility, perhaps the most difficult concept in demographics. The change in fertility is assumed to depend on the age distribution of the population and on one free parameter, α, that determines the speed at which fertility responds

to the age distribution. The free parameter is assumed to depend on external economic, sociological, cultural, political, and biological drivers that do not appear explicitly in the model. More precisely, the free parameter may be a function of non-demographic variables such as the level of women's education, income, urbanization, level of healthcare, family structure, or any of a number of external variables. The fertility assumption can be expressed mathematically as Equation 2.31. For low values of α the movement through the demographic transition is sluggish. The fertility is slow to respond to the shifting age distribution. The population experiences significant growth because fertility is dropping slowly. This is the situation we might expect if women's education is low or the family income is low. As α becomes large, the dynamics become very responsive to changes in age distribution. The population size overshoots the steady state values leading to aging populations. This is a situation in which women are more in control of their reproduction. For values of α greater than approximately two, fertility is very responsive to changes in age distribution. In this case the dynamics become chaotic—the time series appear random at first glance.

- The purpose of any model is to make testable predictions. If the model is based on a set of causal relationships, a successful test of the model reinforces the confidence in the causal relations.

- One prediction of Core Model is that the temporal ordering of events—reduced death rate, increased birth rate, younger population, population growth, reduced fertility, reduced birth rate, aging population, and, finally, saturation of population growth at a greater population size—is consistent with observations of the temporal ordering in actual populations.

- A second prediction is that population aging is a consequence of how rapidly the childhood death rate falls and how responsive fertility is to changing age distributions in the population. The aging population occurs a few generations after the childhood death rate drops dramatically. The actual aging of populations late in the transition, most notably in European populations, is consistent with this prediction. If the model is correctly predictive, then the overshoot is due to the degree and suddenness of the drop in the childhood death rate and the responsiveness of the fertility to the changing age distribution. After aging has occurred, the model predicts that fertility will increase, and the age distribution will become uniform. If the change in childhood death rate is small, then the overshoot and consequently the level of aging in post-transition is also small. Core Model, however, does not yet include the effects of migration, which may be a major player in population rebalancing in aging and developed countries. The model also does not include the effects of increased education, which may lead to increased productivity, which may release economic pressures on aging populations. This released pressure may affect the tolerance for migration into the population.

- A third prediction is that all countries on the planet have entered the demographic transition. OECD countries are in the later stages of the transition, while sub-Saharan African countries are in early stages. The countries cluster by region based on where they are in the transition, with Europe, the offshoot countries of the United States and Australia, and Asian countries in the later stages of transition. Latin American and the Oil countries are in an intermediate stage. Finally, Africa is in an early stage. The dynamic states of the populations are attracted to curves defined by the model known as the Stationary Manifold and the Equation of State. There are two important dimensionless quantities that define the stage of transition, one associated with the level of growth of the population size, the other associated with the age distribution in the population.
- A fourth prediction is that the gross features of the demographic transition can be described by a closed model that includes only demographic variables. External economic, sociological, cultural, political, and biological drivers affect only the childhood death rate and the fertility.
- The success of these predictions increases our confidence in the hypothesized causal relationships in the model.
- What are the context-dependent and context-independent drivers of the demographic transition? The Core Model is coupled to economics through the drop in childhood death rates. Is this coupling context-dependent or -independent? What are the drivers of the economy?

I came into the room, which was half dark, and presently spotted Lord Kelvin in the audience and realised that I was in for trouble at the last part of my speech dealing with the age of the earth, where my views conflicted with his. To my relief, Kelvin fell fast asleep, but as I came to the important point, I saw the old bird sit up, open an eye and cock a baleful glance at me! Then a sudden inspiration came, and I said Lord Kelvin had limited the age of the earth, provided no new source (of energy) was discovered. That prophetic utterance refers to what we are now considering tonight, radium! Behold! the old boy beamed upon me.

Sir Ernest Rutherford

The model is subject to criticism. Core Model does not accurately treat timescales shorter than a lifetime. All of sociology and economics is buried in external drivers and a free parameter. Migration is not included in the model, nor is education and productivity. Core Model assumes the maximum possible life span is a constant. This may not be accurate. The ratio of life expectancy to median age is a coarse measure of population aging. The approach taken in this paper is not the standard research approach in demographics. These are open discussion and research items. Despite the possible criticisms, Core Model attempts to capture the essence of the demographic process, and seems to provide some insight into and predictive power for the demographic transition.

2.5.19
EXERCISES: AGING AND ECONOMICS

What helps with aging is serious cognition—thinking and understanding. You have to truly grasp that everybody ages. Everybody dies. There is no turning back the clock. So the question in life becomes: What are you going to do while you're here?

Goldie Hawn

The purpose of this exercise is to demonstrate the interaction of complex systems and show how an extreme event in one system can lead to extreme events in other systems.

- Assume the common economic assumption that supply balances demand.

$$S = D \qquad\qquad (2.60)$$

$$pN_\omega = cN \tag{2.61}$$

$$\frac{c}{p\omega} = 1 \tag{2.62}$$

where w is the fraction of the population who are workers

$$\omega = \frac{N_\omega}{N}. \tag{2.63}$$

- Divide the consumption into three pieces: consumption by children, consumption by workers, and consumption by elderly.

$$c = c_c \frac{N_c}{N} + c_\omega \omega + c_e \frac{N_e}{N} \tag{2.64}$$

$$1 = \left(\frac{c_c}{p\omega}\right)\left(\frac{N_c}{N}\right) + \left(\frac{c_\omega}{p\omega}\right)\omega + \left(\frac{c_e}{p\omega}\right)\left(\frac{N_e}{N}\right) \tag{2.65}$$

where c_c, c_w, and c_e are the consumption by children, workers, and elderly, respectively. Here, N_c and N_e are the number of children and elderly, respectively.

- Assume the Core Model illustrated in Figure 2.17. Assume the workers are those people from age

$$\frac{T}{2} - \omega \frac{T}{2}$$

to

$$\frac{T}{2} + \omega \frac{T}{2}.$$

The children make up the younger ages, and the elderly make up the older ages.

- Run the demographic transition model for various values of c_c, c_w, and c_e. How does the fraction of consumption in each age group change as the population passes through the demographic transition?
- Where would one find data to test these predictions?
- Many countries are concerned that their populations are aging. There may not be enough workers to supply the health and retirement benefits of the elders. What can you say about this from this exercise?

BIBLIOGRAPHY

2014b. http://www.oecdbetterlifeindex.org/topics/health/.

Bernardus, Henricus and Maria Hilderink. *World population in transition: an integrated regional modelling framework.* PhD thesis, University of Groningen, 2000.

Bongaarts, John and John Casterline. "Fertility Transition: Is sub-Saharan Africa Different?" *Population and Development Review* 38, Issue Supplement (s1) (2013): 153–168.

Burch, Thomas K. "Data, models, theory and reality: The structure of demographic knowledge." In *Agent-Based Computational Demography,* edited by F. C. Bullari. Heidelberg: Springer-Verlag, 2003b.

Burch, Thomas K. "Demography in a new key: A theory of population theory." *Demographic Research* 9(11) (2003a): 263–284.

Burch, Thomas K. Private Communication, 2014.

CIA birth rates, 2014d. https://www.cia.gov/library/publications/the-world-factbook/rankorder/2054rank.html.

CIA death rates, 2014a. https://www.cia.gov/library/publications/the-world-factbook/rankorder/2066rank.html.

CIA fertility rates, 2014e. https://www.cia.gov/library/publications/the-world-factbook/rankorder/2127rank.html.

CIA life expectancy, 2014b. https://www.cia.gov/library/publications/the-world-factbook/rankorder/2102rank.html.

CIA median age, 2014c. https://www.cia.gov/library/publications/the-world-factbook/fields/2177.html.

Darwin, Charles. *The Origin of Species.* New York: Bantam, 1999.

Diamond, J. *Collapse.* New York: Penguin Books, 2005.

Dyson, Tim. *Population and Development: The Demographic Transition.* New York: Zed, 2010.

Edelman, R. Edelman trust barometer, 2013. http://trust.edelman.com.

Einstein, Albert. *Relativity: The Special and General Theory.* New York: Crown, 1961.

Ferguson, N. "Turning Points." *New York Times Magazine,* November 2012.

Goldman, D. *How Civilizations Die.* Washington, D.C.: Regnery Publ. Co, 2011.

Goldstein, J. R., T. Sobotka, and A. Jasilioniene. "The end of 'lowest-low' fertility?" *Population and Development Review* 35(4) (2009): 663–699.

Gourieroux, Christian and Alain Monfort. *Time Series and Dynamic Models.* Cambridge: Cambridge, 1997.

Hirschman, A. O. *Exit, Voice and Loyalty.* Cambridge, Mass: Harvard University Press, 1970.

Jones, Roger D. "Mathematical model for the dynamic behavior of the demographic transition." July 2014. http://xcenternetwork.com/wp-content/uploads/2014/07/140705-demographic-transition.pdf.

Kahneman, D. *Thinking, Fast and Slow*. Macmillan, 2011.

Kirk, Dudley. "Demographic transition theory." *Population Studies: A Journal of Demography* 50(3) (1996): 361–387.

Kuran, T. and C. R. Sunstein. "Availability cascades and risk regulation." *Stanford Law Review* (1999): 683–768.

LeBaron, B., W. B. Arthur, and R. Palmer. "Time series properties of an artificial stock market." *Journal of Economic Dynamics and Control* 23 (9) (1999): 1487–1516.

Notestein, Frank W. "Population: The Long View." In *Food for the World*, edited by Theodore W. Schultz. Chicago: University of Chicago Press, 1945. Oecd, 2014a. http://www.oecd.org.

Orlov, D. *The Five Stages of Collapse*. Gabriola Island, British Columbia: New Society Publishers, 2013.

Rosling, Hans. "Religions and Babies." Technical report, TED Talks, 2012.

Palmer, R., W. B. Arthur, J. H. Holland, B. LeBaron, and P. Taylor. "Artificial Economic Life: A Simple Model of a Stock Market." *Physica D: Nonlinear Phenomena* 75(1) (1994): 264–274.

Quinn, J. "At World's End—The Five Stages of Collapse." *The Market Oracle*, September 2013.

Rowland, Donald T. *Demographic Methods and Concepts*. New York: Oxford, 2003.

Silver, N. *The Signal and the Noise: Why So Many Predictions Fail—But Some Don't*. Penquin, 2012.

Surowiecki, J. *The Wisdom of Crowds*. Anchor, 2005.

Thompson, Warren S. "Population." *The American Journal of Sociology* 34(6) (1929): 959–975.

Timmermans, Jos, Hans de Haan, and Flaminio Squazzoni. "Computational and mathematical approaches to societal transitions." *Comput Math Organ Theory* 14 (2008): 391–414.

Willenius, M. and J. Casti. "Seizing the x-events: The sixth k-wave and the shocks that may upend it." *Tech. Forecasting and Social Change*, in press.

3
UP CLOSE AND PERSONAL

3.1
THE ONE AND THE MANY

On the night of November 12, 1993 at McNichols Sports Arena in Denver, Royce Gracie was the last man standing in an eight-man martial arts tournament, which is now known as "The Beginning." These fights were more like a street brawl with no rules, other than no biting and no eye-gouging. This tournament was televised on pay-TV, and served to introduce the new phenomenon of "ultimate fighting," which turns out to have a huge worldwide following, as evidenced that by 2011 the Ultimate Fighting Championship (UFC) was estimated to be worth around $2 billion by *Forbes* magazine. Commentators have noted that the fascination with this form of combat dates back to ancient Greek and Roman gladiators who fought in the Roman Colosseum and elsewhere for the entertainment of spectators. It would appear that over the last several millennia people have not lost the urge to see violent combat between two humans engaged in a battle to the death. These ultimate fights serve as extreme examples of both complexity mismatches and social mood bias at the level of individual interaction. Let's see why.

At the 1993 Denver tournament, spectators were astonished to see Royce Gracie come out as the winner since he was both smaller and lighter than all the other fighters. But Gracie employed a fighting style developed in Japan called "jujitsu," which turned out to be superior to what all the other competitors were using. So with these skills Gracie prevailed and set the stage for what was to follow over the next couple of decades. Complexity theorists will recognize that what was going on that night in Denver was an interaction between two systems (Gracie and his opponent), each of whom possessed a certain level of complexity (different fighting techniques they could employ). But Gracie's complexity level was simply greater than the level available to the competition, sufficiently greater to push the complexity mismatch to a level at which Gracie could easily prevail despite his lighter weight and smaller size than his opponents.

As for social mood bias, that is a property more of the spectators at the Ultimate Fighting events than the participants. At the time of the Denver "Beginning" in 1993, the social mood as measured by the Dow Jones Industrial Average was setting a new record high. It was a time for expansion, joining together and exploring new forms of activity—including fighting. But by 2010 the UFC was participating in the turn of social mood to the negative, and its $2 billion valuation from *Forbes* in 2011 had shrunk by half in 2012—a 50 percent devaluation. But as the financial markets moved upward at a dizzying rate in 2013 and the first half of 2014, so did the fortunes of UFC, which at the time of writing is again valued at about $2 billion. Such is the power of social mood to move mountains (of flesh, in this case).

The same sorts of arguments regarding complexity and social mood also apply to the activities of groups rather than individuals. Here's an example.

In times of negative social mood when a population believes tomorrow will be worse than today, there is a natural inclination to put off having children. A lot of factors enter into such a decision, including fear of losing a job, uncertainty about availability of housing big enough to accommodate another family member, aversion to bringing a child into a world of turmoil, and so forth. But these factors can all be subsumed into the overarching rubric "fear of the future." An excellent illustration of this line of reasoning is a 2011 report in the *New York Times* headlined "Dip in Birth Rates Reflects Recession, Report Suggests." That report stated that a study by the Pew Research Center showed that birth rates in the United States declined sharply during the recession. Data from 2010 showed a drop to 64.7 births per thousand women in the age group 15–44, from 69.6 per thousand in 2007, the year the recession began. The report showed this declining birth rate phenomenon even more clearly at the regional level. The state of North Dakota, with one of the lowest unemployment rates in the country in 2008, was one of only two states (the other was Maine) to show a slight increase in birth rate from 2008 to 2009. On the other hand, Arizona had the highest decline in birth rate, 7.2 percent. Not coincidentally, Arizona was one of the states hardest hit by unemployment during the recession. Interestingly, the report also notes that the only age group that showed an increased birth rate was for women in the 40–44-year-old category. These are women who cannot put off childbirth any longer. So social mood didn't enter into the choice for them; it was now or never.

Note again that this report was for the period right at the beginning of the Great Recession. Since early 2009 things began to look up, as the social mood meter rose precipitously during the next five years. A 2013 article in *Bloomberg News* headlined this sea change: "Baby Boom in Stronger States Signals US Birth Recovery." Not to belabor the point, the article recounts how the birth rate in states like South Dakota, where unemployment is very low, were on the rise causing demographers to anticipate an upturn in the overall birth rate for the entire country.

The foregoing examples show that the drivers of context in social processes, complexity gaps, and social mood can and do affect people in their personal lives at both the individual and group levels. The balance of this chapter will showcase this fact in different areas, ranging from "middle"-type crises to happiness and on to the ever-vexing problem of personal and group inequality.

3.1.1
EXERCISE: X-EVENTS AT THE PERSONAL LEVEL

That digression business got on my nerves. I don't know. The trouble with me is, I like it when somebody digresses. It's more interesting and all . . . . lots of time you don't know what interests you most till you start talking about something that doesn't interest you most . . . . I like it when somebody gets excited about something.

J.D. Salinger, *The Catcher in the Rye*

Take the authors of this book out for single-malt whiskey. Ask them to relate their personal X-events. What did they learn from the X-Events? Tell them your stories.

3.1.2
DISCUSSION QUESTION: ASHBY'S LAW

Personally, I rather look forward to a computer program winning the world chess championship. Humanity needs a lesson in humility.

Richard Dawkins

Discuss Royce Gracie's win in terms of Ashby's Law of Requisite Variety discussed in Chapter 1.

3.1.3
DISCUSSION QUESTION: HAMLET

Ghost: Do not forget. This visitation
        Is but to whet thy almost blunted purpose.

William Shakespeare, *Hamlet*, Act 3, Scene 4

Discuss the story of Hamlet in terms of personal X-events, mood, and random triggers. How did trend-following lead to a larger disaster than if the problem of the melancholy prince had been dealt with sooner?

3.2
"MIDDLE" CRISES

One of the most talked-about films of 2014 was Richard Linklater's epic *Boyhood*, which gives a blow-by-blow account of the maturing of a young man in twenty-first-century America. While the film covers over 4,000 days of the growing-up of the film's star, Mason Evans, Jr., the actual filming took just 39 days of shooting. Linklater describes his film as an "epic of the intimate," which is very descriptive as we see the hero deal with various life trials that a young man confronts in early twenty-first-century America.

As Anand Giridharadas remarked in a piece about *Boyhood* in the *New York Times*, many of these trials that Mason Evans encountered involved dealing with "ephemeral, adult relationships" he is forced to address in his early years from infancy to pre-teen. Mason is raised by a single mother, Olivia, who engages in—and fails—at four different relationships during his first 12 years. Each of the men presents a very different style of abusiveness to her, each form of abuse presenting difficulties and challenges to Mason in the development of his character. Again, as Giridharadas states, "the movie is about various responses to this male confusion . . . and Mason's own resistance to traditional heteronormative American maleness."

In by-now-familiar terms, what Mason faces is a "complexity gap," in that the outside world, principally his mother and her abusive partners, present him with an environment of very high complexity, while the complexity of his own inner resources for interacting in a suitable and constructive fashion with this environment are quite low. The result is not difficult to predict: forces beyond Mason's control combine with a highly unstable social environment giving rise to a highly stressful, difficult path in reaching a middle-class American life.

One might compare the account of childhood a la Linklater with the popular TV series from the early 1960s *Leave It To Beaver*, which recounts the daily adventures of "Beaver" Cleaver at home, in school and around his suburban middle-class American neighborhood. The show gives a glimpse of a 1950s-style middle-class, white American boyhood and the challenges it posed to a young man like Mason—but from a couple of generations earlier. Even though many episodes of the series revolve about Beaver's parents debating approaches to child rearing, the home environment for Beaver is one of great stability and parental concern. In this version of the American middle-class, parents always have time for their children, no one is ever drunk out of their minds, mothers are always married, and fathers are eternally patient, relatively passive, and totally non-abusive. Reverse all these fantasies and fast-forward 50 years to end up at Linklater's vision of middle-class America and the challenges it poses for growing up as a young male in the early twenty-first century. In the 1950s, the complexity levels between what the young man's resources could supply and what society required were far more in balance than what we see today. Here's another view of Western society today that tells much the same story.

For as long as anyone can remember, the Western middle-class has always been composed of people who had a professional identity. In other words, people chose professions that suited their self-perceived identity. So, for instance, nuts-and-bolts types become travel agents or perhaps accountants. These professions then reinforce their identity. Those days are now drawing to a close. The on-going economic crisis in the Western world, coupled with the rapid pace of technological change as robots take over every type of routine job, leads to fewer and fewer people gaining any satisfaction from their job or even remaining in the same profession. In short, the connection between people and their job has been severed. So instead of having their job reinforce their already existing identity, this disconnection has forced people to find new identities. A good example of this identity restructuring is in academia. This was a field that used to attract people who liked ideas. But as the pressure to publish almost totally meaningless papers and scrounge for pennies from research granting agencies mount, academics have become nose-to-the-grindstone types digging deeper and deeper into smaller and smaller corners of the intellectual landscape.

One of the most evident results of this type of identity change is that a person's story about who they are collapses. As one's job status changes, so does their sense of self-esteem and the way they are viewed by their friends and family. No wonder being unemployed makes people far more unhappy today than in an earlier era. Instead, re-employment today generally leads to a job that involves serving people, such as a waitress, taxi driver, or bank clerk. It's very difficult to create a sense of purpose and identity from such a job. One of the principal reasons for this is that these are very low-complexity jobs. Yet a meaningful sense of self-worth almost always involves projecting an image of someone who's "complicated" and involved in the complexities of modern life. And unless you command a set of very specialized skills that are generally the result of years, if not decades, of training, the skill set of a bank clerk or travel agent is just too low complexity to match up with a high-complexity self-identity.

According to a fascinating account of this loss of identity for today's middle-class, Simon Kuper argues that people who cannot choose their job and thus create an identity from a satisfying, generally non-servile occupation, must create their identity in another manner. Kuper presents the case that one way to do this is via consumption. Such people "become" their favorite make of automobile or their favorite football team or their favorite smart phone. Another way Kuper notes is via social media. For those who do not have a professional identity, their Facebook page becomes their identity through which they present themselves to the world. It can be argued that a large share of the success of sites like Facebook and Twitter is due to the fact that more traditional sources of identity have weakened.

So in both the case of Mason Evans, a growing youngster, and in the case of a former middle-class denizen who lost his professional identity, the difficulties in making their way in modern society can be traced to a growing gap between the level of complexity that society requires and the level that they themselves command. As the gap widens, the social stresses grow. Sometimes there is a technological solution to the problem as with the Facebook identity. Other times no such quick fix presents itself, as with Mason Evans. In the latter case, the stresses mount to the point where an X-event ends the process, often in a dangerous and brutal fashion.

The end result of both of the complexity gaps just chronicled is a dramatic withering away of the traditional American middle-class. As we have just noted, many of the assumptions about American culture—fairness, progress, opportunity—are being questioned. One of the most central assumptions upon which many of the others rest involves the economy and how its largess is distributed among American workers. It will come as no secret to know that this distribution has changed dramatically over the last couple of decades. For example, the median inflation-adjusted family income in the US peaked in the year 2000 at $64,232. Over the next twelve years it fell nearly 6 percent—and is still falling.

The two primary reasons for this decline are the slow economic growth over the past few years, together with the way the economic pie has been divided. The first cause leads to a generally shrinking pie to begin with, while the second is giving an increasingly larger piece of the pie to the now-infamous "top 1%." Figures 3.1 through 3.3 tell this sad story, together showing just how dramatic the situation really is.

So who's to blame for this depressing story? According to findings by the Pew Research Center, middle-income earners target US lawmakers, banks, and big business as the prime reasons why they are poorer today than two decades ago. But others have argued that the real culprits lay in a very different direction. The basic reason they say is that the lack of jobs stems directly from increased productivity due to technology. In other words, the US has mechanized and computerized the labor force into obsolescence.

This notion is by no means new, of course. As long ago as the early nineteenth century, skilled textile workers in England labeled themselves the "Luddites" and went on a machine-bashing attack against technology. Economists

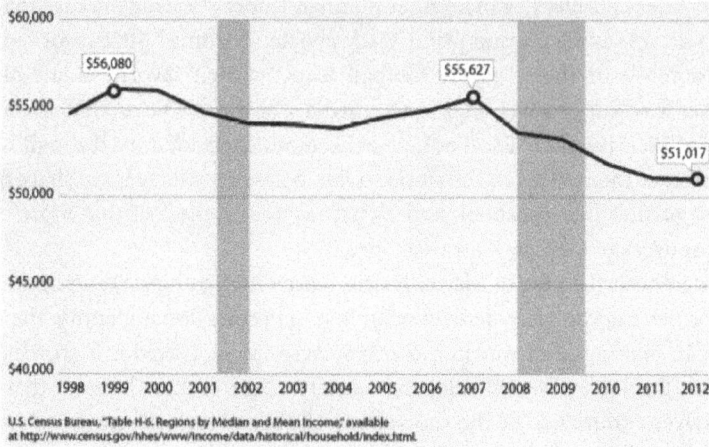

U.S. Census Bureau, "Table H-6. Regions by Median and Mean Income," available at http://www.census.gov/hhes/www/income/data/historical/household/index.html

Median Household Income, 1998–2012.

Figure 3.1

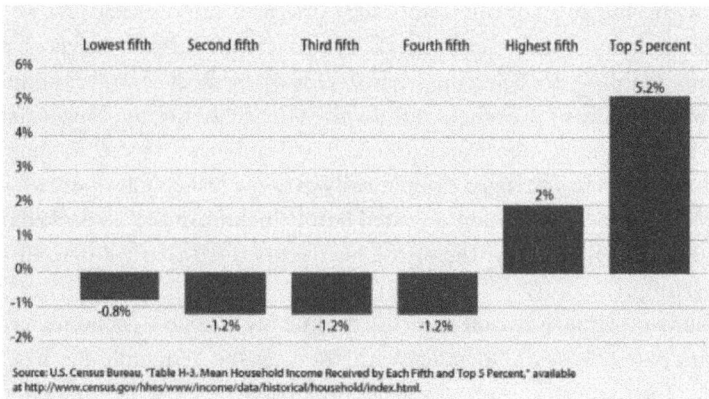

Source: U.S. Census Bureau, "Table H-3. Mean Household Income Received by Each Fifth and Top 5 Percent," available at http://www.census.gov/hhes/www/income/data/historical/household/index.html

Figure 3.2

decry the false notion that an increase in labor productivity by itself necessarily reduces employment. While it is true that there is only a finite amount of labor to carry out, technological change generates new products and services that ultimately increases overall demand for labor. In other words, jobs lost to technology are more than compensated for by jobs gained from the technology. They are just different types of jobs. The machines have simply boosted the demand for workers who can perform "non-routine" tasks, those that complement rather than compete against the jobs now done by the machines. These tasks come at both ends of the job spectrum.

The first type of non-routine task are abstract work calling for problem solving, intuition, creativity, and the like. These are the sorts of things

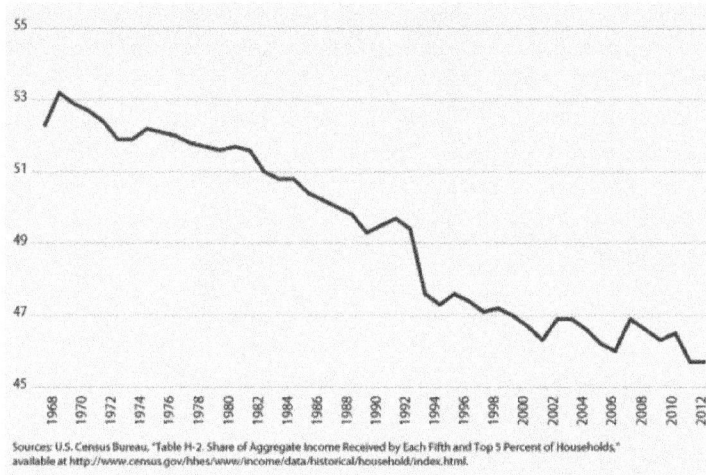

Sources: U.S. Census Bureau, "Table H-2. Share of Aggregate Income Received by Each Fifth and Top 5 Percent of Households," available at http://www.census.gov/hhes/www/income/data/historical/household/index.html.

Share of National Income by the Middle 60 Percent

Figure 3.3

associated with professional jobs like medicine, engineering, and design. At the other end are manual jobs such as driving a truck, cleaning a house, or cooking a meal. Such jobs are difficult to transfer to a computer but rather easy for humans to carry out. The downside is that they involve skills that a large number of people possess, hence don't carry a very hefty paycheck.

So what we are seeing as a consequence of technology is a hollowing-out of the middle. Technology creates lots of jobs at either end of the employment spectrum, but eliminates just those sorts of employment opportunities that previously served to support the middle class, what we might term the "routine" jobs. The end result is job growth in the highly paid and low-paid ends of the job market, while middle-income jobs have gone into free fall. Put compactly, computerization has degraded the quality of jobs for a major slice of the work force.

From the complexity gap line of argument we have been using in this book, the highcomplexity and low-complexity ends of the work force are doing fine, at least insofar as employment goes, if not in terms of actual income at the lower end. But there is a huge gap in the middle. Using the rubber-band stretching metaphor we employed earlier, the band has been stretched beyond the breaking point, and now all we have left are one part of the band in each hand. But the situation is not hopeless, and some commentators have argued that middle-skill jobs will still be available, just not in the traditional blue-collar and white-collar type of positions. Rather, we are likely to see a middle-income group, what some term the "new artisans," consisting of jobs like licensed practical nurses, teachers, repair and support technicians, and personal trainers come to the fore in the decades ahead. Right now, though, we are in the uncomfortable position of being in a transition period where the new artisans are only beginning to emerge as the old middle class dies off.

Much of this middle-class angst over inequality is focused at the individual level, since that's where the actual jobs reside. But there is also inequality at the entire social level, an inequality that threatens the very fabric of modern social and political life as we have known it for the past century or more.

3.3
DISCUSSION QUESTION: HERO'S JOURNEY

Teiresias to Odysseus: When, though, you have killed the Suitors in your palace, by cunning or openly, with your sharp sword, then pick up a shapely oar and travel on till you come to a race that knows nothing of the sea, that eat no salt with their food, and have never heard of crimson-painted ships, or the well-shaped oars that serve as wings. And let this be your sign, you cannot miss it: that meeting another traveller he will say you carry a winnowing-fan on your broad shoulder. There you must plant your shapely oar in the ground, and make rich sacrifice to Lord Poseidon, a ram, a bull, and a breeding-boar. Then leave for home, and make sacred offerings there to the deathless gods who hold the wide heavens, to all of them, and in their due order. And death will come to you far from the sea, the gentlest of deaths, taking you when you are bowed with comfortable old age, and your people prosperous about you. This that I speak to you is the truth.

Homer, *Odyssey*, Book XI

The Hero's Journey is a *monomyth* identified by American scholar Joseph Campbell that describes a set of possibly universal details of personal X-events. The journey is divided into several stages.

3.3.1
STAGES OF THE JOURNEY

> I'm saying to be a hero means you step across the line and are willing to make a sacrifice. So heroes always are making a sacrifice. Heroes always take a risk. Heroes are always deviant. Heroes are always doing something that most people don't and we want to change—I want to democratise heroism to say any of us can be a hero.

Philip Zimbardo

The Ordinary World The hero is uncomfortable or unaware.

The Call to Adventure The hero must face the beginnings of change.

Refusal of the Call The hero fears the unknown and tries to avoid the call.

Meeting With the Mentor The hero meets a seasoned traveler who helps the hero obtain coping skills. The traveler may be internal to the hero.

Crossing the Threshold The hero commits to adventure.

Tests, Allies, and Enemies The hero is tested.

Approach The hero prepares for the major challenge.

The Ordeal The hero confronts death or faces his or her greatest fear. Out of the moment of death comes a new life.

The Reward The hero takes possession of the treasure won by facing death.

The Road Back The hero is driven to complete the journey and return home.

The Resurrection The hero is tested once more on the threshold of home. The conflicts from before the journey are resolved.

Return With the Elixer The hero returns with the reward that has the power to transform the world.

1. Describe the Hero's Journey in terms of complexity mismatch and beliefs about the future.
2. Does the Elixer represent the learning from an X-event?
3. Describe the Star Wars films in terms of the Hero's Journey.

3.4
INEQUALITY KILLS EVERYTHING

American political scientist Francis Fukuyama announced the "end of history" in his essay of the same name published in 1989. In that article, Fukuyama argued that communistic social and economic principles collapsed along with the Soviet Union thus leading to a victory for liberal-democratic capitalism in their decades-long battle. What many people missed in Fukuyama's essay was the part in which he wondered whether citizens in the West would proceed to lose moral and spiritual purpose now that the Cold War had ended the East-West ideological conflict.

In point of fact, what we have seen over the past quarter of a century is that the market system can happily coexist with many sorts of political ideologies, today's China and Russia both illustrate this fact by maintaining systems that are economically capitalistic but politically authoritarian, with both also being highly nationalistic in ideology. As Michael Ignatieff has noted, what we see here is an experiment to answer the question: can a regime continue to exist when it allows its citizens private freedoms but restricts their public freedoms? Put in the terms of this book, what we have here are two systems in interaction: the private enterprise-based economic system and the very publicly-based political system. From a Western point of view, these two systems are in conflict and cannot peacefully coexist for any extended period. By thinking of the complexity levels of these systems, we can rephrase the question as whether the complexity gap between the two systems can be maintained at a level small enough to ensure that no X-event (coup, revolution, or civil war) will take place to break the connection between the two systems.

In his 2014 book *Political Order and Political Decay*, Fukuyama states that "there is a clear directionality to the process of political development," claiming that democracy is where political history is headed. If he's right, then the complexity level of the political system will increase so as to close the gap with the economic system. This process will, in turn, reduce the stress in the overall social system allowing it to at least persist, if not necessarily thrive, for an extended period. In other words, for today's Russia and China to survive, their political ideologies must move toward becoming more democratic.

A necessary condition for Fukuyama's argument to work is a rise in the world-wide middle class. The reason is that as incomes rise, people demand the rule of law to protect their property. They then also demand political participation to preserve and protect their social status, both for economic and moral reasons. As Ignatieff observes, "People become insulted when authoritarian systems of rules treat them as disobedient children."

The United States is perhaps the most clear-cut challenge to Fukuyama's thesis as we have seen a dramatic decline in the American middle class by all measures over the past several decades. This, in turn, seriously challenges American democracy as conceived more than two centuries ago by the founding fathers of the country. We saw this steady disappearance of the middle class in America in the three graphics presented earlier. Just to hammer home the point, here are four additional pointers showing the downward trajectory of the American middle class.

Income Inequality versus Income Tax Rates: Figure 3.4 shows the changes in the share of national income versus the top marginal income tax rates since 1960 for 18 of the world's largest countries in the developed world. What we see here is the change in share of income for the top 1 percent correlates very strongly with decreases in the top tax rates, with the United States prominently leading in this particular race to the bottom (for tax rates versus share of income).

Rich-Poor Employment Gap: The rate of unemployment for the lowest-income families, those earning less than $20,000 per year, topped 21 percent in 2013, almost as high as the total unemployment rate for the Great Depression of the 1930s. But those from households having an income of $150,000 or more, the unemployment rate was just a bit over 3 percent—more than seven times lower, and a level normally considered as "full employment." As noted by Andrew Sum, director of the Center for Labor Market Studies, "One part of America is in depression, while another part is in full employment."

Neighborhood Segregation: A 2013 study by Kendra Bischoff and Sean Reardon found that the segregation of families by socionomic status, i.e., the

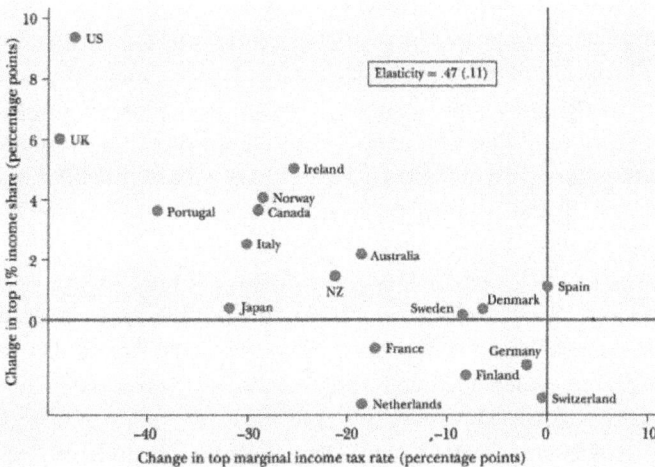

Change in Share of National Income versus Change in Top Income Tax Rates, 1960–2013.

Figure 3.4

rich living with the rich, the poor with the poor, had greatly accelerated in recent decades. Thus, the percentage of families living in middle-income neighborhoods dropped to 42 percent in 2009 from 65 percent in 1970. By way of contrast, the percentage of families living in wealthy neighborhoods more than doubled from 7 percent to 15 percent over the same time period, as did the fraction of families living in poor neighborhoods, which jumped to 18 percent from 8 percent previously.

Downward Mobility: The Baby Boomer generation grew up in a world (the mid 1950s–1970s) of massive individual choices and opportunity. It was a highly individualistic culture, prizing the idea that you could really build yourself. Their children not only inherited this mind-set, but even in the face of today's uncertain economy and daily crises are leading lives dominated and shaped by personal, not collective, values. There will almost surely be a day of accounting for this cognitive dissonance between what people think the world owes them and what the world is prepared to actually hand over. To illustrate this point, Lisa Kahn of the Yale School of Management studied the relationship between growing up in a poor economy and the financial impact that has for young people later in life. Her study found that for each percentage point increase in unemployment, income levels fell by around 6 percent. The most salient point, though, is that this decrease persisted for over 15 years. So graduating from college at the wrong time, economically speaking, means that the graduates will never fully recover and move into higher-paying jobs after the economy comes back to life.

What these facts add up to is that if you grow up when the economic growth is low and unemployment is high, you are already on the slippery slope to downward mobility in every aspect of life. And no amount of self-help books and motivational seminars are going to change this state of affairs. The problem with downward mobility is that it runs against the entire post World War II faith in onward and upward prosperity. Such a world view became a kind of secular religion. And if popular expectations are washed away, the population begins fearing the future rather than welcoming it—the very definition of negative social mood. That, in turn, may well lead to a kind of death spiral for the entire welfare state.

While no country is entitled to economic success, the future is not entirely cast in concrete. As noted by Robert J. Samuelson in a very perceptive and detailed account of this entire process, there are three factors that must be taken into account when making the argument that US prosperity will decline in the coming years.

First, as Niels Bohr once stated, forecasting is very difficult—especially about the future. The graveyard of history is filled with the corpses of forecasts that were simply wrong. For example, many economists thought that there was no engine available to drive the US out of the economic stagnation of the Great

Depression. But they failed entirely to anticipate the Baby Boom expansion following the Second World War, and the technologies that drove the expansion into the suburbs in the 1950s.

A second factor to bear in mind is that perhaps economic growth by itself will not be valued so highly in coming years as in the past. Perhaps Americans will voluntarily cut back on the massive over-consumption of goods and services that has driven the American way of life for the past 50 years or more. Perhaps tomorrow's middle-age American will feel perfectly comfortable with a life with fewer material possessions and more time for their personal lives.

The last item on Samuelson's list is the observation that we are not helpless. We might well be able to soften, if not totally neutralize, the demographic, political, and global economic forces that are driving the middle-class decline. He notes that perhaps the realization that we will live longer lives will motivate people to work longer. And perhaps people will acknowledge that wealthier retirees should not receive subsidies from less well-off younger workers.

These rather bleak facts about the middle class address the question of "What?" But the underlying reason for this hollowing out of the middle class, the "Why?", remains unclear. Let's take a look at what some have proposed for an answer.

Fukuyama believes the basic problem underlying this steady erosion of the middle class rests in a growing distrust in government. To function, the US political system requires that politicians from both sides of the aisle trust one another, at least to the extent that they will generally engage in political compromise. The way things are structured today, the complexity level of the government has way too many political players (i.e., too high complexity) who can each veto any proposed rules. Courts lead the list, but there are also congressional committees, lobbying interests like the American Medical Association, regulatory agencies, and the like. In the end, too many can veto, while too few can act. This is complexity mismatch in action, leading to a state of paralysis.

The foregoing scenario can be summed up by saying there is too much law and too much democracy relative to the capacity of the country to accommodate it. In short, a complexity mismatch, and one that is growing greater by the day. Fukuyama lays this difficulty at the doorstep of the rise of "adversarial legalism," a polite term for way too much formal litigation in the courts and way too few quiet consultations and back-room compromises in the halls of Congress. So paradoxically, we see that too much transparency and public accountability can actually impede the process of government by making politicians loathe to be seen wheeling and dealing in smoke-filled rooms if those wheelings and dealings are going to be on the national news later in the evening. Politicians need some measure of privacy and discretion to do their work and make things happen. And that is exactly what cannot happen if investigative reporters, whistle-blowers, intrusive bloggers, and the like are looking over their shoulder at every moment. To sum it up, less democracy means less veto holders, thus less paralysis in the day-to-day business of government. Put another way, downsize or die!

So Fukuyama's argument is sociologically-based: lack of trust in government and other institutions. But there is a technical argument as well leading to the same conclusion. That is the ever-increasing role that technology plays in everyday life. We alluded to the impact this development has on the core issue in the demise of the middle class, the polarization of the job market. Let's reprise this argument from a slightly different perspective.

A surprise best-seller in the bookstores in the spring of 2014 was a 700-page tome with the unpromising title *Capital in the Twenty-First Century* written by French economist Thomas Piketty. The author states that wage inequality in the United States is "probably higher than in any other society at any time in the past, anywhere in the world." That seems to cover the issue clearly and definitely from all space-time directions! As noted above, the rapid pace of technological developments in the US and elsewhere over the past few decades resulted in the elimination of traditional middle-class jobs. What was left was demand for either highly skilled technically trained workers or low-skill, lowly paid laborers. Piketty's argument says that this process by itself is not sufficient to account for the enormous wealth inequality in the US today. His claim is that it is also driven by the fact that at pay-setting institutions like banks and large corporations, "Above a certain level it is very hard to find in the data any link between pay and performance." Piketty also points a finger at laxity in corporate governance, another contributor to the large-scale mistrust people have today in such organizations.

A central argument in Piketty's book is that when the rate of return on capital becomes greater than the economic rate of growth, then the money that the rich make from their wealth piles up while wages grow much more slowly, if they grow at all. This fact implies that the US is entering a period that will be dominated socially and politically by people with huge amounts of inherited wealth. Piketty calls this a "Jane Austen world" in which people's lives are determined by their inheritance, not their talents and hard work. He goes on to claim that "The belief that technological progress will lead to the triumph of human capital over financial capital and real estate, capable managers over fat-cat stockholders, and skill over nepotism is largely illusory."

But some economists question Piketty's rather pessimistic arguments. For example, Erik Brynjolfsson of MIT says that technology is the main driver in the rich-poor gap and is concerned that even as digital technologies expand overall income, an ever-increasing share of the workforce will not participate in this largesse. He argues that "technology-driven economy greatly favors

a small group of successful individuals by amplifying their talent and luck."
Brynjolfsson also distinguishes between Piketty's "supermanagers" and what
he terms "superstars." The distinction is important, as the superstars obtain
their high income directly from the technology they create, not simply from
moving money and people from one side of the desk to the other. In essence,
Brynjolfsson's argument is that the economy will be increasingly driven not
by managers but by a small elite that innovates and creates. So the forces
that drive the income inequality are primarily the demand for highly-skilled
workers, while those with less expertise get left behind.

In either the Piketty or Brynjolfsson paradigms, though, the essential element is a growing complexity gap between one segment of the workforce (the
supermanagers or skilled elite) and the rest (the worker bees or the unskilled).
This gap widens daily. And as it does, the social stresses grow in just the same
way that the stresses increase between two tectonic plates as they slowly move
in different directions. In both cases, the stresses ultimately must be released.
The typical form of that release is a rapid break or crash. In the social realm,
that usually takes the form of a revolution of some type; in nature, the form
is an earthquake. And in both cases, a huge amount of damage is done to
the social or physical structure. Of course, the landscape that remains after
the crash has many new hills and valleys that the surviving "organisms" can
exploit. In the next chapter, we will take up this point in detail.

For now, though, let's close out our discussion of inequality by report-
ing briefly on the role negative social mood has played recently in the with-
drawal of young people from traditional forms of social interaction. While
these examples are not specifically within the domain of inequality, income
or otherwise, they again illustrate better than any social theory just how the
landscape of social interaction is and has changed in America over the past few
decades. Our first example harkens back to the downward mobility factor that
we discussed a moment ago, while the second involves the way young people
are "hooking up" in the eternal search for a soulmate. As Stephen Stills put it,
"There's something happening here."

Traditionally, Americans are noted for their social and geographic mobility, not to mention being ready to take a risk to move up in the social hierarchy.
But sometime in the past couple of decades, young Americans have reversed
that trend—they have become positively sedentary and risk-averse. For example, the likelihood of someone in their twenties moving to a new state has
dropped by more than 40 percent in the last 30 years. And this is not just for
uneducated high-school dropouts. The very same numbers apply to the col-
lege-educated, as well.

Even more stunning is the fact that a steadily increasing number of teen-
agers are not even bothering to get their driver's license any more. In the early
1980s, 80 percent of 18-year-olds obtained a license. By 2008 that number had
dropped to 65 percent. And this is not due to the Great Recession, or rising

gas prices. Rather, researchers suggest that Facebook and its associated social media clones bear a much greater share of the reason, as several studies have shown that young people spend more time on the Internet than they do on the road.

As an example of this reversal of the American historical tradition, we note that in the mid-1970s when every high-school male and many females too opted for their driver's license and a chance to hit the road, Bruce Springsteen recorded his breakthrough album *Born to Run*. But a couple of decades later, Mr. Springsteen's offerings have a much more somber tone, epitomized by the dead-end dirge "The Ghost of Tom Joad," referring to the main character in John Steinbeck's masterpiece, *The Grapes of Wrath*. This is just what one would expect to see if the young people were in a mind-set that saw the future as a fearful place rather than an environment where opportunity lay around every street corner. In short, in a world in which negative social mood is the dominant belief.

As a capstone to this relentless story of negative social mood and its impact on American life, both at the collective and individual levels, we find that in today's world even the most elemental activities have been "outsourced" to technology. In the film *Her*, a computer so convincingly mirrors human thought, emotion, and speech that the film's male lead, Theodore Twombly, initially dismisses the idea of falling in love with his computer's operating system. Of course, that's exactly what happens. And why? Mostly because when flirting and falling in love with other humans, people usually feel insecure and vulnerable. But when you do it with a machine or by remote control via a social networking site, you can hide. So there is no chance of being judged and rejected.

According to Daniel J. Jones, editor of the Modern Love page in the *New York Times*, the most commonly written about topics in his periodic essay contests were either the theme of trying to figure out "How to navigate a sexual relationship that excluded emotion, or figuring out how to navigate a personal relationship that excluded sex." So nowadays, young people engage in cyberintimacy! Instead of meeting in person at the local bar or fitness club or rock concert, students today spend their evenings on Skype or in chat rooms, exchanging messages deep into the night with their e-lovers. The strange thing is that e-lovers do occasionally actually meet. But when/if that occurs, as often as not the relationship goes up in flames. It seems that being together physically just doesn't "feel right." Jones offers two possible explanations for this.

The first is that perhaps the two e-lovers didn't really get to know each other as well as they had imagined. Instead, what they got was a collection of images, text, and perhaps audio. So the messy parts of a relationship are never on display, only ideal versions of themselves. The personal encounter yanks away that version almost immediately, a very uncomfortable and jarring emotional experience, one that most such e-relationships cannot survive.

A second explanation Jones puts on the table is that the urge to find pleasure through a machine rather than through a person who's in the same room might be a habit difficult to break. In short, the grass always looks greener on the other side of the street. Or in this case, perhaps on the other side of the world.

The role of social mood in this movement from the personal to the mechanical in the romance department is easy to see. When people start fearing the future they are more inclined to withdraw into themselves for protection from an increasingly hostile environment. One way of doing this is not to take chances by putting your inner thoughts, feelings, and emotions on the line for someone else to shoot down. Rejecting rather than welcoming is one of the polarities that dominates in a world of fear. Machine romance is simply one manifestation of that dichotomy.

3.5
DISCUSSION QUESTIONS: PRODUCTIVITY, INCOME INEQUALITY, AND THE JOBLESS RECOVERY

> *Being lazy does not mean that you do not create. In fact, lying around doing nothing is an important, nay crucial, part of the creative process. It is meaningless bustle that actually gets in the way of productivity. All we are really saying is, give peace a chance.*
>
> Tom Hodgkinson

3.5.1
PRODUCTIVITY

> *In an industrial society which confuses work and productivity, the necessity of producing has always been an enemy of the desire to create.*
>
> Raoul Vaneigem

Repetitive jobs are easy to automate, whether the repetition is in either time or space. Repetitive work on an assembly line can be handled by robots. This replaces factory workers. Economists argue that the robots need robot maintenance workers, so that there is not necessarily a net loss of jobs. However, robot maintenance is less repetitive and more creative work than that done on the assembly line and requires workers who are able to perform creative work that is difficult for computers.

Assembly-line work represents repetition in time. There are also jobs that are repeated in locations all over the world simultaneously. An example of this is teaching basic college courses. The same lectures on acids and redox reactions are being given in chemistry classes in many countries. This process is being automated by Massive Open Online Courses (MOOCs)—online courses in economics, science, humanities, and art. Students can go online and view lectures from the world's experts on almost any topic. They can also receive online feedback. This will soon be a tremendous productivity enhancement as fewer professors are needed to teach basic college courses. Professors will still be needed, however, to teach creative non-repetitive skills such as laboratory work, creative writing, undergraduate and graduate-level research, and critical thinking. These are all creative skills that are difficult to teach online.

3.5.2
INCOME INEQUALITY

The ability of the 1 percent to buy politicians and regulators is nothing new in American politics—just as inequality has been a permanent part of our economic system. This is true of virtually all political and economic systems.

Eric Alterman

Productivity in the US has increased steadily since 1947 when measurements began. Verify this. Increased productivity has taken the blame for the rise in income inequality that has occurred since the 1970s. Verify this. What other factors may be responsible for the rise in income inequality?

1. Income inequality was as high as it is today in the first few decades of the twentieth century. Income became more equal in the middle of the twentieth century. By the beginning of the twenty-first century, income inequality had risen again. What was the main source of income for the rich in the early twentieth century, labor or capital? How does this differ from the income sources in the twenty-first century?

2. What was the level of income inequality in 1929 just before the Great Depression? Just before the Great Recession of 2008? Are there periods of high income inequality that did not lead to an X-event in the economy?

3. How is income inequality related to social mobility? There are strong indications that mobility decreases as inequality increases. Verify this. It is a common belief in America that opportunity exists for all—that any person has the opportunity to become a millionaire. Does social mobility data support this belief?

3.5.3

THE JOBLESS ECONOMIC RECOVERY

There's a whole generation of young people who are faced with the so-called "jobless recovery." Necessity is the mother of invention. They are out there, all around the world, creating new companies.

Don Tapscott

1. After the recession that ended in 2009, the US experienced several years of jobless recovery, economic recovery with simultaneous high unemployment. Companies were making money, but they were doing it with fewer employees. How did increased productivity contribute to the high unemployment?

2. As the recovery proceeded, companies once again started hiring, but a common complaint among employers was that it was very difficult to get employees with the more-creative skill set that was needed. Is there a business opportunity in education and re-education? Can creativity be taught? Will creativity be learned?

3. What are the implications for economies of scale in business? Will companies increase in size or shrink as a result of the changing skills of the workforce?

4. Most people would agree that a successful person probably had to work hard to become successful. The American national mythology flips this statement around and claims the converse is true. If you work hard, you will become successful. Some people take this a step further and claim that if you work hard at anything, then you are entitled to become successful. College graduates who cannot find work often feel betrayed because they "followed the rules," but the "promised" outcomes did not occur. The national mythology is being challenged by reality. Deeply held beliefs are being attacked. Does this lead to cognitive dissonance? What are the implications for peoples' behavior? What are the implications for the probability of an X-event?

3.6
POLARIZATION AND SOCIAL MOOD

If there is any period one would desire to be born in, is it not the age of revolution, when the old and the new stand side by side and admit of being compared, when the energies of all men are searched by fear and by hope, when the historic glories of the old can be compensated by the rich possibilities of the new era?

Ralph Waldo Emerson, 1837

Let's take a closer look at a simple model for the dynamics of social polarization. For simplicity, we only consider mood polarization, the optimistic or pessimistic attitude of the population. We focus on the situation in which there is not a single zeitgeist in the population, but the case in which there are two moods, a subpopulation of optimistic people and a subpopulation of pessimistic people. In this model we allow people to be influenced by themselves and by their connections. We do not consider income inequality. That topic is saved for discussion questions and follow-on work.

We base the model on the observation that people's moods are influenced by their current mood and the moods of the people in which they are connected. People are captured by the *groupthink* of their cohort. We look at the phenomenon of *homophily*, people choosing to connect with people of similar mood, in the exercises.

We also consider the situation based on the observation that happy (optimistic) people tend to have more connections in their networks than unhappy (pessimistic) people. Happy people are willing to have more complex networks than pessimistic people because they feel less risk in social interaction. We can think of this as happy people have more opportunities because of their connections, while unhappy people have fewer opportunities in their lives.

3.6.1
EXAMPLES: STABLE STATES

Let's look at a few examples. Consider the case in which everyone is happy.
This can be represented by the expression

$$...,h,h,h,h,h,h,h,h,h,h,h,h,... \qquad (3.1)$$

where h indicates a happy optimistic person. All of each person's neighbors are happy. Therefore, at the next time step, the state of the system will remain unchanged; everyone will still be happy. A similar thing occurs if every person is sad. The state is completely sad.

Now consider what happens when one person is an outlier; there is one sad person among many happy persons.

$$...,h,h,h,h,h,s,h,h,h,h,h,h,... \qquad (3.2)$$

The sad person has happy neighbors. The happy neighbors outnumber the single sad person, so, at the next time step, the sad person will flip to a happy person. The happy people also have mostly happy neighbors, so they will remain happy. Similarly for a happy person in the presence of sad people.

What happens if there are large numbers of happy and sad people? Let's assume for the moment that people are clumped; happy people are mostly neighbors of happy people, and sad people are mostly neighbors of sad people. We can represent this situation by

$$...,s,s,s,s,s,s,h,h,h,h,h,h,... \qquad (3.3)$$

There is an interface where sad people have happy neighbors and vice versa. In physics this interface is known as a *domain boundary*. There are two domains, a sad domain and a happy domain.

Far from the domain boundary the situation reduces to our previous example; sad people remain sad and happy people remain happy. We need only consider people in the vicinity of the domain boundary in order to determine the short-term dynamics of the system. Consider the sad person just to the left of the domain boundary. The neighbors to the left of this person are sad. The neighbors to the right are all happy. If the sad person has equal number of neighbors to the right as to the left, then the net mood of the cohorts of the sad person at the domain boundary is neither sad nor happy. The sad person at the boundary must rely on his or her own experience to determine mood. In that case, the sad person breaks the tie of the cohorts by continuing in the current mood, sad in this case. Therefore, there is no change in dynamics at the domain boundary due to the sad domain. By the same argument, the happy domain cause no change of state. Therefore, a domain boundary in which the domains have greater extent than the neighbors of people at the boundary is stable and unchanged.

One conclusion would be that, according to this model, large groups of happy (optimistic) people can coexist stably with large groups of sad (pessimistic) people.

3.6.2
EXAMPLES: MIXING OF OPTIMISTS AND PESSIMISTS

Now let's consider an example in which the polarity of the mood changes rapidly. This is a situation in which each person has several friends of the opposite polarity and several friends of the same polarity. Our state may look something like this.

$$\ldots,h,s,h,s,h,s,h,s,h,s,h,s,\ldots \tag{3.4}$$

In this example, half the people are sad, and half the people are happy.

Pick out a sad person. Now assume that the sad person is connected to one neighbor on the right and one neighbor on the left. Then the connected neighbors are happy and the sad person is sad.

Therefore, in the next time step, the sad person becomes happy. Similarly, if a happy person is connected to one neighbor to the left and to the right, then the happy person becomes sad. The state of the system then "flashes." people alternate between being happy and sad.

Suppose now, however, that a sad person is connected to one neighbor on each side, and a happy person is connected to two neighbors on each side. Then a majority of a happy person's connects are happy. Therefore all the happy people remain happy. The sad people, however, do not remain sad. They also become happy. After one time step, everyone is happy. This is a stable state.

Now suppose that the sad people are connected to two neighbors on each side, and the happy people are connected to three people. Then the state after one time step will be all sad, again a stable state.

In general, by these same arguments, one can see that, for the initial condition specified by Equation 3.4,

1. If both sad and happy people are connected to an even number of neighbors on each side, the system is stable.
2. If both sad and happy people are connected to an odd number of neighbors on each side, the system oscillates.
3. If one group is connected to an even number of neighbors, while the other group is connected to an odd number, then in one time step, the system moves into the stable state in which all people are happy or all people are sad.

The details of the final states, in this example, whether stable or oscillating, are not important. The important thing to note is that the final states are very dependent on the details of the number of neighbors with which sad and happy people are connected. When optimists and pessimists mix, the outcome is unpredictable.

3.6.3
EXAMPLES: COMPETITION BETWEEN UNIFORM AND MIXED DOMAINS

Now consider what happens when a uniform domain abuts a mixed domain as illustrated by this set of initial conditions.

$$\ldots s,h,s,h,s,h,s,h,h,h,h,h,\ldots \qquad (3.5)$$

Suppose that the sad people are connected to one neighbor on each side, and the happy people are also connected to one neighbor on each side. Then using the previous logic the state at the next time step is

$$...h,s,h,s,h,s,h,h,h,h,h,h,h,... \tag{3.6}$$

The mixed domain has started flashing, and the uniform domain has encroached one person into the mixed domain. This process continues until the system is completely happy. The happy domain has subsumed the mixed domain. A similar conclusion is reached if the uniform domain is sad.

Now consider the case in which sad people are connected to one neighbor on each side, and happy people are connected to two. If the initial conditions are given by Equation 3.5, then in one time step, the state of the system becomes entirely happy.

If, on the other hand, the initial uniform domain is sad,

$$...h,s,h,s,h,s,h,s,s,s,s,s,s,s,... \tag{3.7}$$

then the system evolves in one time step to the stable state containing two uniform domains.

$$...h,h,h,h,h,s,s,s,s,s,s,s,s,... \tag{3.8}$$

If the happy people have three neighbors on each side and the initial conditions are given by Equation 3.7, then the sad domain slowly eats the mixed domain.

The takeaway heuristic from this example is that clusters of people that contain optimists and pessimists are unstable. When these clusters encounter uniform clusters of either optimists or pessimists, the mixed clusters eventually disappear leaving uniform clusters of optimists and/or pessimists.

3.6.4
DISCUSSION QUESTION: RED COUNTIES AND BLUE COUNTIES

Byrdes of on kynde and color flok and flye allwayes together.

William Turner, 1545

Can these observations be translated to politics? It is claimed that people of similar politics tend to inhabit the same geographical locations. Is this claim well-founded? If so, does our simple model inform this observation?

3.6.5
THE MODEL

Let's generalize these results beyond heuristics. We translate our assumptions,

1. Peoples moods are influenced by their current mood and the moods of the people in which they are connected. People are captured by the groupthink of their cohort.
2. Happy people have more network connections than sad people.

into mathematical language.

Consider N nodes located on a circle. Each node can have two values, designated 1 for a *happy* node and -1 for a *sad* node. Sad nodes are connected to m neighbors on each side. Happy nodes are connected to $n \geq m$ neighbors on each side. Therefore, sad and happy nodes are connected to $2m$ and $2n$ other nodes, respectively. The *state* of the system at time t is given by vector $x_i(t)$ where each component of the vector is either happy ($x_i(t) = 1$) or sad ($x_i(t) = -1$). The rule for updating the state from time t to time $t + 1$ is

$$x_i(t+1) = \theta[z_i(t)] \tag{3.9}$$

where

$$z_i(t) = \frac{1}{2n+1} \sum_{j=i-n}^{i+n} x_j(t) = h_i(t) \tag{3.10}$$

for $x_i(t) = 1$,

$$z_i(t) = \frac{1}{2m+1} \sum_{j=i-m}^{i+m} x_j(t) = s_i(t). \tag{3.11}$$

for $x_i(t) = -1$. Here, θ is defined such that it is 1 if its argument is greater than zero and -1 otherwise.

The update rule simply states that a happy(sad) node is happy(sad) at time $t + 1$ if the majority of the nodes the happy(sad) node is connected to including itself were happy(sad) at time t. If the majority was sad(happy), then the happy(sad) node turns into a sad(happy) node. Since $n \geq m$ the happy nodes are connected to the same or greater number of other nodes than sad nodes.

3.6.6
SIMULATION RESULTS

The results for equal values of n and m are displayed in Figure 3.5. It can be seen that all states settle to a fixed value. States that start out happy become somewhat more happy. States that start out sad become somewhat more sad.

The results for unequal values of n and m are displayed in Figure 3.6. It can be seen that, once again, all states settle to a fixed value. The fixed-state values, however, are a bit more complex than in the case of $n = m$. We are able to classify these states with a simple theory.

3.6.7
FIXED POINTS OF THE SYSTEM

We can find the final states, or *fixed points*, of the system with a simple approximation. If we define the mean of $x_i(t)$ as

$$\langle x_i(t) \rangle = \frac{1}{N} \sum_{i=1}^{N} x_i(t) \qquad (3.12)$$

then, in the Mean Field Theory Approximation $\left(\langle \langle f(x) \rangle \rangle \approx f(\langle x \rangle) \right)$, the fixed points of the system are given by (from Equation 3.9)

$$\langle x_i(t+1) \rangle = \langle x_i(t) \rangle \qquad (3.13)$$

$$p - (1-p) \approx p\,\theta_h + (1-p)\,\theta_s \qquad (3.14)$$

where p is the ratio of happy nodes to total nodes and

$$\theta_h = \theta \left[\langle h_i(t) \rangle \right] \qquad (3.15)$$

$$\theta_s = \theta \left[\langle s_i(t) \rangle \right]. \qquad (3.16)$$

One might think that θ_h might be always equal to one, and θ_s might always be equal to negative one. We saw in the examples, however, that this is not always the case.

n=m=2

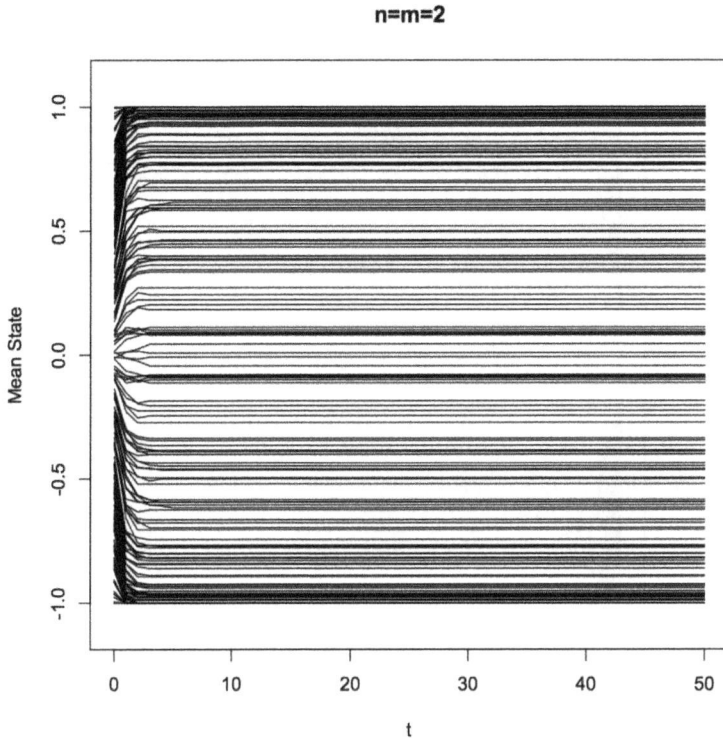

Figure 3.5 Plot of the mean value of a state as a function of time for n = m = 2. The initial values of the mean states were chosen from 1 to 1. The state vectors were of length 500. The actual configuration of each state was chosen randomly. It can be seen that all states settle to a fixed value. States that start out happy become somewhat more happy. States that start out sad become somewhat more sad.

3.6.8
FIXED POINTS SOLUTIONS

There are four possible solutions for the fixed points, one for each of the possible combinations of θ_s and θ_h.

$$p = 1 \qquad (3.17)$$
$$\langle h_i(t) \rangle = 1$$
$$\theta_h = 1$$
$$\theta_s = 1$$

n=50, m=2

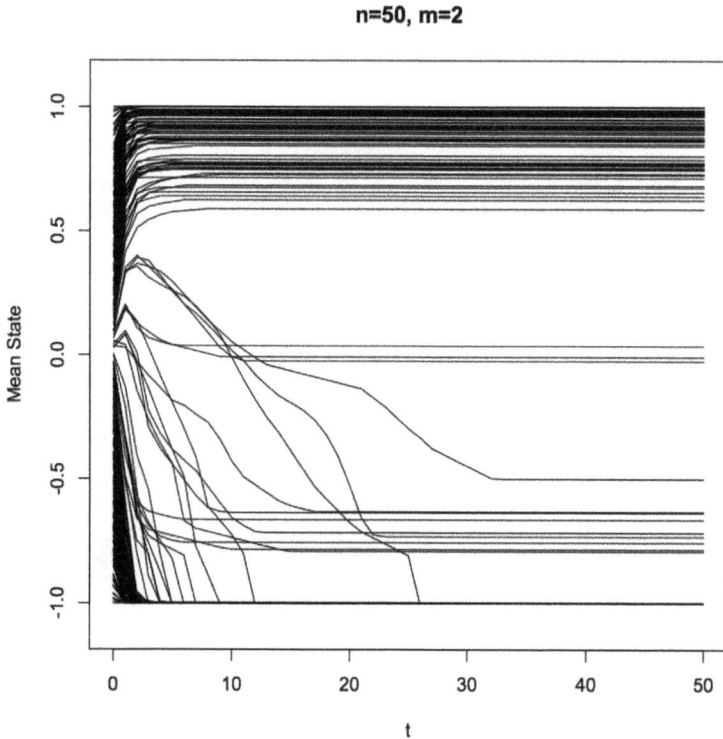

Figure 3.6 Plot of the mean value of a state as a function of time for n = 50 and m = 2. The initial values of the mean states were chosen from 1 to 1. The state vectors were of length 500. The actual configuration of each state was chosen randomly. Mean field theory defines four classes of states: all happy, all sad, states of equal numbers of happy and sad, and states with random fixed points. All four of these classes appear in the figure.

$$p = \frac{1}{2}$$ (3.18)
$$\langle h_i(t) \rangle = 0$$
$$\theta_h = -1$$
$$\theta_s = 1$$

$$p = 0$$ (3.19)
$$\langle h_i(t) \rangle = -1$$
$$\theta_h = -1$$
$$\theta_s = -1$$

The fourth solution ($\theta_h = 1$ and $\theta_s = -1$) states that any value of p can be a fixed point.

We label the first three fixed points, respectively, as the Happy fixed point in which every node is happy, the Tranquil fixed point in which half the nodes are happy and half are sad, and the Sad fixed point in which all the nodes are sad. We label the fourth solution as the Whatever fixed point.

Given our examples, we might speculate on the character of each of the fixed points. Equations 3.17 and 3.19 are clearly uniform happy and sad states respectively. We have seen that these states are stable. The Whatever fixed point must then correspond to states of multiple stable domains, such as a happy domain abutting a sad domain. Equation 3.18 must then correspond to a mixed or similar state. We have seen that this state is unstable and evolves into a state with multiple uniform domains.

3.6.9
EXERCISE: CHARACTER OF FIXED POINTS

Build your own simulation and verify or discredit the speculations of Section 3.6.8.

3.6.10
STABILITY OF FIXED POINTS

Alliances and partnerships produce stability when they reflect realities and interests.

Stephen Kinzer

The fixed points may be stable, the system is attracted by them. This is like a ball being attracted to the bottom of a round bowl. They may be unstable, the system is repelled by them. This is like a ball balanced on top of an inverted round bowl. One small nudge and the ball rolls down the side of the bowl. Each attractive fixed point has a basin of attraction, a set of system parameters, and initial conditions from which the system is driven to the fixed point.

These results can be understood intuitively. In the case $n = m$, the values of the final fixed points are dominated by the initial values for small values of n and m. Take the extreme case of $n = m = 0$. Each person has no friends. In that case there are no friends to persuade a person to change moods, and the final average state is given by the initial mood of the population. Each person has his or her original mood. If n and m are small but nonzero, then a happy population tends to increase somewhat in happiness, while a sad population does the opposite.

In the case $n \gg m$, the mood of the population as well as the details of the configuration of the state play a larger role in determining the behavior of happy people because of their increased connectivity. The final behavior of the state is very sensitive on the initial conditions when the initial population of happy and sad people are nearly equal.

3.6.11
EXERCISES: MODELING INEQUALITY

Americans have so far put up with inequality because they felt they could change their status. They didn't mind others being rich, as long as they had a path to move up as well. The American Dream is all about social mobility in a sense—the idea that anyone can make it.

Fareed Zakaria

- Groupthink
  All mass movements, as one might expect, slip with the greatest ease down an inclined plane represented by large numbers. Where the many are, there is security; what the many believe must of course be true; what the many want must be worth striving for, and necessary, and therefore good.

  Carl G. Jung, *The Undiscovered Self*

  1. Reproduce the groupthink calculation.
  2. How do the results vary with n and m?
  3. Are there characteristic patterns in the state vectors that lead to distinct final outcomes?

- Homophily
  Cass Sunstein, an amazing legal scholar, says that one of the dangers of the Internet is that we're only hearing like voices, and that makes us more polarized. Homophily can make you really, really dumb. What's incredible about the net is we have this opportunity to hear more voices than ever. But the tools we tend to build to it have us listening to the same voices again and again. Search in the future needs to lead us to people, to places, to voices. My hope is that in the future we get over homophily and we start looking for really productive serendipity.

  Sahana Chattopadhyay

  Homophily is the observation that "birds of a feather flock together." People choose to be connected to other people with similar outlooks.

  1. Create a model in the style of the groupthink model that describes homophily.
  2. Does your model change the average state of a person? If not, why not?
  3. Combine the homophily model with the groupthink model. Does anything surprising happen?

- Income Inequality
  It is a wise man who said that there is no greater inequality than the equal treatment of unequals.

  Felix Frankfurter

  Generalize the social-mood models to include income inequality.

3.7
DISCUSSION QUESTIONS: PERSONAL X-EVENTS

A revolution is coming—a revolution which will be peaceful if we are wise enough; compassionate if we care enough; successful if we are fortunate enough—But a revolution which is coming whether we will it or not. We can affect its character; we cannot alter its inevitability.

Robert Kennedy, Speech in the United States Senate (9 May 1966)

3.7.1
BIPOLAR DISORDER

Where would the memoir be without bipolar writers? I mean, that's what —that whole oversharing thing is really a very clear symptom of bipolar disorder. And I'm not saying that every, you know, I'm not accusing every memoirist of being bipolar. But I think in a way it's kind of a gift.

Ayelet Waldman

1. What is bipolar disorder?
2. How is bipolar disorder on an individual scale similar to or different from social polarization due to income inequality?

3.7.2
NATURE VS. NURTURE

One brain's blueprint may promote joy more readily than most; in another, pessimism reigns. Whether happiness infuses or eludes a person depends, in part, on the DNA he has chanced to receive.

Thomas Lewis, *A General Theory of Love*

There is literature that indicates that each person is genetically disposed to happiness or unhappiness. Identify the literature on the topic. What does this imply for the likelihood of persuasion being an important factor in changing mood?

3.7.3
EVIDENCE-BASED BELIEFS

I would never die for my beliefs because I might be wrong.

Bertrand Russell

1. Do people base their beliefs/mood on evidence?
2. What does the scientific literature say about this topic?
3. What happens when people's self image and beliefs are challenged—cognitive dissonance? What is cognitive dissonance? Is cognitive dissonance a type of personal X-event?
4. What are the implications of evidence and non-evidence-based beliefs for people management in various organizational structures? Corporate? Military? Entrepreneurial? Artistic? Academic? Government? Non-Profit?

3.7.4
CHANGING RELIGIOUS DEMOGRAPHICS IN THE UNITED STATES

Religion is what keeps the poor from murdering the rich.

Napoleon Bonaparte

• Demographers have made the observation that as a population advances through the demographic transition (see Chapter 2) the population becomes more secular and less religious. They attribute this to the premise that people become more in control of their lives as the demographic transition advances, and they rely less on a personal deity. Is this a way of saying that individuals become more complex and the complexity mismatch between the individual and the individual's environment is reduced? Does this make sense? Are there other possible explanations?
• The Pew Research Center published survey results that indicated that the number of Christians in the United States has dropped 8 percent in the period 2007 to 2015. The number of people not affiliated with a religion has increased by 6 percent in the same time period. This is

consistent with the demographers general observations. In this time period evangelical Christians have become very vocal and show signs of being threatened. There is talk of a "War on Christianity."

- In this same period there was a dramatic reversal in public opinion regarding same-sex marriage. The population as a whole became more tolerant of the practice. Much of the opposition to the reversal came from evangelical Christians.
- Is this religious polarization related to the polarization due to income inequality? Does this represent a mood/belief polarization? Is change occuring too quickly for many people's comfort? Is this an indicator on an impending X-event? Are we in an X-event?

3.8
DISCUSSION QUESTIONS: POLITICAL X-EVENTS

Let us not seek the Republican answer or the Democratic answer, but the right answer. Let us not seek to fix the blame for the past. Let us accept our own responsibility for the future.

John F. Kennedy

3.8.1
POLITICAL LEADERS

Politics is the art of looking for trouble, finding it everywhere, diagnosing it incorrectly and applying the wrong remedies.

Groucho Marx

Consider the following to be a true statement: political leaders tend to have above average capabilities, but not exceptional capabilities. How would you explain this statement in terms of complexity mismatch? Can you find studies in the literature that argue the truth or falsehood of the statement? How would mood affect the degree to which this statement is true?

3.8.2
SOCIAL MOOD AND THE 2014
US MIDTERM ELECTION

Win or lose, we go shopping after the election.

Imelda Marcos

US presidential elections occur every four years. Members of one house of the legislative branch, the House of Representatives, are elected every two years. One third of the members of the other house, the Senate, also are elected every two years. Thus the term of a House member is two years, and the term of a senator is six years. The president, Barack Obama, who belongs to the Democratic Party, was halfway into his second term and was not facing re-election in 2014. At that time, the Senate was controlled by the Democratic Party, and the House of Representatives was controlled by the Republican Party. With the election late in 2014, the Republican Party took control of the Senate and increased control of the House. The executive branch of the government was then controlled by the Democratic Party, and the legislative branch was controlled by the Republican Party.

By the election all imaginable indicators of mood except one were positive.

- The Dow Jones Industrial Average was at an all-time high.
- The unemployment rate dropped below 6 percent from a high of 10 percent in October of 2009.
- There was steady job growth from January 2010 through the election of 2014.
- In six years the budget deficit had been reduced by half.
- The Consumer Confidence Index was the highest in six years.
- Oil production nearly doubled from its low in 2008.

The one indicator that was negative was income inequality. In 1976 the top 1 percent of households received 8.9 percent of all income. By 2012, this number was more than 22 percent.

The key observation is that the 2014 midterm election did not seem to obey the rule that presidential elections seemed to follow. The presidential outcomes data indicated that the rising stock market indicated good expectations for incumbents. Yet, in the 2014 legislative races, incumbents fared badly.

- Does this mean that the stock market is a bad indicator of social mood?
- Is this an example of belief-based voting rather than evidence-based voting?
- Does this mean that income inequality trumps all other indicators of social mood?
- Income inequality can be thought of as a complexity mismatch in the social fabric. Can a competition between complexity mismatch and social mood exist? Are the two independent measures of context, or are they correlated? In this example, why would social mood disagree with income inequality?
- In the situation of large income inequality, do stock traders still represent the entire mood of the population?

3.8.3
TEXAS POLITICS

We oppose the teaching of Higher Order Thinking Skills . . . critical thinking skills and similar programs that are simply a relabeling of Outcome-Based Education . . . which focus on behavior modification and have the purpose of challenging the students' fixed beliefs and undermining parental authority.

2012 Platform, Republican Party of Texas

In the US, congressional districts are redrawn at least every ten years after the national census. The districts may be redrawn more often. Each district is entitled to elect one member of the House of Representatives of the United States. There are two major political parties in the US, the Republicans and the Democrats. The demographics of the parties are such that the Republicans tend to be older and Caucasian males, while the Democrats tend to be younger, female, Hispanic, African-American, and other minorities. The districts are often redrawn to benefit one political party or the other by taking advantage of these demographic differences. In extreme cases, the process of redrawing district boundaries to benefit one party or the other is known as *gerrymandering*.

The state of Texas has a long history of gerrymandering. In the 1990s, the Democrats redrew district boundaries to benefit the Democratic Party. In the 2000s, the Republican Party gained a majority in the Texas legislature and redrew district boundaries to benefit their party. The ensuing political fight led to many Democratic legislators leaving the state so that there would not be a quorum for the vote on redistricting—thus making Texas politics a great source of entertainment for the rest of the US.

The Republican majority also passed legislation to require picture IDs from citizens before they would be allowed to vote. On the surface, this does not seem to favor one party over the other, however, discrimination surfaces when one digs deeper. For instance, the law permitted, as legal identification, expired gun licenses from other states, while not permitting student IDs and social security cards. This favored the Republican demographic.

By modern American standards, this behavior seems extreme. What are the forces driving this polarization? It turns out that the overall demographics of the state are changing. In 2000, 52.4 percent of the population was Caucasian according to the 2000 census. By the 2010 census, this number had dropped to 45.3 percent. Moreover, 65 percent of the population growth was Hispanic, which tends to vote Democratic. The Democratic base is increasing, while the Republican base is decreasing, leading to a loss of political power by the Republicans and a more visible polarization of the Texas population.

Change is bad for Texas Republicans in this scenario. The changing demography is driving behavior designed to prevent change—any change—from occurring in Texas. In 2012, a plank of the Republican platform opposed the teaching of critical thinking in Texas schools. Critical thinking was "challenging the students' fixed beliefs and undermining parental authority."

Is the picture presented in this section factually accurate? The picture is one of cultural polarization, which expresses itself as political polarization. Is there polarization in mood—optimistic and pessimistic? Is an X-event imminent? Is the political process sufficient to contain the X-event? Are Texas politics an indication of a complexity mismatch in the entire US?

3.9
DISCUSSION QUESTIONS: UTILITY

Anything that won't sell, I don't want to invent. Its sale is proof of utility, and utility is success.

Thomas A. Edison

The standard prescriptive model for rational decision making under uncertainty is utility theory. Under utility theory a risk-neutral decision maker, i.e., one who is indifferent to risk, faced with selecting from among multiple alternatives with uncertain outcomes would always choose the alternative with the highest expected value. However, humans are often not risk-neutral. Depending on the circumstances they will exhibit either risk-seeking or risk-averse behavior. Risk-seeking behavior means that given a choice between a sure thing and a gamble with an equal expected value, the decision maker will choose the gamble. This is the behavior that people exhibit when they gamble in casinos. The gamble favors the house, but people play anyway. Risk-aversion is the opposite. Given the same choice, a risk-averse decision maker will choose the sure thing. This is the behavior that people exhibit when they purchase insurance. They essentially pay the insurance company to take the risk away.

The way utility theory captures risk attitudes is by encoding them in a function. The principle is based on the fact that convex functions of a random variable shift the expected value up while concave functions shift the expected value down. Thus, a risk-averse person would have a concave utility function (assuming an attribute where more of it is preferred). This effectively lowers the expected value of a gamble relative to the value of a sure thing. Another way to think about it is that it discounts the value of an opportunity based on the level of risk. This effectively increases the threshold expected value required in order for the risk-averse person to take a risk.

3.9.1
RISK AVERSION

The fear of death is the most unjustified of all fears, for there's no risk of accident for someone who's dead.

Albert Einstein

In this chapter, the suggestion was raised that people may be becoming more risk-averse.

- If that is true, what does utility theory tell us about the number of risky economic and technology opportunities people are willing to exploit?
- If we assume that economic growth is the aggregate result of a very large number of people attempting a very large number of new things, then from an economic standpoint, we are concerned about maximizing expected value because the losses and gains will average out due to the law of large numbers. What does utility theory suggest about economic performance over time if people become more risk-averse?
- Does increasing risk aversion mean decreasing flexibility both among individuals and organizations?
- Does decreasing flexibility mean an increasing complexity gap relative to the economy and the environment?
- If so, does increasing risk aversion contribute to social fragility and increased susceptibility to X-events? How might this be explained via utility theory?

3.9.2
PROSPECT THEORY

Failures of perspective in decision-making can be due to aspects of the social utility paradox, but more often result from simple mistakes caused by inadequate thought.

Herman Kahn

As was noted above, utility theory is a prescriptive theory for decision making. That is—it defines how people should make decisions, not how they actually do. Prospect theory was developed in order to better reflect how people actually make decisions. One of the key insights is that people tend to focus on gains and losses relative to a reference point rather than the absolute value of an attribute. For example, utility theory would predict that a risk-averse but very wealthy person would not be very concerned with the risk of losing $100 because relative to his or her absolute wealth, the amount is trivial. In reality, people don't make decisions based on their absolute wealth, they make it based on a reference point. So the wealthy person would view the situation as losing $100 as opposed to going from $1,000,000,000 to $999,999,900. Framing the problem this way could result in different decisions because people tend to weigh losses much more heavily than gains.

- One of the results of prospect theory is that it explains how people can be risk seeking when there is a low probability of a gain and risk-averse when there is a low probability of a loss. How does this relate to observations made in this chapter with regard to risk aversion? In particular, the notion that those with very little view everything as a gain and are willing to take big risks while those with a lot view everything as a loss and thus, are risk-averse. Does this comport with your experience? Does this comport with the traditional notion of people's behavior when they have "nothing to lose"?
- Could we view an X-event as having the effect of changing the reference point, and consequently altering people's risk preferences?

3.9.3
PROBABILITY ADJUSTMENT

Money has no utility to me beyond a certain point.

Bill Gates

Under both utility theory and prospect theory, the decision maker chooses the alternative with the highest adjusted expected value. Up until this point we have discussed how we modify the value portion to adjust for risk attitudes, but the other component of expected value is the probability distribution of outcomes. Under utility theory, a probability distribution is applied directly to weight the utilities of a different outcome. However, it is well known that people tend to overweight low-probability events and underweight high-probability. Prospect theory includes a weighting function to adjust probabilities for this effect.

- What does this suggest about human responses to low-probability events that will incur a loss? Will people over allocate resources to avoid or mitigate such events?
- The probability of dying in a terrorist attack is incredibly low relative to other risks such as the probability of a fatal automobile accident. Do people's responses to the risk of terrorism comport with this idea of overinvesting in response to low-probability events?
- Is such behavior consistent with the ideas of Joseph Tainter that were discussed in Chapter 1?
- How would such resource allocation decisions affect the ability of one to respond to unexpected events such as X-events?
- If resources, i.e., wealth, are heavily concentrated in a small percentage of a society's population, then those in that group are faced with the potential for very large losses due to low-probability, adverse events (they have a lot to lose). This would suggest risk-averse behavior. Does this imply that the overall aggregate resource allocation behavior of a society with substantial income inequality should be fairly risk-averse? What does it imply with regard to the resilience of such a society?

BIBLIOGRAPHY

Atwater, Peter. "Colloquium presented at the Center for Complex Systems and Enterprises." Stevens Institute of Technology, October 2014.

Brynjolfsson, E., and A. McAfee. *Race Against the Machine*. Cambridge, Mass: Digital Frontier Press, 2012.

Fukuyama, F. *Political Order and Political Decay*. New York: Farrar, Strauss and Giroux, 2014.

Giridharadas, A. "Observations on America's Middle-Class Malaise." *New York Times*, September 2014.

Gonglof, M. "The U.S. has the worst income inequality in the developed world, thanks to Wall Street." Study, June 2013.

Ignatieff, M. "Doubling Down on Democracy." *Atlantic*, September 2014.

Jones, D. "Romance at Arm's Length." *New York Times*, February 2014.

Kahneman, D., and A. Tversky. "Prospect Theory: An Analysis of Decision Under Risk." *Econometrica: Journal of the Econometric Society* (1979): 263–291.

Keeney, R. L., and H. Raiffa. *Decisions with Multiple Objectives: Preferences and Value Tradeoffs*. Cambridge, United Kingdom: Cambridge University Press, 1993.

Kuper, S. "The Great Middle-Class Identity Crisis." *Financial Times*, November 2013.

Marrone, P. "The Ultimate Fighting Championship: A New Variety of Primitive Spectacle." *American Thinker*, November 2010.

McWhinnie, E. "3 Charts Revealing America's Disappearing Middle Class." *Wall Street Journal*, October 2013.

Pew Research Center. "America's Changing Religious Landscape," May 2015 http://www.pewforum.org/2015/05/12/americas-changing-religious-landscape/.

Piketty, T. *Capital in the Twenty-First Century*. Cambridge, Mass: Belknap Press, 2014.

Samuelson, R. "The Withering of the Affluent Society." *The Wilson Quarterly*, Summer 2012.

Von Neumann, John and O. Morgenstern. *Theory of Games and Economic Behavior*. Princeton, New Jersey: Princeton University Press, 1947.

4
STAYIN' ALIVE

4.1
TIME FOR A CHANGE

In the mid 1860s, mining engineer Fredrik Idestam established two ground wood pulp mills on the Nokianvirta River near Tampere, Finland giving rise to the name of the firm we all know today as Nokia. How that company transformed itself from a wood pulp company producing paper products to what was up until a few years ago the world's largest cell phone manufacturing firm is a circuitous tale. This story is a fascinating account of how alert management can shift the focus of an entire organization in time with changes in the outside world so as to more effectively deploy available resources. At one time or another, Nokia proceeded from the production of paper to producing rubberized cables for telephone and electrical firms, as well as bicycle tires, and rubber boots. In the mid-twentieth century, Nokia expanded its repertoire to include consumer electronics by manufacturing electricity generation machinery, personal computers, and communication equipment. In 1992, the firm decided to abandon consumer electronics and focus solely on the rapidly growing telecommunication sector. This decision sowed the seeds of Nokia's early dominance of the cell phone business when the company used its expertise to develop the GSM technology, which was later adopted as a de facto standard for mobile telephony in the 1990s. It's estimated that by 2008 worldwide GSM connections were growing at a rate of over one million per day.

The opportunistic path from a small wood pulp manufacturer to the world's largest cell phone company is a textbook example of how a firm can adapt to a changing environment and consumer needs. Of course, nothing lasts forever, not even a sense of how to shift product lines in tune with the changing winds of fortune. The beginning of the end of Nokia's dominance of the cell phone market was the launch of the iPhone by Apple in 2007. And by 2010, the Apple iOS and Google's Android-based phones pushed Nokia out of the top spot in the world's cell phone sales. By then, Nokia's slide was clear to see as they failed to really penetrate the North American market with its Symbian-based smart phone. And in early 2011, Nokia and Microsoft announced a business partnership, and from early 2011 through 2013 Nokia fell from first place in global smart phone sales to number ten. Finally on September 2, 2013, Microsoft acquired all of Nokia's mobile device business, effectively putting Nokia totally out of the cell phone business.

While Nokia's story of rags to riches and back to rags again is particularly dramatic, the annals of business are filled with similar stories of firms that began their life with a product line that dramatically shifted over the course of time to something entirely different. Here are a few examples:

- *Avon*: This firm began in 1886 with founder David McConnell selling books door-to-door. He always gave perfume samples to the women who bought a book from him. When he realized how much the ladies liked the perfume, McConnell started the California Perfume Company and hired female sales reps since he believed that they would be better at networking with female customers. The rest is history.
- *Samsung*: Samsung Sanghoe formed his firm as a trading company in 1938. His business then was shipping dried Korean fish, vegetables, and their private brand of noodles to customers in Manchuria and Beijing. No electronics, no cars, no high-tech, simply very low-tech food products. But times change—and so did Samsung!
- *Wrigley*: We're all familiar with chewing gum and the Wrigley name stands at the top of the list of suppliers of such staples as Juicy Fruit, Orbit, and the like. But Wrigley started its life in 1891 as a firm that sold a product that you certainly would keep as far from your mouth as possible: soap!
- *Colgate*: At its founding in 1806, Colgate was a manufacturer of soap, candles, and starch. It made its first toothpaste only 67 years later.

So what do these stories tell us? Mostly, they chronicle how a company with a forward-looking management can jump from one line of business to something quite different and make a huge success of it. In general, the companies started small and adapted to the market as times changed. The management of all the firms understood one simple principle: to grow as a firm, you have to adjust with the times. This is the essence of adaptation. In just a bit more detail, the corporate management had to combine two lines of thought into one by answering the following pair of questions: 1) What resources—human, financial, operational, and otherwise do I have at my disposal? 2) What kind of products could I produce with these resources that could more well serve the market today and tomorrow better than the market of yesterday? All of these stories illustrate successful answers to these questions. Of course, there are no guarantees in life and there certainly exist many examples of wrong answers to the questions, too. How to separate the right from the wrong is part of our story in this chapter. So by way of contrast, let's recount a few of those wrong answers just to see how things can go off the tracks instead.

4.2
FAILURE IS ALWAYS AN OPTION

During the second half of the twentieth century, if you'd asked anyone who was the world's leading photo-imaging company they would have looked at you like you'd just dropped in from outer space. The answer to that question was so obvious that to even ask the question marked one as a cultural illiterate. Anyone who even faintly understood the term "photo imaging" would have instantly replied, "Kodak, of course." And indeed it was that obvious. There were no contenders within sight even for second place. Kodak was it. And almost everyone would have imagined that the Soviet Union would collapse before Kodak. But times change, both for companies and for countries. And by 2012 the USSR was but a distant memory—and Kodak was in the bankruptcy courts on its way to oblivion. Perhaps it's not accidental that the reasons why both the USSR and Kodak collapsed are about the same. So as the story of this chapter is business, not geopolitics, let's look at Kodak, not the Kremlin.

Strangely, Kodak was not only the chief producer of image technology ranging from cameras to film to industrial imaging products, it was the inventor of almost all the technology that it ultimately transformed into commercial products. These inventions even included the very digital technology that was ultimately Kodak's undoing. Basically, Kodak didn't keep up with the digital innovations its patents pioneered. Instead, other firms like Canon and Nikon moved commercialized digital photography, while Kodak remained mired in its analog-imaging culture. At the same time, mobile phone pioneers led by Apple and Samsung added digital photographic capabilities to their phones, removing the need for people to carry a separate camera to capture their "Kodak moments." Thus ended Kodak's reign as the name synonymous with photography. But Kodak was far from the first company to come undone as a result of not paying attention to a changing world. So let's look a bit beyond the simple imaging-based reasons for Kodak's failure and try to understand the larger lessons at play leading to its corporate demise as chronicled by Koren Simon in her blog *Roots of Resilience*.

Lesson 1: Lack of a Clear Vision Kodak's vision statement says it will "help consumers, businesses, and creative professionals unleash the power of pictures . . . " Compare this statement with the vision statement of Apple: "At Apple, great ideas have a way of becoming great products . . . " See any difference? In case you didn't, notice that the Apple vision talks about "great products" that the firm will produce to help their customers. By way of contrast, the Kodak vision says nothing even semi-specific about what it will do to help their customers, only that somehow they will help them unleash the power of pictures. In short, the Kodak vision statement is vague and fuzzy, perhaps because the company was involved in too many different things— cameras, film, film developing, printing, and so forth. The company's vision did not evoke the idea of a firm that was on top of current technology and would harness that technology for its customers. Instead, it was a vision that offered to facilitate, not lead.

Lesson 2: Lagging Behind the Trend Curve Technology is always on the move, and never more so than today. So even the leading firm can quickly become a follower if it doesn't keep its eyes and ears open to new trends, looking to see how its existing resources can be deployed to lead the trend, not follow it. The big question here is how did Kodak, the developer of the first hand-held camera, end up lagging other imaging innovators?

Lesson 3: Failure to Guard Your Interests As noted, Kodak was the developer (and patent holder!) for much of the digital technology that other firms like Apple, Samsung, Sony, and Fujitsu used to take the lead in the world of digital imaging. Instead of keeping this technology to itself, Kodak licensed it to these firms who then used it to bury Kodak, not praise it. In fact, following Kodak's filing for bankruptcy these patents were the main asset the corporation still held. And court calendars around the world are still filled with various lawsuits in progress against the leading firms in the digital technology business. If only Kodak had used their own IP and developed it instead of selling it to these other firms, the world of digital technology would look vastly different today at least insofar as who the leading players are.

From the standpoint of the principal themes of this book—social mood, complexity overload, and resilience—the second lesson, lagging behind the trend, is a classical example of complexity overload. Technology was marching on; Kodak wasn't. As the world of digital technology became increasingly complex, Kodak stuck to what it knew: analog technology, which as far as Kodak was concerned was something simple that they understood. There was no time taken to learn an entirely new way of imaging the world. Unfortunately (for Kodak), the gap reached a breaking point early in the twenty-first century and the road has been straight downhill to the bankruptcy court ever since.

The other two lessons, having a vision that's too vague and guarding your interests, are more properly matters for the next chapter on resilience. What we can say here is only that the rapid emergence of digital imaging was an X-event for Kodak. But the firm's inability/unwillingness to roll with that punch instead of trying to resist it sent the firm down for the ten-count. In short, Kodak did not display the kind of organizational resilience needed to see how to deploy their resources in the new environment created by the X-event. That inability turned out to be fatal for the company.

Returning to the question of why Kodak let digital cameras drive the firm into a penny-stock company, it's useful to consider the observation of Jeff Stibel, formerly a cognitive scientist from Brown and now an entrepreneur who has engineered turnarounds at several companies including Dun & Bradstreet Credibility Corporation. He says, "Once the human mind has set out to do something, or has gotten into the habit of doing something, changing it is very hard." And it's not simply that people resist change. What's astounding is how many companies drive at top speed into the brick wall of corporate disaster. Another turnaround specialist, Thomas Kim of the Turnaround Management

Association, says that it's only when the situation reaches the point that the firm can't make the payroll or make a loan payment or the cheques start to bounce that the sense of urgency becomes great enough that people become ready to change. But why do they have to wait until the chances to make meaningful change are so small?

One reason offered by Michael Hannan and John Freeman in their book *Organizational Ecology* is that inertia is "in their genes." In fact, it's a gene that made many of these companies successful to begin with. The authors argue that companies rarely change their fundamental structural features. Change is risky, since it involves doing something that isn't already working. They note that even lackluster product lines have some customers. So a company that engages in frequent changes is far more likely to kill itself off with bad choices than firms that resist change.

Hannan and Freeman further argue that in today's economy accountability and reliability select against constant radical experimentation. A quintessential example of this is McDonald's, whose most characteristic feature is that their food, décor, and service will be reliably the same wherever in the world you find their store. And the bigger and older the company, the heavier is the selection bias toward stability. Kodak is a textbook example of this phenomenon.

To quote Thomas Kim on the matter of corporate inflexibility, "There are companies that perform reasonably well, and are completely dysfunctional." Then the market changes. "In companies that we see that hit the wall, that dysfunctional corporate culture really becomes a problem." And even a dysfunctional culture, once established, is amazingly efficient at reproducing itself. Gabriel Rossman, a sociologist at UCLA, notes that if new entrants simply assimilate to the majority and enter the system slowly, the founding culture can persist over time even if in the long-run they constitute a vanishingly small minority. In sociology, Rossman says this is what's called "The Founder Effect." In corporations, it has a different name: "How We've Always Done Things." And now you see how companies fail!

What we see here are two conflicting forces at work: a conservative, inertial resistance to change and herding behavior giving rise to speculative bubbles. The bubbles involve big risks that would not be undertaken using conventional risk/reward, cost-benefit analysis. The bubbles give rise to the X-events we've spoken about many times, and ultimately clear out social and economic structures that are no longer functional. This clearing process creates new "eco-niches" that provide opportunity for entrepreneurs and innovators to offer new products and services. This process is what the Austrian-American economist Joseph Schumpeter termed "creative destruction." Let's take a harder look at what he had in mind and try to relate it to the story we've told thus far about corporations, business, and economics.

4.3
OUT OF THE ASHES

The idea of creative destruction as argued by Schumpeter is that the capitalistic system exists in a constant state of ferment, a system continually reinventing itself through the process of innovations regularly destroying existing firms and enterprises and building new ones. While this is perhaps a good elevator sales pitch for Schumpter's big idea, it is woefully incomplete in a number of ways. For instance, if we take the foregoing description at face value we'd be led to think that innovators simply and inevitably just push aside the established order of things in a kind of "out with the old, in with the new" fashion. The picture that this conjures up is a kind of relentless death of existing firms and the birth of new ones.

A big problem with this picture is that the power structure in most capitalistic societies consists of the political ruling class(es) and the business/financial establishment. As a general rule, the last thing this power structure wants is dramatic, meaningful, lasting change. Rather, it has a vested interest in just the opposite, namely, maintenance of the status quo. The tools at the disposal of the powers that be to maintain the existing systems are enormous, both legislative and financial. This is why it's no joke to talk about the nonstop "Express Shuttle" between Capitol Hill and Wall Street. It's not a fiction of a conspiracy theorist's imagination.

So how does an innovation ever get off the ground when the very social, political, and economic fabric of society is massed against it? The answer is not that the innovations are so spectacular and so irresistible that they overcome all obstacles put in their path. Rather, the innovations move into the mainstream in the same way that a chemical reaction is accelerated by the presence of a catalyst that speeds up the reaction several hundredfold. In the case of the economy, that catalyst that gives life to Schumpeter's vision of creative destruction is an X-event. In short, some unavoidable, uncontrollable event has to take place that blasts the existing social structure apart. This might be something globally quick and destructive like a world war, a massive earthquake, volcanic eruption, or even global warming. But it may be something more nuanced like a financial crash, an epidemic, or a political revolution. Any of these things can blow away existing structures, creating new "niches" to be filled by innovators with new products and services.

The above picture shows that in one sense, Schumpeter was right. The innovators do replace the existing establishments. But they don't do it directly; they do it with the essential help of the X-event that creates the niches giving their innovation space in which to develop. So the role of innovators in this picture is to continue to develop their innovations, but also to keep their eyes open for new niches that open up the chance for their innovation to "breathe." If the timing is not right and no X-event takes place, then the innovation will die on the vine. The innovation will also die if the innovator is looking the other way when the right niche appears. When opportunity knocks, you have to be there to open the door. So when Schumpeter argues that it is entrepreneurs who drive economies, he's right. But those entrepreneurs don't do any driving without an X-event to smooth their way.

The creative destruction aspect of Schumpeter's message is what seems to have caught the fancy of the capitalistic class. In their ardor for creation of new ideas and firms, the capitalists ignore the second part of Schumpeter's argument. That is that as innovation becomes mechanized in corporate labs, entrepreneurs will disappear. The implication of this argument is that the very success of capitalism leads to socialism! That is exactly what happened in Japan. But some argue that in the United States those with an entrepreneurial leaning simply leave their current situation, raise venture capital, and start a new company. If the government creates an environment, legal and financial, that's favorable to this process, then socialism can be averted.

The philosophy and concepts underlying creative destruction a la Schumpeter are intimately intertwined with the notion of resilience that we've spoken about in passing earlier in the book. We'll defer a discussion of these connections to the next chapter, since resilience will be the piece de resistance for that chapter. But to give just a flavor of how creative destruction and resilience interact, let's take another look at the way complex systems—and complex companies—collapse.

4.3.1
DISCUSSION QUESTION: BAILOUTS

> *You know Americans are obsessed with life and death and rebirth, that's the American Cycle. You know, awakening, tragic, horrible death and then Phoenix rising from the ashes. That's the American story, again and again.*
>
> Billy Corgan
>
> After the financial crisis of 2008, the Federal government bailed out the automobile industry in the US. The industry made a satisfactory recovery. Some people made arguments that the industry should have been allowed to fail. Discuss.

4.4
MIRROR VISION AND COMPLEXITY OVERLOAD

On March 27, 1977 the greatest airline disaster in history took place at Los Rodeos Airport on the island of Tenerife in the Canary Islands. Two 747 aircrafts, KLM Flight 4805 and Pan Am Flight 1736, collided in fog. The crash killed 583 people, with just 61 survivors. The accident has been analyzed in depth and the conclusion is that it was caused by a cascade of errors in both communication and human nature.

The communication aspect was probably exacerbated by the fact that much traffic, including the two airliners involved in the crash, had been diverted from the major airport on the island, Gran Caneria Airport, due to the explosion there of a terrorist bomb. This overload of traffic certainly increased the volume of communication between the airport tower at Los Rodeos and the flight crews, which many felt led to much greater confusion than usual in the aircraft crews following the tower's instructions.

On the human nature side, KLM pilot Jacob van Zanten was eager to get his plane off the ground, since he and his crew were nearly at the limit of their on-duty time. If they didn't take off soon, they would have to stay in Tenerife overnight and the flight would be postponed until the next day. Van Zanten made a fatal mistake by beginning his takeoff when he heard the message, "You are clear" from the tower. His wish to get into the air likely caused him to overlook the fact that he needed a second clearance before he could take off. But van Zanten's failure to wait for that clearance before beginning his takeoff required yet one more confusion to give rise to the devastating accident.

As the KLM flight was beginning its takeoff, the Pan Am flight was attempting to find its assigned taxiway. But in the heavy fog, the Pan Am crew overshot that taxiway and as they hunted for the right path they ended up directly on the same runway that the KLM flight was using for takeoff. As the Pan Am plane emerged from the fog, van Zanten tried to get his plane into the air but his attempt was just a bit too late. The Dutch plane bounced off the top of the 747 upper cabin, ripping it from the Pan Am plane and sending the KLM plane more than 100 feet into the air before it crashed down and exploded into a ball of fire. The Pan Am plane was also sliced to pieces and caught fire.

So what we have here is a case of communication complexity overload, aided and abetted by the sense of urgency on the part of the KLM crew to get their plane into the air. If any one of these factors had not been present, there would have been no accident. Almost the very same statement can be made for the overwhelming majority of airplane accidents. The details, of course, are different. But the structure of the story is always the same. A constellation of individual mistakes and misunderstandings combine to create a horrific accident that could otherwise have been avoided. So let's distill this pattern for airline accidents into some general principles for complex systems.

Airplanes, corporations, banks, and many other organizations have detailed plans for how to address what might be termed "single-point failures." That is, failures that arise from a single problem. For dealing with such "simple" failures, systems have redundant controls, backup systems, manual overrides, warning systems, and the like to compensate and address failures.

The real problem with complex systems, though, is that the very complexity of the system generally means that failures occur when many things go wrong at once. The Tenerife air disaster is a textbook example of this kind of failure. In that case, no single safety measure, compensating redundancy or fail-safe mechanism put in place to address just one of the failures leading to that accident would suffice. As we saw, the crash required several different types of failures to all occur in order for the failure to take place. Can we do better than to simply protect against single-point failures? James Reason and Dante Orlandella of the University of Manchester in the UK thought so and developed what's now termed the Swiss Cheese model for accident analysis—and prevention—in several areas, including aviation.

The Swiss Cheese model can be thought of in the following terms. First, complex systems have several ways to defend against failure. Each one of these procedures can be thought of as a slice of Swiss cheese with the holes in each slice corresponding to a point-failure within the system. It is a type of failure that that slice *cannot* defend against. So to see the entire defense, you stack up all the slices. Then for a total systemic failure to occur, a hole on each slice must line up with holes on all the other slices. Therefore, as long as the positioning of the holes on each slice is more-or-less independent of the others, a failure will be averted. So the basic idea is to have many defenses, each protecting against a particular point-failure. Unless the holes are strongly dependent, i.e., the slices only look different and are actually protecting against roughly the same failures, the totality of the stacked slices will protect against cascades of the sort that brought down the two planes in Tenerife.

To close this section, let's now return to the question with which we began, namely, how can a corporation continue to prosper in the face of a continually changing environment? Perhaps the best way to see the answer is to look at a couple of examples of firms that dominating their niche—until they collapsed—and analyze why they went into terminal failure.

4.4.1
DISCUSSION QUESTION: SWISS-CHEESE MODEL

Luck is a very thin wire between survival and disaster, and not many people can keep their balance on it.

Hunter S. Thompson

The greatest safety emerges when the locations of the holes in the Swiss-Cheese Model are uncorrelated. What mechanisms will correlate the locations of the holes in real situations? How might the holes become correlated without people becoming aware of the correlations?

4.5
OVER THE EDGE OF THE TECHNOLOGY CLIFF

In the latter half of the twentieth century, two of the highest-flying tech firms were Wang Laboratories, manufacturer of word processors, and Research in Motion (RIM), a Canadian company that produced the famed Blackberry, which took the world of cell phones and electronic email by storm. It's instructive to look at the timeline of these two companies, both in terms of technology and revenues, to see how things can go very badly very quickly for a company operating in a fast-changing environment.

According to columnist Joe Nocera of the *New York Times*, the growth of Wang Laboratories was so steep that the company's founder An Wang kept a chart in his office showing when he expected the firm to overtake IBM. Wang thought it would be sometime in the mid-1990s. But he ran afoul of one of the principal rules of corporate survival: don't ever believe that tomorrow will be just like today—only a little better. In other words, avoid falling into the trap of optimistic trend-following. And when IBM released the first personal computer the handwriting was on the wall for Wang. An Wang simply didn't take the personal computer seriously. The firm failed to recognize that people wanted more from a computer than for it to be a glorified word processor. And even though the company tried to play catch-up once they caught on to this fact of technological life, the rest of the world was already a million miles down the road and Wang could never catch up. By 1992 Wang Laboratories was bankrupt.

At just about this same time that Wang was sinking into a financial black hole, RIM's flagship product, the Blackberry, was dominating the cell phone and wireless email market. And as recently as five years ago, the company still had over 20 percent of the smart phone market. Now it's less than two percent and still falling. What happened? The easy answer is that Apple's introduction the iPhone in 2007 and similar devices from other competitors like Samsung sounded the death knell for the Blackberry. But the real story is a bit more nuanced than that.

To begin with, the founders of RIM made the same mistake about Apple that An Wang made about IBM: they just didn't take the iPhone seriously. They thought the touch screen was inferior as an input device than the keyboard on the Blackberry and that long, detailed business memos and emails that were the specialty of the Blackberry crowd could not as easily be created with a touch-screen input. Obviously, they never envisioned "apps" that would appear to solve all these sorts of problems.

Even worse, the Blackberry management fell in love with their existing customers and did everything possible to protect this base of loyal clients. So when a new competitor like Apple steps forward with a new technology instead of embracing that technology and building it into their own product, the firm stood paralyzed and instead focused all their resources on protecting what they'd already built. As with Wang, Blackberry finally bit the bullet and tried to play catch-up with Apple, Samsung, Sony, and all the other smart phone manufacturers. And again as with Wang, Blackberry could never catch up.

These two stories can be multiplied several-fold, raising the question of whether the collapse of a company dominating an industrial sector is inevitable. Basically, the answer is yes. Occasionally we see a firm like Burberry or General Electric cited as examples of firms that successfully reinvented themselves. But these are the exceptions that prove the rule. Companies like Wang and Blackberry are the rule, not the exception.

4.5.1
EXERCISES: COMPLEXITY MISMATCH IN BUSINESS AND POLITICS

> *An organization's ability to learn, and translate that learning into action rapidly, is the ultimate competitive advantage.*
>
> Jack Welch

Suppose you were an idiot, and suppose you were a member of Congress; but I repeat myself.

Mark Twain

You can lead a man to Congress, but you can't make him think.

Milton Berle

1. Describe the relationship between complexity and risk in a business, political, or social situation. What is the likely outcome if a low-complexity vendor tries to deliver product to a high-complexity customer? What if the opposite were true—a high-complexity vendor delivers product to a low-complexity client? What would happen if the complexity of a political system were more complex than the constituency? What would happen if there was a complexity mismatch between a health-delivery system and the health needs of patients?
2. Consider the following to be a true statement: political leaders tend to have above average capabilities, but not exceptional capabilities. How would you explain this statement in terms of complexity mismatch? Can you find studies in the literature that argue the truth or falsehood of the statement? If politicians are accurate representatives of their constituencies, then is there complexity mismatch between the complexity of the constituents and the problems that governments need to address?

4.6
HOW MOOD AFFECTS THE NATURE OF PRODUCTS

I invented nothing new. I simply assembled the discoveries of other men behind whom were centuries of work. Had I worked fifty or ten or even five years before, I would have failed. So it is with every new thing. Progress happens when all the factors that make for it are ready, and then it is inevitable. To teach that a comparatively few men are responsible for the greatest forward steps of mankind is the worst sort of nonsense.

Henry Ford

The momentum of the mind can be vexingly, involuntarily capricious.

Gregory Maguire, *A Lion Among Men*

4.6.1
COMMODITIES

In economics, the simplest product is a commodity, a product in which the decision to buy is based solely on its price or cost. The canonical commodity is a bushel of corn. For many purposes, such as feeding cattle, one bushel of corn is the same as another, except for how much it costs. There are buyers who would like to purchase a bushel (Demand) and sellers who would like to sell a bushel (Supply). The price of the transaction is negotiated or is the consequence of a bidding process.

4.6.2
RISK IN COMMODITY PRODUCTION

Corn, however, has another property: it is planted in the spring and harvested in the fall. Its value has a temporal or risk component. The corn seed in the spring has less value than the harvested corn in the autumn. Moreover, the buyers of the corn, e.g. the cattle producers, may have different needs for corn at different times of the year. Therefore, their willingness to pay a certain price for the corn varies throughout the year. In order to reduce the risk of both buyers and sellers, a new product, called a future, was developed. A future is simply a guarantee that the corn will be sold at a certain price at a given time in the future. Buyers or sellers can purchase this future at a fixed price from the seller of the future, and the future seller absorbs the risk of price fluctuations. Since corn has been grown for many years, the future seller can calculate the risk he or she bears and can price the future accordingly. The transaction of buying and selling a bushel of corn has just increased in complexity from simply consideration of the price at a given time to consideration of the price now and the price at some future time.

4.6.3
PRODUCT QUALITY

We do not, however, make our purchasing decisions based solely on price and risk. We also base it on the quality or value of the particular product. For instance, a Mercedes Benz automobile is usually perceived to have higher value than a Chevy; thus we may be willing to pay more for the Mercedes than the Chevy. This is different than the time dependence of the value. This difference in value is due to workmanship, reliability, company reputation, social perceptions, and other characteristics of the product. A purchasing or selling decision that takes price, time, and value into account is more complex than a simple commodity transaction. The components of the more complex sales transaction are of three types: 1) a component associated with cost or price, 2) a component associated with quality or value, and 3) a temporal component associated with risk. Risk can be mitigated by speed. For instance, if a bushel of corn could be grown in one day, there would be little need for a future's contract associated with the product.

4.6.4
MOOD AND COMPOUND PRODUCTS

We can think of the bushel of corn, the quality of the corn, and the risk associated with producing the corn as a single product. The social mood can affect the composition of the product. If, for instance, the mood is optimistic, then the perceived value of the risk of producing the product may be smaller than if the mood is pessimistic. This may reduce the farmer's willingness to pay for a futures contract. If several farmers feel the same way, then the risk profile of the market is altered. If the supply of corn is unusually high at the end of the season, then the farmers may take in less revenue than they expected. The fact that they did not properly hedge their bets can be attributed directly to their optimistic mood.

4.6.5
META-PRODUCTS

A product can become more complex. The futures can, themselves, be regarded as a product. They are a quantity that has a price. The price fluctuates with the market. If a speculator feels that the price of futures will increase, then the speculator may buy futures. This is called a *long sale*. If the speculator feels the price will decrease, then he or she may sell futures. This is called a *short sale*.

More complexity is possible. Options are a right, but not an obligation, to buy or sell a product at a future time at a given price. A *call option* is the right to buy a product at a given price. A *put option* is the right to sell at a given price. A farmer may purchase a put option to sell the bushel of corn at a certain price at a certain date in the fall. If the market price is favorable, then the farmer will probably choose to exercise the option. The futures are also products. Speculators may decide to buy call or put options on futures based on their belief in market trends.

Another layer of complexity is added with derivative products. Options can be bundled together to make financial instruments, derivatives, that can hedge against even more risk than an increase or decrease in price of an underlying product asset. For instance, excessive fluctuations in price of the underlying product can be hedged.

Our simple bushel of corn has turned from a single product into layers of products: bushel of corn, future on the price of corn, option on the price of corn, option on the price of a future of corn, and derivatives based on the price of options on the price of a bushel of corn and on the price of futures on the price of corn. As the complexity of the product is increased, the market for the more complex products decreases. There are many more people who would like to buy a bushel of corn than there are people who would like to buy a financial derivative that hedges against exotic characteristics of the price fluctuation of corn.

Our simple bushel of corn has turned into a complex risk product. The price of risk management is determined by the mood of the market. The complexity of the product is also affected by the mood of the market.

4.6.6
DISCUSSION QUESTIONS: RISK, MOOD, AND COMMODITIES

> Hedge funds, private equity and venture capital funds have played an important role in providing liquidity to our financial system and improving the efficiency of capital markets. But as their role has grown, so have the risks they pose.

Jack Reed

- What is the *triple constraint*, and how is it related to product complexity?
- What are the conditions in which the owner of a call or put option should exercise the option?
- What happens if there is no market for a complex product? Discuss how product complexity that is greater than market complexity can lead to an extreme event.
- The standard method of pricing futures, options, and derivatives is with the Black-Scholes method. A key assumption in the method is that a market exists for the underlying product asset, and that standard statistical laws apply to the market. As the products become more complex and the market shrinks for the products, these assumptions break down. The break-down of the assumptions increases the uncertainty of the pricing with the Black-Scholes method. Uncertainty increases risk. We therefore have the paradox that increasingly complex products that are intended to reduce risk actually increase risk. Look at the derivation of the Black-Scholes method. Identify where the assumptions of market and statistics enter.
- Discuss the concept of *price*. When is price determinable? What if you have a product and wish to sell it? There are one or two people in the world who might buy the product. You have no competitors.

What price do you charge? What price should the buyer pay? Should the price be based on the value to the buyer? How would that be determined? Is the concept of price meaningful in this situation?

- What happened with Long-Term Capital management in the late 90s?
- What is a mortgage-backed security? What role did these securities play in the financial crash of 2008? What role did Black-Scholes play in creating uncertainty in the value of advanced financial products?

4.7
HOW STABILITY OF COMPANIES LEADS TO INSTABILITY OF COMPANIES

There is nothing stable in the world; uproar's your only music.

John Keats

4.7.1
STABILITY AND MIDDLE MANAGEMENT

Stability, which is not the same as resilience, is a form of risk reduction. As a company grows, the company becomes more complex. Large companies can employ tens of thousands of people. If each of these people were a node in our complexity network and behaved independently, the complexity of the company would far exceed any simple product or market. This complexity mismatch would lead to an extreme, and probably disastrous, event for the company. There must be a simplifying mechanism that reduces the complexity of the company, at least on the scale at which the company interacts with the market. There must be emergent phenomena that lead to coherent behavior of the company's workforce. Typically one attributes coherent behavior to the management, Dilbert jokes notwithstanding. How does this stability come about? The workers in the company are charged with delivery of products and services to clients. The senior management is charged with strategic direction of the company and meeting shareholder goals. What is the role of middle management, and why are there so many middle managers? Intuitively, one could claim that the role of middle management is to execute directions of the senior management. Surprisingly, however, middle managers take actions counter to the interests of the company as defined by senior managers. For example, it may be a strategic mandate of the company to collect data on the effectiveness of the sales force in order to optimize market spend. It is not necessarily in the interest of a sales manager to accurately provide that information because of the potential career-limiting aspects of having his or her sales force reduced if the data is not favorable. We see that while it may be in the company's interest for a particular change to occur, it may not be in the middle manager's interest. This suggests that a role of middle management is to promote stability of the company by opposing change to the company just as friction opposes change to movement.

4.7.2
NEGATIVE FEEDBACK

Let's see how opposition to change can be stabilizing by looking at some analogs in physics and economics. Friction, the force that brings balls to rest, is basically opposition to change. Frictional force is in a direction that is opposite to velocity, which is the change in position of an object. If the velocity of an object changes, then the frictional force changes to oppose the motion. The net effect is to bring all objects to rest. If a marble, for instance, is moving on the surface of a curved bowl, we can safely predict that eventually the marble will come to rest at the bottom of the bowl. If the bowl is bumped or perturbed, we know that, at some time, the marble will return to the bottom of the bowl. We can claim that the stable state of the ball is at rest in the bottom of the bowl. In control theory, the generalized concept of friction is known as *negative feedback*.

Let's consider a proper economic model with negative feedback. The Federal Reserve is charged in the US with keeping inflation and employment stable. One of the ways it does this is by controlling interest rates for short-term loans. If, for instance, the economy is heating up and prices start to rise, the Fed increases short-term rates making money more expensive and investment more difficult thus leading to a slowing down of the economy. If unemployment rises, then the Fed lowers interest rates, encouraging investment and hiring. This negative feedback loop is designed to keep inflation and unemployment within stable levels.

If we use these examples as analogies, it may not be unreasonable to claim that middle management, certainly unintentionally, uses opposition to change, i.e., negative feedback, to stabilize their companies and promote stable profit. This is the emergent phenomenon that reduces the complexity of a company that may have tens of thousands of employees.

4.7.3
THE EXAMPLE OF KODAK

Stability can end up being a major problem for a company, however. Kodak is a striking example of this. The company was so stable that it was unable to adapt to the change in the marketplace brought about by digital photography despite the fact that innovators in the company proposed changes that would have adapted the company to the new market. Kodak experienced an X-event and no longer exists for any practical purpose. Stability is stickiness to a certain way of doing business and is opposed to adaptability. Resilience is the ability to move to some stable state, not necessarily the original stable state, and is reliant on adaptability. The complexity of the marketplace exceeded the complexity of Kodak, which was knocked out of its stable profit stream. Unfortunately for Kodak, it was stable but not resilient. It was unable to adapt to the new situation and find a new viable state for the company. The only available state for the company was the bankrupt state. The instability of the company resulted from the excessive stability of the company.

4.7.4
DISCUSSION QUESTIONS:
STABILITY OF COMPANIES

> People are looking for stability in a shaky world. They want something they can get hold of that's firm and sure and an anchor in the midst of all of this instability in which they're living.

Gordon B. Hinckley

- Discuss how stabilizing a company can lead to an extreme event for the company. Discuss how not stabilizing a company can lead to an extreme event for the company.
- What happened to Kodak? It was a major US company; now it does not exist. Were the senior managers not able to see the potential of digital photography with its ability to destabilize the film market? Did middle management block innovation that would have allowed the company to adapt to the changing market? Did company stabilization lead to the extreme event of the demise of the company? Can short-term stabilization lead to an extreme event that is destabilizing? Is the Kodak case an example of how extreme events come about in economics?
- What is the difference between stability and resilience?
- How does the concept of *creative destruction* apply to companies like Kodak, Apple, KFC, and Microsoft?
- The observation was made in Chapter 3 that the role of the middle class is diminishing. Can we identify middle management with middle class? If so, how does this affect the stability of large companies?
- If the reduction in the role of the middle class results in a reduction in middle management, does this imply that company size in the future will be smaller than today? Is economy of scale changing? Can an economy of smaller firms succeed? Are there currently successful economies composed of smaller firms? Is Italy an example of a successful economy composed of smaller firms?

4.7.5

DISCUSSION QUESTIONS: PHOTOGRAPHY AND VISUAL ARTS

> *The aim of art is to represent not the outward appearance of things, but their inward significance.*
>
> Aristotle

- What effect did the rise of Kodak and the popularization of photography have on the visual arts? Did Kodak precipitate an X-event in the visual arts?
- Discuss the advent of Impressionism, Pointillism, Fauvism, Cubism, Expressionism, Photo-Realism, and Abstract Expressionism in relation to the popularization of photography.
- What was the Armory Show of 1913, and how is it related to the popularization of photography?

4.8

THE BEER GAME

> *Behold the rain which descends from heaven upon our vine-yards, there it enters the roots of the vines, to be changed into wine, a constant proof that God loves us, and loves to see us happy.*
>
> Ben Franklin

What are the effects of communications delay? We take the MIT Beer Game, a simple *supply chain* model, as our model for business communication. The Beer Game was used by one of the authors (JC) in a previous book, *Complexification*, to demonstrate principles of complexity. It is also well suited to demonstrate the onset of X-events in business environments. It is a very good example of how changes in context drive changes in structure of an organization. The first part of our discussion follows the discussion in *Complexification* closely.

4.8.1
THE BEER SUPPLY CHAIN

Industries employ a hierarchical distribution system of products with dealers at many different levels. The basic hierarchy of a demand-supply system for beer distribution, for instance, is composed of the following:

- A *distributor*, who receives the beer from the factory and ships it to the main markets
- Regional *wholesalers*, who receive the beer from the distributor and allocate it to local outlets like supermarkets, liquor stores, and bars
- *Retailers*, who disperse the products to the consumers

We'll call this collection of beer suppliers the *dealers*.

Each dealer maintains an inventory to prevent unpredictable fluctuations in demand and supply. The hierarchical distribution is intended to ensure the availability of beer to the consumer. The supply chain functions as a buffer to protect the production line from fluctuations in consumer demand.

The process works as follows. Each week customers order beer from the retailer, who ships the requested quantity out of inventory. The retailer adjusts the order that it places with the wholesaler in response to variation in customer demand and to other pressures. As long as the retailer has sufficient inventory, the wholesaler ships the beer that's been requested. Orders that cannot be met are kept in backlog until delivery can be made. Similarly, the wholesaler orders and receives beer from the distributor, who in turn orders and receives from the brewery. And to keep things as simple as possible, we'll assume that orders cannot be canceled nor can deliveries be returned.

4.8.2
PLAYING THE BEER GAME LIVE

Business students play the Beer Game by taking on the role of one of the four dealers in the distribution chain. The players try to minimize their cumulative costs over the duration of the game, which is typically taken to be 40 weeks.

The decision made by each player each week is the amount of beer to be ordered from that dealer's immediate supplier. The dealers can base their ordering decisions on all information locally available to them (e.g., the current level of their inventory/backlog, previous values of these quantities, expected orders, and anticipated deliveries). In addition, the dealers can use their overall conception—their mental model—of the way the distribution chain works.

Figure 4.2 displays a typical outcome of the Beer Game, showing the variation in effective inventory (i.e., the actual inventory minus the backlog) for the different sectors. Note that a negative effective inventory represents a backlog of unfilled orders.

Generally speaking, a play of the Beer Game is characterized by large-scale oscillations that grow in amplitude from the retailer to the wholesaler and from the wholesaler to the distributor. So by the time the original stepwise increase in customer orders reaches the brewery, it typically leads to an expansion of production by a factor of six or more. Another feature of these games is the increase in orders, which propagates in a wavelike fashion down the chain, depleting the inventories one by one until it's finally reflected at the brewery, at which point the large surplus of orders placed during the out-of-stock period is produced. These features clearly suggest a strong amplification mechanism at work in the system. At the same time, the behavior is restricted by various disproportionalities (i.e., nonlinearities). For instance, we have a pronounced nonlinear relationship between orders and shipments. Together with the relatively high number of state variables, these nonlinearities can generate an extraordinary variety of complex dynamical behaviors.

The amplification process seen in the beer distribution chain is connected with the built-in time delays involved in communicating from one sector to the next. Assume that a particular sector suddenly experiences a significant increase in demand. To discover whether the change in demand is of a more permanent character, players usually hesitate a little before adjusting their own orders by a similar amount, since the very purpose of maintaining an inventory is to absorb rapid changes in demand. However, because of this hesitation the built-in communication and shipping delays ensure that the demand then exceeds inventory replacements for several weeks. So during this period the inventory level goes down. As a result, the players must increase their orders beyond the level of the immediate incoming orders to build the inventory back up to its desired level. As the players come to realize that the increase in demand is of a more enduring nature, they generally increase their orders even more with an eye toward rebuilding their inventory.

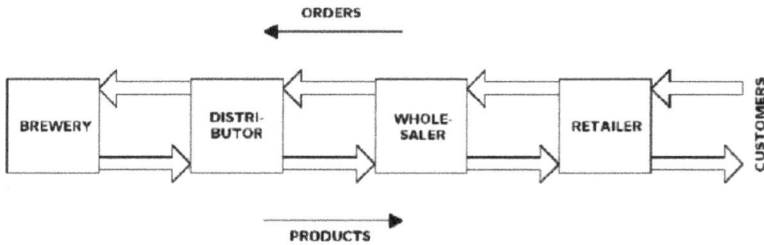

Figure 4.1 Supply Chain. The basic structure of the simplified beer distribution system, or supply chain, that we'll consider here. Orders for beer propagate from right to left, while products are shipped from stage to stage in the opposite direction. Since the processing of orders and the production and shipment of beer involves time delays, we'll assume there is a communication delay of one week (one time-period) from one stage to the next. In the same way, we assume it takes one week to ship beer between two adjacent sectors. Finally, we take the production capacity of the brewery to be unlimited, with a production time of three weeks from the time an order is received from the distributor. To keep things as simple as possible, all the results reported here assume a customer demand of four cases of beer per week until week five, at which time demand increases to eight cases per week. It is then maintained at this level for the rest of the process. At the beginning of the process, there are assumed to be twelve cases of beer in each dealer's inventory. Because of the costs of holding inventory, stock levels should be kept as low as possible. On the other hand, failure to deliver immediately may force customers to look to alternative suppliers. For this reason, penalty costs are assessed for accumulating a backlog of unfilled orders. Therefore, each stock manager must attempt to keep his inventory at the lowest possible level while at the same time avoiding a "stockout." If the inventory begins to fall below the desired level, extra beer must be ordered to rebuild the inventory. If stocks begin to accumulate due to a falloff in demand, the order rate must be reduced. In the experiments discussed here, inventory holding costs are taken to be $0.50 per case per week, while the cost of a backlog is set at $2 per case per week.

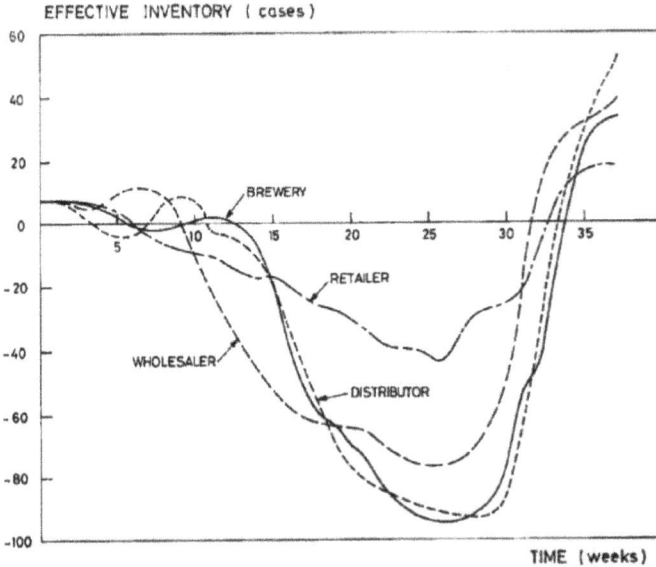

Figure 4.2 Typical Beer Game behavior

4.8.3
STABLE OPERATION OF THE LIVE BEER GAME

The amplification phenomenon in the beer system is a direct consequence of the structure of the distribution chain. But it's important to realize that the beer-distribution chain can be operated in a stable manner. In fact, experience shows that many players are capable of doing just that, and only about a quarter of the participants use ordering policies leading to chaos. Large-scale oscillations are always observed in the transient behavior leading to the system's attractor, however. And in all cases the ordering decisions turn out to be far from optimal, incurring costs exceeding the theoretical minimum by more than a factor of four! Now let's look at some results arising out of a dynamical model created to formalize much of the empirically observed results obtained in more than three decades of play.

4.8.4
SIMULATION OF THE BEER GAME

First of all, we define a stock adjustment parameter α. This quantity represents the fraction of the inventory shortfall that the participants order in each round. So, for example, if the retail demand is for 100 cases and only 50 cases are available in the inventory, the shortfall is 50 cases. A stock adjustment value of $\alpha = 0.4$ would then result in an order of 20 cases (0.4 × 50). Initially, you might wonder why a dealer wouldn't always order what's needed to cover the current shortfall, a policy that corresponds to setting $\alpha = 1$. The reason is that there's a penalty to be paid for overshooting the anticipated future demands, thus building up too large an inventory.

Similarly, we define the quantity β to be the fraction of the supply line, starting from the brewery, that dealers take into account when placing their orders. So, for example, if $\beta = 1$, the players fully recognize the supply line and do not double order, while if $\beta = 0$ orders placed are forgotten until the beer arrives. Now for the promised results.

The Beer Game dynamical system contains 27 state variables, quantities such as expected demands, inventory levels, and order rates for each of the dealers. Compared with real managerial systems, the model is a vast simplification; but compared with most physical systems investigated in the world of nonlinear dynamics, the model is very complicated. In certain regions of values for α and β, the distribution system has three positive *Lyapunov exponents*; positive Lyapunov exponents are indicators of instability of the system. Therefore we might expect the system to display an unusually complicated spectrum of behaviors. Figure 4.3 shows the distribution of behavior types in the α-β plane. Here the results are plotted using a gray-scale code: light gray indicates stable behavior, dark gray represents aperiodic behavior, and black denotes periodic behavior.

A closer inspection of Figure 4.3 shows several regions of unstable behavior separated by "fjords" of stable behavior. For instance, in the regions around $\beta = 0.50$ and $\beta = 0.70$ the model is stable for all values of α, while the narrow peninsula near $\beta = 0.72$ contains only small-amplitude periodic solutions. The other regions of unstable behavior are dominated by large-amplitude fluctuations. The occurrence of unstable behavior is most clearly seen in the lower right corner, where α is large and β relatively small. Therefore, to stabilize the

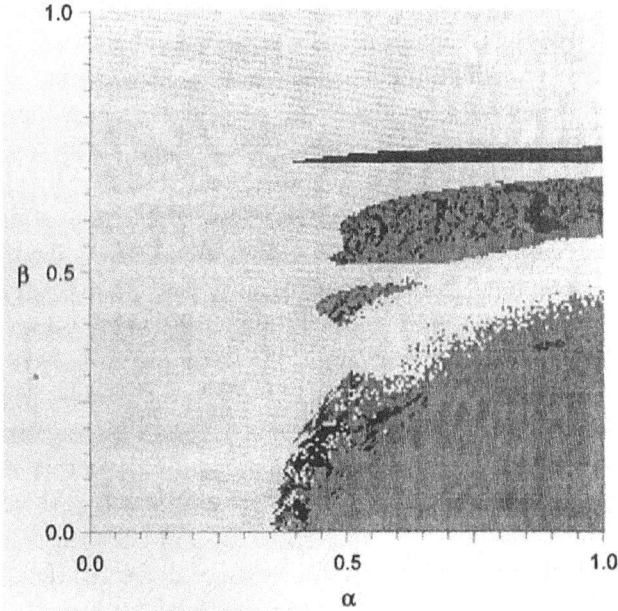

Figure 4.3 Parameter Space for the Beer Game Simulation

distribution chain it's necessary to use an ordering policy in which inventory discrepancies are adjusted relatively slowly and a significant fraction of the supply line is taken into consideration. However, β should not be too large, since a large value of β increases the costs. This is because the system will then stabilize in a state for which the inventories are negative.

4.8.5
SIMULATION PARAMETERS AND CONTEXTUAL DRIVERS

This concludes the treatment of the Beer Game from *Complexification*. Let's see how this treatment translates into the language of X-events that we present in this book. The two parameters α and β correspond to the mood of the dealers and the complexity of the dealers' knowledge of the state of the orders. Low values of α, the shortfall parameter, indicate that the dealers are expecting demand to hold steady or decrease. High values correspond to expectations of increased demand. Low values correspond to pessimistic attitude of dealers, while high values indicate optimism.

The quantity β is the size of the memory of the dealers. Low β indicates that previous orders have been forgotten. High β indicates that all orders back to the brewery are taken into account in the ordering decision. Therefore, low β is an indication of low dealer complexity. High β is the opposite. In this version of the Beer Game, the complexity of the supply chain is held fixed and the complexity of the dealers is variable. The complexity mismatch results from the difference in the two complexities. Here, α and β define the hills and valleys of the landscape of this version of the Beer Game.

4.8.6
ANALYSIS OF A BEER GAME SIMULATION WITH VARIABLE CHAIN LENGTH

It makes sense to look at a version of the Beer Game in which the complexity of the dealers is held fixed and the complexity of the supply chain is variable. This can provide a different insight into the instability of the supply chain. We start by relaxing the requirement that there are three dealers: the retailer, the regional distributor, and the wholesaler. We allow for any number of dealers in the supply chain.

Let's assume that our beer market is very upscale and that the consumers are intolerant of backorders. This means that there is a very high penalty for a dealer not to be able to fulfill an order when it is placed. Backorders are unacceptable. With this assumption, the inventory I of a dealer at time $(t + 1)$ weeks is related to the inventory at t weeks by the relation

$$I(t+1) = I(t) + D(t) - C(t) \tag{4.1}$$

where $D(t)$ are the deliveries made to the dealer at time t, and $C(t)$ are the orders the dealer fills at time t. Backorders are not permitted. If a dealer must make a backorder, the supply chain has failed.

We can now establish the dealer ordering strategy. We specify that, at time t, the dealer places an order O that is proportional to delivery that has just been made.

$$O(t) = mC(t) \tag{4.2}$$

where μ is the proportionality constant. If $\mu = 1$, then the dealer expects future demand to be the same as the current demand. If $\mu <$ 1, then the dealer expects the demand to decrease, and if $\mu > 1$, then the dealer expects demand to increase. Therefore, μ is a measure of the mood of the dealer.

The delivery D at time t is simply the order O placed at time $(t - \tau)$ where τ is the length of time an order has to work its way through the supply chain.

$$D(t) = O(t - \tau) = mC(t - \tau) \qquad (4.3)$$

The greater the length of the supply chain, the larger is τ. Therefore τ is a measure of the complexity of the supply chain. We can vary the complexity of the supply chain by varying the size of τ. The complexity of the dealer is fixed by Equation 4.2 where the dealer is only aware of current orders and current expected deliveries. The dealer is quite simple. This situation corresponds to $\beta = 0$ in the *Complexification* discussion. Therefore, in this model, the complexity mismatch between dealers and supply chain is driven by the complexity of the supply chain. Equation 4.1 simplifies to

$$I(t+1) = I(t) + mC(t - \tau) - C(t) \qquad (4.4)$$

Equation 4.4 has a fixed point in which the inventory remains unchanged if

$$mC(t - \tau) - C(t) = 0. \qquad (4.5)$$

Let's focus on the retailer for simplicity. The retailer takes orders directly from the consumers. Equation 4.4 is a very simple equation that is gravid with meaning. It contains dealer mood with μ and supply chain complexity with τ. Let's start our exploration of its meaning by considering the very simple case of unchanging consumer demand $C(t) = C$. In that case, Equation 4.4 becomes

$$I(t+1) = I(t) + (m-1)C. \qquad (4.6)$$

It is very easy to see from Equation 4.6 that the inventory remains unchanged when $\mu = 1$. When the dealers are optimistic, $\mu > 1$, then the inventory grows despite the fact that the demand is constant. When the dealers are pessimistic, $\mu < 1$, the inventory shrinks. If the mood remains unchanged for $\mu \neq 1$, then the inventory will either disappear and the retailer cannot supply his or her customers, or the inventory grows to such a large value that storage costs put the dealer out of business. This is displayed for all three dealers in Figure 4.4. Note the

Constant Demand

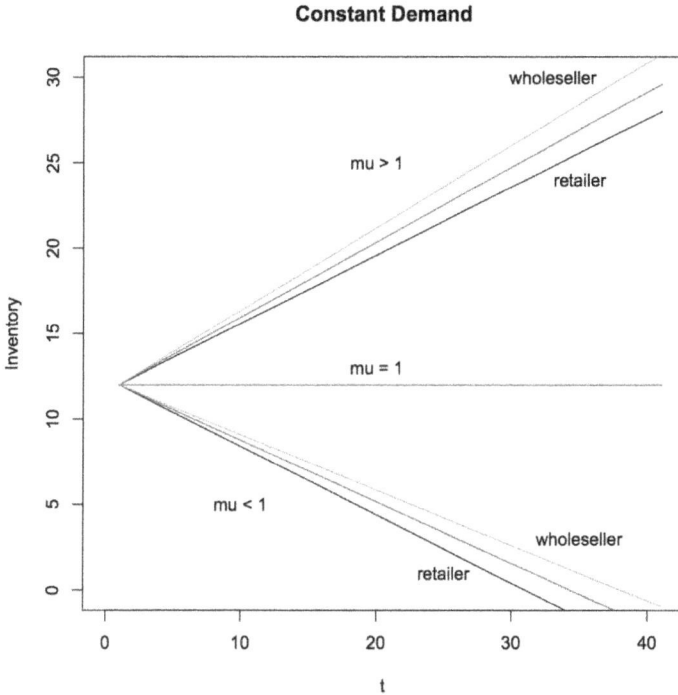

Figure 4.4 Different Moods, Constant Demand. Three cases are displayed for μ = 0.9, 1.0, 1.1 and for three dealers. The graph is colored in the electronic version of this book. The retailers are in black (labeled "retailer"). The wholesalers are in green. The regional distributors are in red (unlabeled). Note that in the optimistic case μ > 1 that the wholesaler inventory increases faster than the retailer inventory. The retailer actions are amplified as the dealers are closer to the brewery. This is known as the bullwhip effect. In the pessimistic case μ < 1 the opposite effect is seen. The effects of retailer actions are damped. The wholesaler inventory does not shrink as fast as the retailer inventory.

bullwhip effect for the optimistic case. The bullwhip effect is a consequence of the size of orders being amplified as the orders proceed down the supply chain to the brewery. The retailer thinks the demand will increase, so he or she orders extra beer. The regional distributors also think the demand will increase, so they order even more beer than has been ordered. By the time the signal reaches the wholesaler, the order to the brewery is much larger than the original retail order. The opposite effect occurs for a pessimistic $\mu < 1$ set of dealers.

The case for eight dealers is displayed in Figure 4.5. We see that the bullwhip effect is enhanced for the longer supply chain, the supply chain with the greater complexity. The instability of the optimistic supply chain is therefore enhanced when the complexity mismatch between the supply chain and the dealers increases—when the supply chain gets longer.

We emphasize the main point of this section. **The mood μ and the complexity τ of the supply chain define the landscape. In this particular version of the Beer Game the supply chain sits on a peak with $\mu = 1$. Any perturbation on the mood will drive the supply chain to either zero or infinite inventory. The further μ is from 1, or the larger τ is, then the narrower, and more dangerous, the peak.**

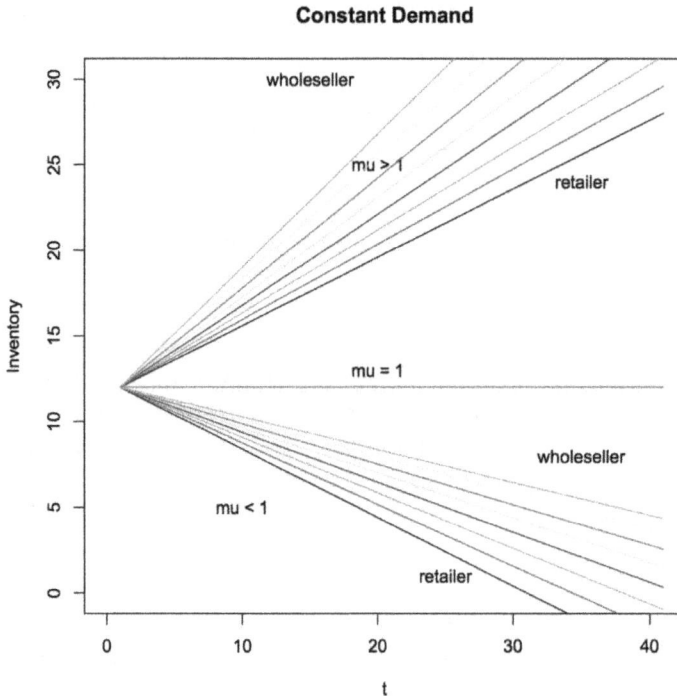

Figure 4.5 Different Moods, Constant Demand. Three cases are displayed for $\mu = 0.9, 1.0, 1.1$ and for eight dealers. In the electronic version of this book, the retailers are in black. The wholesalers are in gray. Note that in the optimistic case $\mu > 1$ that the wholesaler inventory increases faster than the retailer inventory and much faster than the case of the wholesaler for a supply chain of length three. The bullwhip effect is more pronounced for the longer supply chain with the greater complexity. In the pessimistic case $\mu < 1$ the damping is enhanced.

4.8.7
DISCUSSION QUESTION: COMMUNICATION DELAY

The single biggest problem in communication is the illusion that it has taken place.

George Bernard Shaw

Communication errors were instrumental in the Tenerife disaster. Correct, but delayed, communication can also create complexity mismatch. Discuss the Beer Game developed at MIT in the 1960s to model a supply chain. What happens when communication is delayed? What happens if there is no delay in communication? We will discuss the Beer Game in greater depth later in this chapter.

4.8.8
EXERCISES: THE BEER GAME

The gods had condemned Sisyphus to ceaselessly rolling a rock to the top of a mountain, whence the stone would fall back of its own weight. They had thought with some reason that there is no more dreadful punishment than futile and hopeless labor.

Albert Camus

1. Reproduce the Beer Game in code. Assume the inventory is determined by Equation 4.4. Neglect backorders.
2. Reproduce the results of this section.
3. What happens if the consumer demand varies rather than remains constant?
4. Set $\mu = 1$. Add some noise to the consumer demand. What happens to the inventory? What is a random walk? Use the theory of the random walk to estimate when the inventory is likely to go to zero or to double. Does the presence of noise destroy the one stable point $\mu = 1$ for the system?
5. Create other rules for placing orders in the Beer Game. What are the results? Can you identify mood and complexity gap in the new rules?

4.8.9
DISCUSSION QUESTIONS: THE BEER GAME

A mountain is composed of tiny grains of earth. The ocean is made up of tiny drops of water. Even so, life is but an endless series of little details, actions, speeches, and thoughts. And the consequences whether good or bad of even the least of them are far-reaching.

Swami Sivananda

The Beer Game models an X-event in one part of a single company. A company is, of course, much more complicated than just its supply chain. Moreover, a company sits within an industry that is undergoing X-events. The industry sits in an economy, and so it goes like a Russian doll. Is prediction possible in such an environment? Can any individual foresee the spectrum of X-events that are constantly occurring at multiple scales? Is prediction of future events an adequate strategy for managing a company? What about building resilience to perturbations?

4.9
THE BUSINESS OF US HEALTHCARE

You're in pretty good shape for the shape you are in.

Dr. Seuss

Up to this point in the chapter, we have focused on individual companies and a small piece of an industry, the supply chain. We have not looked at complexity mismatch and mood at the industry level. This section drills down into a particular industry, healthcare in the US. We see that there are forces on the industry as a whole and forces on segments of the industry. We drill down into a particular segment, the pharmaceutical industry, to examine the complexity mismatches at that level.

4.9.1
US HEALTHCARE IS POISED FOR AN X-EVENT

The brutalities of progress are called revolutions. When they are over we realize this: that the human has been roughly handled, but that it has advanced.

Victor Hugo, 1862

Healthcare in the US is complicated. There are dozens of components.
- Providers
  - hospitals
  - specialized physicians
  - general physicians
  - physician assistants
  - nurses
  - chiropractors
  - hospices
  - assisted living facilities
  - nursing homes
  - wellness centers
  - home care, pharmacies
  - pharmaceutical companies
  - medical device manufacturers

- Regulators
  - Food and Drug Administration
  - Patent Office
  - Payors

- Payors
  - Medicare
  - Medicaid
  - private insurers
  - self insurers
  - employers
  - self-employed

- Conditions
  - chronic conditions
  - acute conditions
  - emergency conditions
  - end-of-life conditions
  - rare diseases

- Treatment Modalities
  - personalized medicine
  - cosmetic surgery
  - concierge medicine
  - alternative medicine

The complication is impossible for any single person to penetrate or understand. Why is healthcare so complicated? Well . . . human bodies are complicated. In the early twentieth century bodies were simpler. At that time, people tended to die from acute conditions before their health became Gordian from chronic conditions. Medicine was simpler. It consisted almost solely of providing comfort to those at the end of their lives. Medicine has added years to our life expectancies with the consequent increase in healthcare complication. The higher population densities of today have also added complexity by providing rich biological cultures for infectious diseases. Moreover, personalized medicine is making life bewildering. Sequencing an individual genome is now inexpensive enough for every person to be able to identify his or her own disease susceptibility spectrum, which must be understood and managed individually.

The healthcare market is experiencing significant cost and quality pressures that suggest large changes may occur rapidly. Healthcare costs are increasing at a 6.7 percent annual rate—much higher than the current (2014) inflation rate of 1.7 percent and the current GDP growth rate of less than 2 percent. In 2010, healthcare costs of $2.6 trillion consumed 17.9 percent of the US GDP. This is the highest rate in the world. At the same time, the quality of care fell behind most industrialized countries.

One of the drivers of healthcare costs is technology advancement. Advancements have been in the area of more advanced procedures and testing at the expense of better information management. The lag in information management is placing pressure on the system.

Healthcare costs are also driven by *sudden cessation* of technology advancements. Development for new drugs has slowed, putting pressure on pharmaceutical margins. Several blockbuster drugs went off patent in 2012 with no replacements in the pipeline.

Healthcare costs can be driven by inequities in how the care is being paid. The rate of uninsured in the US was 18 percent in 2013. The uninsured are not denied healthcare, so the costs must be covered by the insured, placing pressure on the system.

Finally, differences among healthcare systems in other countries place pressure on the US system as biopharma and medical-device companies compete globally.

It is clear that the US cannot continue its current course in which healthcare costs are more than 17 percent of GDP and outcomes are significantly behind the rest of the world. The US is poised for an X-event in healthcare.

Some of the material in this section has been condensed from blogs written by one of the authors (RDJ).[Jones, 2013]

4.9.2
WHY IS HEALTHCARE NOT A COMMODITY?

Nothing that has value, real value, has no cost. Not freedom, not food, not shelter, not healthcare.

Dean Kamen

The concept of supply and demand is the cornerstone of economic theory. For simple commodities, the theory predicts that the demand for a product decreases as the price of the product increases and consumers are unwilling to pay the higher price. The supply increases as the price increases and suppliers increase production to capture increased profits. The actual price of the product is a compromise between the desires of consumers and the acumen of suppliers.

This simple equation breaks down when applied to the healthcare market. A person at the end of his or her life may be willing to spend an entire life savings on a few months of extended and more comfortable life. The demand for those healthcare services that can satisfy this desire is effectively infinite. Traditional economic theory would say that the supply would meet the demand and the price of healthcare products and services would become effectively infinite.

Healthcare differs from simple commodity economics in another key aspect. For simple commodities, the user of the commodity is the buyer and the supplier of the commodity is the seller. In healthcare in the US, there are three players rather than two. The person who prescribes the product or service is the provider; the person who uses the product or service is the patient; and the person who pays for the product or service is the insurer.

Why is the cost of healthcare not infinite? In many countries, such as the UK, the cost is regulated. Americans, however, tend to prefer market solutions to government regulation. Market solutions have not been effective at controlling costs in the United States. Healthcare costs are increasing at a 6.7 percent annual rate—much higher than the current inflation rate of 1.7 percent and the current GDP growth rate of less than 2 percent. In 2010, healthcare costs of $2.6 trillion consumed 17.9 percent of the US GDP. This is the highest rate in the world. At the same time, the quality of care fell behind most industrialized countries. Healthcare costs in the US are rising to meet the demand. About one-quarter of Medicare outlays are for the last year of life.

Healthcare in the US is not in a state of equilibrium in which supply meets demand. Supply is lagging behind demand. What is holding back supply? One answer is the pace of invention. Over the last half century a number of life-extending procedures have been developed, from open-heart surgery to advanced chemotherapy. A common property of these procedures is that they are expensive. It has taken time to develop these procedures. As more expensive procedures are invented, healthcare costs will rise to meet the demand. Unfortunately, these costs are becoming a larger proportion of GDP, which adversely affects the ability to pay for other activities that make life worth living.

Medicare and Medicaid were established in 1965 to manage the healthcare of the elderly and poor. In the early 70s, Health Maintenance Organizations (HMOs) emerged as the dominant decision maker. These are organizations controlled by payors that can employ physicians directly or indirectly and that control the flow of patients among those physicians. In 1982, Diagnosis-Related Groups (DRGs) were developed to capitate the costs of hospital treatments. This enhanced the decision-making focus of the payors. Then, providers banded together in Planned Provider Organizations (PPOs) to enhance the negotiating power of the providers with respect to payors. Point of Service Plans (POS) evolved as hybrids of HMOs and PPOs, thus setting up a pick-two process in which the payors and providers are favored over patients. In 2010, the Affordable Care Act (ACA) provided for the creation of Accountable Care Organizations (ACO) to shift the focus to the patients, specifically to basing reimbursement on patient outcomes. The complexity of insurance has increased with time. Several experiments have been done; none have been very successful.

As we can see from technology innovation and the changes in payor dynamics over the last half century, healthcare economics in the US is not in a stable state of supply/demand equilibrium. In fact, if equilibrium of supply and demand existed, it would make the cost of healthcare so high that Americans would not be able to spend their income on anything except healthcare. Equilibrium exists, but it is not based on anything as simple as traditional supply-and-demand economics. One might expect an equilibrium involving three entities rather than two. We already see the beginnings of this tripartite equilibrium. Patients represent demand, providers represent supply, and payors are the third and regulating party in the triad.

4.9.3
TWO VISIONS

Vision is the art of seeing what is invisible to others.

Jonathan Swift

In December 2012 one of the authors (RDJ) attended the Forbes Healthcare Summit in New York City. Over 200 healthcare leaders converged at Lincoln Center to discuss and forecast the future of healthcare in the US. Two different visions for the future of US healthcare emerged at the conference. The first vision is an extension of our current trajectory in which space-age technology yields dramatic, but expensive, health outcomes. The second vision is one in which common-sense medicine produces low-cost very good health over a large segment of the population, but is not necessarily designed to accommodate specialized high-technology procedures.

Gov. Rick Perry of Texas championed the high-technology vision. Perry outlined how certain policies in Texas, such as tort reform and no income tax, attracted high-end medical specialists to the state. This set the state up as a destination for medical tourism that attracted very sick patients from all over the US and wealthy patients from all over the world. This provided the state with a healthy income. When asked whether this process should be implemented nationally, he claimed that the federal government was not able to deliver on a vision like this. It was clear, however, that implementation at the national level would degrade Texas' competitive advantage over the other states. When asked about non-specialized medicine and primary care in Texas, Perry was candid that many Texans were not receiving adequate primary healthcare. He gave as an example the population along the Rio Grande that had to travel several hours to access prenatal care. He mentioned that Texas was looking into some loan forgiveness for Texas medical students who were willing to spend five years in rural settings, but clearly, when he talked about this, the sparkle was missing from his eyes.

Bradford Berk, CEO of the University of Rochester Medical Center, and David Klein, CEO of The Lifetime Healthcare Companies, a healthcare funder in the Rochester area, championed the second vision. They described a collaborative system that focused on providing low-cost high-quality healthcare at a community level. This system emerged as a cooperative arrangement between large local employers, such as Kodak and Xerox, and a first-rate medical school at the University of Rochester. Of course, Kodak and Xerox are shadows of their former selves in Rochester, but the system they helped create still exists. The key observation was that, contrary to traditional economic theory, increased healthcare supply increases costs. This cynical view is that medical entrepreneurs increase the number of hospital beds, and then prescribe to fill the beds. The Rochester team decided to right-size the supply of healthcare in the community and to focus on outcomes. This was possible because of the economic motivations of the community businesses who were funding the healthcare and the cooperation of the medical school that drove the vision through its training and hiring policies. The Rochester community succeeded in its goal of providing low-cost high-quality healthcare. Of course, if an upstate New York resident needs a very exotic procedure, he or she may need to fly to Texas.

The two visions for healthcare that were presented at the Forbes Healthcare Summit are almost caricatures, however. There is opportunity for creative individuals and institutions. Technology has not been applied evenly in healthcare. While the US can be proud of its innovations in high-technology procedures, its adoption of information technology is not even at the level of the pizza industry. Both visions emerged as a result of economic incentives, one to increase revenue, as was the case in Texas, and one to reduce costs, as was the case in upstate New York. The question now is how do we shift the incentives to create the proper mix of outcomes, cost, and risk?

4.9.4
DISCUSSION QUESTION: PHYSICIAN COMPENSATION

The good physician treats the disease; the great physician treats the patient who has the disease.

William Osler

- What is the average income of a primary care physician in the US?
- What is the average income of a specialist physician in the US?
- What are the current criteria for physician compensation in the US? Activity based?
- Which type of physician benefits most from compensation of procedures?
- What would be the criteria for physician compensation in an outcome-based system such as the Rochester system?
- How would the relationships between primary care physicians and specialists change in an outcome-based system?
- How would the practice of primary care change in an outcome-based system?
- How would hospitals change in an outcome-based system?

4.9.5

TECHNOLOGY-DRIVEN COMPLEXITY MISMATCH

The very first requirement in a hospital is that it should do the sick no harm.

Florence Nightingale

It is clear that technology is driving much of the complexity mismatch in US healthcare. Technology can also *reduce* the complexity mismatch. We illustrate this with two personal anecdotes, originally presented in a blog of one of the authors (RDJ).

I would like to start this blog with a story about my college-age daughter. Like most college students, she likes pizza. Beth, because she is a modern child completely comfortable in the information age, orders her pizza over the internet. She can monitor the progress of her pizza online. She knows when the cheese has been applied and also the pepperoni. She knows when the pizza has been placed in the delivery car, and she knows, within a few seconds, when the delivery-man will knock on our door. She also knows the delivery-man's name.

Let me contrast this with another personal anecdote. My mother, while living at home some distance from where I live, had a chronic and potentially lethal bowel infection. She had an incident in which she needed to go to the emergency department. The emergency doctor, who had no health records for my mother and who did not consult her primary-care physician, diagnosed her as having a rotavirus and sent her home. Two days later, she was admitted to the hospital with the serious bowel infection for which she was being treated by her primary-care physician and that had nothing to do with a rotavirus. She remained in the hospital for several weeks and had near-death experiences. Her life was saved by the skill of her physicians and high-technology expensive procedures.

A few weeks after her return home, she had a recurrence of the infection and went again to the emergency department, where the same emergency doctor once again diagnosed her as having a rotavirus. Once again she was sent home, and once again she was later readmitted to the hospital and treated for bowel infection. This time she came much closer to death. At one point, I was told she would not live through the night. After another heroic and expensive life-saving procedure, she did live. After a few weeks in the hospital and rehabilitation, I admitted her into an assisted-living facility. My mother has not had a recurrence of her infection in the two years she has been in the assisted-living facility. She has gained weight and is, in general, in good health for someone her age. The reason her health has improved is because, now, her health information is being better managed. A nurse has complete knowledge of her medical conditions and vital signs. Her medication is properly administered. Her doctors' appointments are coordinated. In my mother's case, there were dramatic and expensive technological procedures that saved her life, but her life would not have been threatened in the first place had her healthcare information been readily available to her healthcare providers. While her entire assisted-living package is expensive, it is much less expensive than the life-extending procedures she underwent because her health information was not being properly managed. The information-management systems are simply not yet in place in large areas of healthcare.

There may be many reasons why modern information management has not yet made it into US healthcare: privacy concerns; size of the problem; physician and hospital compensation designed around procedures rather than outcomes; the emphasis of healthcare training programs; and political issues. In many respects, however, online information management is an essential component of the modern lifestyle. While healthcare information management may not be as easy as pizza pie, Americans are prepped and ready for it.

The story illustrates complexity mismatch in two ways. Initially, the complexity of the healthcare system was greater than the complexity of her disease. Her initial infection could have simply been controlled by a thoughtful application of antibiotics. The system was prepared for a more complex solution, and it worked when RDJ's mother had a more complex life-threatening condition. When her condition improved and simplified, the reduced-complexity solution of improved information management in an assisted-living facility was more effective and less expensive.

A key to managing healthcare costs and outcomes is to manage technology in a manner that reduces complexity mismatch between patients and providers. The next section illustrates one way this is currently done in the pharmaceutical industry—through the use of patents. A more complete picture of how the complexity of the pharmaceutical industry is regulated is presented in a subsequent section.

4.9.6
PATENTS AFFECT COMPLEXITY MISMATCH

Patents are like fertilizer. Applied wisely and sparingly, they can increase growth. But if you apply too many chemicals, or make patents too strong, then you can leach the land, making growth more difficult.

Alex Tabarrok

While patents on medical devices seem normal, patents on drugs and chemical entities may seem like a stretch. I am not sure that the law makers in Venice in 1474, who invented the legal concept of a patent, envisioned the need to patent molecules. In fact, molecules were not even envisioned at that time. We all know that a patent allows an inventor time to commercialize his or her product, but are patents really needed for the economic viability of healthcare? Shouldn't healthcare be all about saving lives and promoting health and not about making money on people who desperately need healthcare? Do patents have a benefit to patients, not just the patent holders? The answer to this question is "perhaps." Patents promote diversity of products in the healthcare market place by forcing inventors to develop drugs outside the domain of currently patented products.

This idea can be illustrated more colorfully with the famous hot-dog vendor example from economics. Consider a beach that contains, in addition to the bathers, two hot-dog vendors located at either end of the beach. There is nothing to differentiate their products, other than their location on the beach. Bathers will purchase from the closest vendor, therefore the value or quality of the product of a particular vendor depends on the number of bathers closer to the vendors cart than the competition. In order to capture market share and value, each vendor moves his cart closer and closer to the other until they meet in the middle of the beach. At this time, each vendor has captured half the market share of the beach, and, since they are in the same location, their differentiation has vanished. Their dogs are now commodities, and the market is driving the price to the cost of production. This is the classic process of commoditization.

Let's apply this to healthcare. A perfect market for a pharmaceutical company is the hyperlipidemia market. Properly treated patients with high cholesterol can live a normally long lifetime, paying the manufacturers of Crestor or Lipitor quite a lot of money for the valuable service. Since this market is large, stable, and profitable, all pharma companies will want to enter this market, which is at the center of the healthcare beach. Diabetes is a similar market. If, however, the makers of Lipitor have a patent, other pharma companies cannot enter the exact same area of the beach as the Lipitor manufacturer. The patent forces the vendors to maintain some distance on our healthcare beach. The other non-Lipitor-producing pharma companies must come up with a product that is sufficiently different from Lipitor to be patented, or they must develop drugs for an entirely different disease, say pancreatic cancer. This forces companies to innovate and provide products for the entire healthcare beach, not just the stable lucrative parts of the beach. The downside for patients is that they must pay more for Lipitor while it is on patent. The upside is that pancreatic patients may receive life-extending treatments they would not otherwise have received.

4.9.7
REGULATION OF THE PHARMACEUTICAL INDUSTRY

Throughout the nineteenth century, when there was a laissez-faire mentality and insufficient regulation, you had one crisis after another. Each crisis brought about some reform. That is how central banking developed.

George Soros

The pharmaceutical market place is not entirely a free market. As we have noted, the extreme demand for lifesaving products can make standard economic assumptions inoperable. Therefore, regulatory mechanisms have emerged to protect patients and to provide patients access to affordable medications. The complexity of the regulation must match the complexity of the market if X-events are to be avoided.

There are three aspects of pharmaceutical operations in the US that are regulated by the government:

- the amount of business risk that a pharmaceutical company is allowed to mitigate and the time interval that the risk is mitigated
- the quality and safety of pharmaceutical products
- and the cost of the products and the efficiency in which products get into the market—these three regulatory goals can be thought of as nodes of a triangle

In the US, the temporal/risk node is controlled by the Patent Office. A pharmaceutical company that develops or licenses a drug has a certain amount of time to market and sell the drug without competition. Upon expiration of the patent, competitors are allowed to sell the drug, and the price of the drug nearly always falls precipitously. The expiration of the patent can be extended under certain conditions, such as significant improvements to the drug protected by follow-on patents.

The Food and Drug Administration controls the quality/safety component of the regulatory triangle. The FDA is responsible for approval of drugs entering the market. Their decisions are based on safety and efficacy of the drug. The approval process is extensive involving several levels of clinical trials and post-launch monitoring. In addition, the FDA regulates the advertising and promotion of the drug.

The cost/efficiency component of the triangle is quite complex. The mechanism of control is through formularies. These are lists of drugs with the requirements for compensation for each drug. The requirements for compensation for the drug are determined by a myriad of entities. About 35 percent of healthcare expenditures are paid through the federal government and the Center for Medicare and Medicaid Services (CMS). Private insurers, which are not regulatory entities themselves, pay for most of the remainder. State governments regulate the private insurers. State regulation of private insurers focuses on solvency of insurance companies, risk spreading, fraud, and ensuring customers are paid benefits.

The interplay of these three regulatory nodes can determine the profitability of a pharmaceutical product, the patient's access to the product, and the risk that patients incur from the product. Pharmaceutical business is as much about navigating the regulations as it is dealing with the competition.

4.9.8
DISCUSSION QUESTION: FORCES ON THE PHARMACEUTICAL INDUSTRY

> *It's easy to complain that pharmaceutical companies place profits over people and apparently care more about hair loss than TB. However, many in the pharmaceutical industry would be glad for the opportunity to reorient their research toward medicines that are truly needed, provided only that such research is financially sustainable.*

Thomas Pogge

The pharmaceutical industry has increased spending on research and development, and it has not paid off. From 2009 through 2012 approximately $60 billion in pharmaceutical sales were lost to the patent cliff, the expiration of drug patents with the consequent drop in prices as cheaper generic drugs replace patented brand drugs. Despite increased R&D expenditure, the drug pipeline has not met the demand for new drugs.

- Verify that pharmaceutical R&D spending increased while the drug pipeline shrank.
- A pharmaceutical company makes the most money providing treatments for chronic conditions that are not immediately life-threatening. These might include hyperlipidemia (cholesterol), hypertension (blood pressure), and diabetes. These diseases provide long-term customers and a steady revenue stream. Curing diseases only creates short-term customers and is less profitable.

This led to the blockbuster model for drugs in which a drug such as Lipitor, which treats hyperlipidemia, generated revenues of billions of dollars a year, which then led to the creation of very large pharmaceutical companies. How will the industry evolve based on current economic pressures?

- How will the pressure on the pharmaceutical industry change the size distribution and makeup of pharmaceutical companies?
- How is a biotechnology company different from a pharmaceutical company? How are the products different?
- What is the future of biotechnology companies?

4.9.9
PERSONALIZED MEDICINE AND INFORMATION MANAGEMENT FOR TREATMENT

The ever quickening advances of science made possible by the success of the Human Genome Project will also soon let us see the essences of mental disease. Only after we understand them at the genetic level can we rationally seek out appropriate therapies for such illnesses as schizophrenia and bipolar disease.

James D. Watson

Personalized medicine will change the way physicians diagnose. With every person able to map his or her own genetic makeup, the possibilities for individuated diagnosis will increase beyond the limits of current human imagination. How will physicians of the future cope? The solution to the problem may start with goats, cars, and game shows.

Several years ago, one of the authors (RDJ) and his colleagues at Los Alamos National Laboratory in New Mexico did a little experiment. They were interested in whether machines or humans were better at unraveling the logic of a non-intuitive problem. They chose the Monty Hall Problem as our prototype problem. The problem is loosely based on the popular game show *Let's Make a Deal* hosted by Monty Hall. Stated simply, the problem is

Suppose you're on a game show, and you're given the choice of three doors: behind one door is a car; behind the others, goats. You pick a door, say Number 1, and the host, who knows what's behind the doors, opens another door, say Number 3, which has a goat. He then says to you, "Do you want to pick door Number 2?" Is it to your advantage to switch your choice?

The answer seems simple. It should not matter whether one swaps doors or not. The probability is 50 percent that the car will be behind either remaining door. This answer is, however, incorrect. The correct answer is that one should always switch doors. The chance of winning a car is 2/3 if one switches and 1/3 if one does not switch. This answer is so non-intuitive that the discussion on the topic made Marilyn vos Savant's column in *Parade* magazine one of the hottest columns of 1990. The great mathematician Paul Erdös refused to believe the answer until it was demonstrated to him by computer simulation.

At Los Alamos, the researchers created their own computer simulation of the problem. They allowed the computer to randomly pick a door. The computer-generated game-show host picked a remaining door that held a goat behind it. And the computer randomly switched doors or not. The outcome was then revealed to the observer. The computer either won a car or a goat. We ran this experiment many times.

They created a second program that observed the outcome of the experiments and whether the computer switched doors or not, and then learned from its observations. They measured how quickly the program learned the correct answer. They then repeated the experiment with humans as observers rather than a computer program as an observer. They measured how quickly the human observers learned the correct answer and compared this with how quickly the computer program learned. The program was unquestionably a faster learner than the humans. The researchers sent this result to vos Savant and it generated even further discomfort and disbelief in her readers.

Why was the computer program able to learn faster than humans? This may be related to what in psychology is called anchoring. Anchoring is a cognitive bias that describes the common human tendency to rely too heavily on the first piece of information offered (the "anchor") when making decisions. In the Monty Hall Problem, the anchor is the belief that the probability of an outcome is inversely proportional to the number of possible outcomes. In other words, if there are three doors that a car can be behind, and the probability is random, then the car is behind any one door with probability of one chance in three. The computer program does not have the human bias. It simply looks at the evidence and makes an unbiased judgment, which is that the probabilities are not equal at all.

This suggests another popular television game show—*Jeopardy*. *Jeopardy* is a quiz show in which questions are inferred given the answers to the questions. In 2011, Watson, an artificial-intelligence computer system capable of answering questions posed in natural language, beat two former *Jeopardy* champions, Brad Rutter and Ken Jennings, who happened to be human. It is interesting to note that Watson had poorer performance compared with the humans in some categories such as those containing short clues containing only a few words. The machine, however, performed better than the champion humans overall. The lack of human learning shortcomings, such as anchoring bias, seems to have complemented and even enhanced our collective ability to organize and interpret information.

Watson is now working in collaboration with Memorial Sloan-Kettering in order to organize diagnostic information. Sloan-Kettering has taken on the task of tutoring Watson in cancer diagnosis. This problem may be a bit tougher than answering Jeopardy clues, but the payoff could be much more real. I quote from a February 2013 *Atlantic* article by Jonathan Cohn:

> "The process of pulling out two key facts from a *Jeopardy* clue is totally different from pulling out all the relevant information, and its relationships, from a medical case," says Ari Caroline, Sloan-Kettering's director of quantitative analysis and strategic initiatives. "Sometimes there is conflicting information. People phrase things different ways." But Caroline, who approached IBM about the research collaboration, nonetheless predicts that Watson will prove "very valuable particularly in a field like cancer treatment, in which the explosion of knowledge is already overwhelming. If you're looking down the road, there are going to be many more clinical options, many more subtleties around biomarkers. There will be nuances not just in interpreting the case but also in treating the case," Caroline says. "You're going to need a tool like Watson because the complexity and scale of information will be such that a typical decision tool couldn't possibly handle it all."

Perhaps machines like Watson will be an answer to the question of how to diagnose in an era of personalized medicine, in which a gene sequence costs $10, and the amount of medical information we have about any patient and his or her family is astronomical—beyond the capabilities of any group of humans without smart machines to make sense of. Good information management is cheaper than expensive medical procedures, particularly if the procedures are not backed by high-resolution information. This is a case of the complexity of treatment increasing as the amount of complex information about the patient increases.

4.9.10
PERSONALIZED MEDICINE AND CLINICAL TRIALS

Life it is not just a series of calculations and a sum total of statistics, it's about experience, it's about participation, it is something more complex and more interesting than what is obvious.

Daniel Libeskind

The adoption of personalized medicine poses a dilemma for those people involved in the development of new treatments. How can the safety and efficacy of a treatment be determined if the treatment is designed for a single individual? Today, safety and efficacy are determined, in large part, by randomized control trials, clinical trials that typically involve hundreds of participants. The large number of patients is required to assure statistical confidence in the outcomes of the treatments. Clearly clinical trials must be designed that are able to build assurance in the predictability of the outcomes and do this with very small test populations. The challenges are at least twofold: confidence is difficult to build with small populations, and the identification and recruitment of the trial participants is quite difficult if the number of eligible participants is very small. This again is a situation in which the complexity of personalized medicine requires an increase in complexity of the providers—in this case drug developers.

The first challenge, building confidence once a small population has been identified, may be aided by adaptive trial-design methods. In adaptive design the rules of data collection and sampling change as data is collected. Adaptive designs allow investigators to start with a small population and change the data that is being collected as data is collected. This speeds the knowledge-accumulation process, allowing for quicker decision-making.

Adaptations to clinical trials can take several forms: adaptive randomization; stopping a trial early due to safety, futility, or efficacy at interim analysis; dropping the losers (or inferior treatment groups); sample size re-estimation; modifications in inclusion/exclusion criteria; evaluability criteria, dose/regimen and treatment duration; changes in hypotheses and/or study endpoints; and modifications and/ or changes made to the statistical analysis plan prior to database lock or unblinding of treatment codes. Clearly this is a major shift in process.

The FDA has encouraged this approach. The FDA released a Critical Path Opportunities List in 2006 that calls for advancing innovative trial designs, "especially for the use of prior experience or accumulated information in trial design." According to the FDA, "the purpose of adaptive design methods in clinical trials is to give the investigator the flexibility for identifying best (optimal) clinical benefit of the test treatment under study without undermining the validity and integrity of the intended study."

4.9.11

INSURANCE-DRIVEN HEALTHCARE COST INFLATION

We first make our habits, and then our habits make us.

John Dryden

There is another driver of high healthcare costs in the US besides technology mismatch—non-uniform distribution of insurance. Nobody is (or, rather, should be) denied healthcare in a civilized society. A person injured in a car wreck or suffering from cancer receives care. If that person does not have insurance or a means to pay, some form of healthcare will still be provided. The costs are borne by those with insurance, whether private or government. This drives up insurance premiums. The higher premiums cause people to leave the ranks of the insured. This raises the cost of the uninsured, which raises premiums further—creating a vicious cycle.

4.9.12
DISCUSSION QUESTION: EMPLOYER-FUNDED INSURANCE

There are worse things in life than death. Have you ever spent an evening with an insurance salesman?

Woody Allen

In the US, health insurance is funded by employers for people under 65 years old. For people 65 and older, health-insurance payments are provided by the government through Medicare. The poor are provided healthcare payments through Medicaid. Employees are not taxed for payments made to private insurance companies by employers on their behalf. Since employees are not taxed for the insurance benefit they receive from employers, employers have tended to view health insurance as *tax-free* compensation to employees—a part of the employee total compensation package. In order to attract good employees, employers have inflated the employee insurance plans with extra features such as low deductibles, vision insurance that pays for eyeglasses, dental insurance that pays for routine teeth cleaning, and payment of routine physicals.

- Employees are discouraged from changing health plans by an insurance requirement—refusal of insurance companies to accept new customers with pre-existing conditions. This encourages employees to remain with their current company. Otherwise they might lose significant insurance benefits. Is this a real effect?
- Insurance companies use the pre-existing condition requirement to raise premiums faster than the inflation rate. It prevents companies from changing insurance plans because the new plan will not cover pre-existing conditions.
- How does the policy of employer-funded health insurance affect the ratio of large businesses to small businesses? Does this discourage entrepreneurship and start-up companies and add to the stability of large businesses?

4.9.13

DISCUSSION QUESTION: AFFORDABLE CARE ACT OF 2010

> *Obamacare is not about improved health care or cheaper insurance or better treatment or insuring the uninsured, and it never has been about that. It's about statism. It's about expanding the government. It's about control over the population. It is about everything but health care.*
>
> Rush Limbaugh

The US Congress passed the Affordable Care Act in 2010 to address the problem of the uninsured. Other parts of the legislation addressed the problems of physician compensation based on expensive procedures as opposed to improved outcomes. Earlier legislation associated with economic recovery addressed the issue of information management and electronic medical records.

1. How were these issues addressed in the legislation? What were the mandated processes of change?
2. The Affordable Care Act of 2010 eliminates the pre-existing condition requirement on changing insurance plans. As you read this, have the issues mentioned here been abated or not? Has there been an effect on small entrepreneurial business?
3. As of your reading of this section, how has the legislation worked?
4. What were/are the criticisms of the legislation? Are the issues of this section addressed in the criticisms? Are other issues that are not addressed in this section addressed by the criticisms?

4.9.14

DISCUSSION QUESTION: COMPLEXITY, MOOD, AND RANDOM TRIGGERS IN HEALTHCARE

- Where in this discussion on US healthcare are there complexity mismatches?
- Where are there cases where social mood will affect outcomes?
- What are the possible random triggers for X-events?

4.10
DISCUSSION AND RESEARCH QUESTIONS

- An article entitled "3000 Raw Ideas Equals 1 Commercial Success," analyzed the success rates for new commercial products, and as one would expect, the failure rate is extremely high. Consequently, if a firm always assumed that each new technology will fail, that firm will be right most of the time. In hindsight, it is always easy to accuse a failed company of lacking foresight when it misses its opportunity to take advantage of a disruptive technology. But what is overlooked in those cases is the fact that the firm was likely correct in dismissing a large number of other disruptive technologies that never came to fruition. Had the firm chased one of these other failed technologies, the company might have collapsed sooner than it did. Consequently, one might reach the conclusion as Hannah and Freeman did that organizational inertia can actually confer a survival advantage.

  - Do you think that organizational inertia is always the most advantageous approach for survival?
  - Are there markets or industries where inertia would be liability?
  - If you were a major institutional investor, would you prefer that the firms you invest in exhibit organizational inertia since you can always manage your risks by investing in multiple firms?
  - Are organizations that are incapable of radical transformation actually an optimal solution for the economy? (i.e., is it better to achieve change by new firms entering than old firms transforming?)

- Enterprise transformation is a popular topic in the business world and is often portrayed as a necessity. Yet the value of transforming an enterprise is largely dependent upon one's point of view. While a CEO of a company may be in favor of transforming that company to ensure its survival, this may not necessarily be the best outcome for shareholders, employees, and the public. Perhaps the public would be better served through the failure of the old company and the entry of new, more innovative companies. It certainly wouldn't be a positive outcome for any employees laid off during the transformation. Thus, it is critical to consider what level of an organization is changing and who are the winners and losers from such a change.

- If a firm transforms by acquiring new business and divesting old ones, did the firm really transform? In other words, the same organizations still exist and provide the same goods and services. They have just been shuffled around among legal entities that we call corporations. Is anything transformative really going on?
- What do you think is better for the economy: allowing declining firms to fail and new entrants to replace them or intermittently transforming established firms?
- What about for employees and middle managers of a firm that is considering transformative changes? Would they be incentivized to resist or impede transformative efforts?
- Now consider the general public. How concerned do you think the public is with whether or not a given firm transforms or fails as long as they still get the goods and services that they desire?
- Which factors affect how much of a burden firm failure and/or firm transformation impose on a government?

• Major changes in organizational structure can occur at different levels of the organization at different times. A firm that divests unprofitable divisions preserves the upper level of the firm, but changes the lower levels. On the other hand, a firm that is taken over by another essentially loses its upper level but preserves the lower levels. We can also extend this to other organizations such as governments. As discussed in this chapter, factors besides innovation can influence whether a portion of an organization is changed or is preserved. Since different stakeholders have different preferences over when and how different organizational levels change, one cannot ignore the resources, influence, and capabilities that each stakeholder has to resist or promote change. Presumably any stakeholders that benefit from the status quo would use their resources and influence to preserve the portions of the organization that benefit them.

- In the short term, do the stakeholders with the greatest power and influence drive when and where an organization changes as opposed to economic efficiency?

- If organization structure is preserved because of parochial interests in the face of external pressure to change, presumably there is a mismatch between the organizational structure and the needs of some external stakeholders. Could the size of this mismatch or complexity gap be characterized by the amount of organizational change that would be needed to close it?
- Does a larger gap mean that it is more likely that a random event will force the organization into a situation that it cannot handle (i.e., there are more possible future states that the organization cannot handle, therefore all else being equal there are more possible ways that the organization can fail)?
- When an unmanageable event occurs, can the status quo be preserved or must either the organization or the external stakeholders change?
- Does a larger gap mean a more rapid reconfiguration in the event that status quo cannot be preserved (i.e., a catastrophic collapse vs. a gradual decline)?
- Are those with the most resources and influence those that most benefited from the status quo?
- If so, will they use those resources and influence to preserve the status quo even when there is external pressure to change?
- Does a larger mismatch between resources and influence among stakeholders make for a bigger gap? (i.e., more resources and more influence means that change can be resisted against greater and greater mismatches)
- Are the resources and influence consumed and eventually exhausted when protecting the status quo against external pressure and does this allow the eventual collapse due to a random event?
- Is the implication here that the greater the difference in resources and influence among stakeholders, the larger the gap will become which will result in a longer period without change, but the change will be larger and more catastrophic when it does occur? How could this idea be tested?

• When considering a layered defense, the Swiss cheese model is a helpful conceptual view. However, to actually identify risk scenarios that involve multiple failures is not so simple. In the world of engineered systems several approaches have been developed to accomplish this such as FEMCA, fault trees, event trees, and Hazop. Each of these methods takes a different approach to identify paths through a system that ultimately result in failure. FEMCA starts with physical breakdown of a system and asks how each component could fail. Fault trees start with an event to be avoided (e.g., a nuclear meltdown) and attempts to find all the paths in a system that result in that event. Event trees start the other way from an initiating event (e.g., a power failure) and follows it through to all possible outcomes. HAZOP starts in the middle and works in both directions. It considers a deviation in a system function (e.g., what if there were too much flow in this pipe?). It then asks how it could be caused and what would the consequences be. Many of these techniques were developed to deal with engineered systems where there is a risk of catastrophic failure such as a nuclear power plant or a chemical plant.

As sophisticated as these techniques are, there are countless cases where unanticipated failure paths found a way through the systems defenses. Consider the various nuclear and chemical plant disasters that have occurred over the years. The techniques described above were developed to find failure paths in physical, relatively well-defined, stable systems. By stable, we mean that a chemical plant doesn't spontaneously reconfigure itself. However, we consider organizations and social systems, we find that while portions remain stable, aspects are frequently reconfiguring and adapting. Not to mention that human beings themselves learn and adapt.

- How effective do you think techniques developed to find failure paths in physical systems will be when applied to social systems that are less well defined and frequently changing?
- If it is challenging to develop an effective layered defense for a well-defined physical system, how challenging do you think it is to develop one for an organizational system?
- Charles Perrow introduced the concept of a normal accident. He argues that for extremely complex systems, such as a nuclear fission plant, failures are inevitable, hence normal. There are simply too many possible ways for them to fail and not all of them can be detected. Do you think that this concept extends to complex human organizational systems? Are failures in organizational systems normal?
- Is this idea of normal accidents related to the complexity gap discussed previously? Does the presence of a complexity gap make failure inevitable?

BIBLIOGRAPHY

Black, Fischer, and Myron Scholes. "The Pricing of Options and Corporate Liabilities." *Journal of Political Economy* 81(3) (1973): 637–654.

Casti, John. *Complexification: Explaining a Paradoxical World Through the Science of Surprise.* HarperCollins, 1994.

Cohn, Jonathan. "The Robot Will See You Now." *Atlantic*, February 2013.

Gawande, Atul. "Overkill." *New Yorker*, May 2015. http://www.newyorker.com/magazine/2015/05/11/overkill-atul-gawande.

Hannan, M. T., and J. Freeman. *Organizational Ecology.* Cambridge, Mass: Harvard University Press, 1993.

Hannan, M. T., and J. Freeman. "Structural Inertia and Organizational Change." *American Sociological Review* (1984): 149–164.

Hull, John C. *Options, Futures, and Other Derivatives, 9th edition.* Upper Saddle River, New Jersey: Prentice Hall, 2014.

Jones, Roger D. "Healthcare as a Complex System," 2013. http://xcenternetwork.com/roger-d-jones-us-healthcare-as-a-complex-system/.

McArdle, M. "Why Companies Fail." *Atlantic*, March 2012.

Moosekilde, E., E. Larsen, and J. Sterman. "Coping with Complexity: Deterministic Chaos in Human Decision Making Behavior." In *Beyond Belief: Randomness, Prediction and Explanation in Science*, edited by J. Casti and A. Karlqvist. CRC Press, 1991 (199–229).

Nocera, J. "How Not to Stay on Top." *New York Times*, August 2013.

Perrow, C. *Normal Accidents: Living with High Risk Technologies.* Princeton University Press, 2011.

Rouse, William B., and Nicoleta Serban. *Understanding and Managing the Complexity of Healthcare.* Cambridge, Mass: MIT Press, 2014.

Schramm, C. "Schumpeter's Moment." *Wall Street Journal*, May 2009.

Simon, Koreen A. "Three Leadership Lessons from Kodak's Misfortune." *Roots of Resilience*, January 2012. http://rootsofresilience.blogspot.com/2012/01/three-leadership-lessons-from-kodaks.html.

Sreedhar, S. "Conquering Catastrophe: The Industrial Internet vs. the Swiss Cheese Model," March 2014. https://www.gesoftware.com/blog/conquering-catastrophe-industrial-internet-vs-swiss-cheese-model.

Stevens, G. A., and J. Burley. "3,000 Raw Ideas Equals 1 Commercial Success!" *Research-Technology Management* 40(3) (1997): 16.

Trex, E. "15 Companies That Originally Sold Something Else." *Mental Floss Magazine*, 2013.

5
EXPECTING
THE UNKNOWN
UNKNOWNS

5.1
THE RESILIENCE OF "RESILIENCE"

In the summer of 1973, one of us (JC) took a position as one of the first scientists at the International Institute for Applied Systems Analysis (IIASA), located at a former hunting palace of the Austrian Empress Maria Theresa, just a few miles south of Vienna in the village of Laxenburg, Austria. IIASA was a joint venture of the US National Academy of Sciences and the Soviet Academy of Sciences, with several junior partners, the countries of eastern and western Europe, along with Canada and Japan. The research structure of the Institute was set up along the lines you'd find in a university, except that the "departments" had names like Energy, Urban Studies, Water Resources, Methodology, and so forth, reflecting the fact that IIASA was set up to study questions common to the industrialized countries of the world.

One of the IIASA projects at that time was Ecology, which was headed by C.S. ("Buzz") Holling, who we met in the first chapter. Holling was a professor of ecology at the University of British Columbia in Vancouver, Canada. Holling arrived with a team of professors and graduate students, all focused on understanding the system-theoreti nature of ecological processes. Earlier that same year, Holling had published a path-breaking article, "Resilience and Stability of Ecological Systems," which sparked off the interest in the idea of system resilience that is so topical nowadays. So it's fair to say that this paper, together with the work begun at IIASA at that time, was the forerunner of the "resilience revolution" we see in the media and on the Internet today.

Formally, JC was a member of the Methodology Project, whose mission was to provide mathematical modeling and computational support to the applied projects. He soon gravitated to a collaborative mode with the Canadian ecologists, a collaboration that lasted several years. At the time, JC had just completed his doctoral dissertation on the stability theory of control systems, so was well-positioned to see the relevancy of resilience as a new system concept, one differing in important ways from the more classical notion of stability as understood by control and dynamical system theorists.

The traditional concept of stability was the idea that if a system is perturbed from its current equilibrium position, it's stable if it eventually returns to that very same equilibrium. More prosaically, a system is stable if any disturbance from its current state eventually washes out and the system eventually returns to that state. This was the idea in JC's head when he ran into Holling. But he soon learned that there was more on heaven and earth than were dreamed of in his mathematical philosophies!

In numerous conversations with Holling over the next couple of years, JC came away with the idea that simple stability, mathematical-style, was totally inadequate to encompass the concept of resilience. According to Holling, a resilient system wasn't necessarily stable at all. Rather, it was a system that could "roll with the punches," so to speak, and continue to perform its function. Moreover, the resilience allowed the system to even change its function as its operating environment dictated, so as to enhance its survivability. JC finally saw the light, realizing that resilience was a new concept in the system theorist's arsenal of weapons for understanding the behavior of the natural world. Now let's fast-forward a few decades and look at what researchers see today as a resilient system.

◆ ◆ ◆

The word "resilience" most likely entered the English language via the Latin verb resaltare, meaning to rebound or bounce back. But as we noted above, in today's world the word is used in a multitude of ways, all of which revolve about the idea of adjusting and adapting to changing circumstances. Note how this differs from the simple notion of stability described earlier. Stability refers to a system that only changes its behavior in reaction to changed circumstances, but does not change its underlying structure at all. It remains the very same system as it was prior to the disturbance. In Holling's work and most of what we see today going under the rubric of resilience, an essential part of a system being resilient is that it be able and ready to restructure and reconfigure itself in reaction to a changing environment. All this being said, the word resilience is still used in slightly different ways in different settings. Let's look at a few of them outlined by Loup Francart in his very illuminating article, "What Does Resilience Really Mean?"

Psychology: The capacity of a person to carry on in an environment that would normally lead to a mental breakdown. In other words, resilience is the capacity to confront trauma without being later affected by it.

Economics: An economy is resilient if it can regain the ability to grow after a crisis.

Biology: An organism's ability to survive in a changing environment and overcome attacks by predators.

Ecology: The ability of an ecosystem to maintain its function in the face of a possibly unexpected disturbance.

Organizations: A firm is resilient if it has the ability to restructure itself so as to withstand a shock, and possibly even be stronger afterwards.

Societies: The capacity of a society to overcome the consequences of an attack while preserving the societal culture.

Geopolitics: The ability to reduce risk from emergencies so that people can go about their business freely and with confidence.

Francart notes that the terminology is now so widespread that even mattress manufacturers use the word to describe the ability of their mattresses to recover their original shape after someone lying on them gets up!

What is the common element in each of these semi-metaphorical uses of the term? Basically, what links each definition is that there must be some kind of shock or crisis, what we are calling an X-event, constituting a major change in the way the system goes about its business. Generally, the X-event overturns previous assumptions about the world and the way the system functions, often accompanied by new uncertainties and dangers.

Putting all these factors together, we will use the following definition of resilience in what follows in this chapter. For simplicity, we'll call it the *Four As*:

Awareness—A resilient system should be monitoring early-warning signals for X-events, and be able to take action to "batten down the hatches" if the X-event seems imminent;

Assimilation—A resilient system will be able to survive the X-event. Maybe the survival will be by resistance to the event, maybe by absorbing the shock into the system's operation, or through some other survival mechanism. But survival is a necessary condition for being resilient;

Agility—A resilient system is able to survey the new landscape that the X-event creates and have the ability to evaluate its resources and see how to deploy them to fill one or another of the new niches that the event opens up;

Adaptivity—The resilient system should be ready to change its way of doing business if it finds that a new niche offers greater potential for growth, development, and survival than its pre-shock activities.

Since the *sine qua non* of the entire notion of resilience rests upon the occurrence of an X-event, and since there are many, many different types of X-events, it follows that any idea of system resilience is necessarily context-dependent. A system may be very resilient to, say, the shock of an earthquake but totally vulnerable to the shock of a solar storm. Thus, in order to properly speak about the "resilience" of a system, we are tacitly assuming that what, precisely, the X-event is that the system is resilient against. And any notion of measuring the overall resilience of a system must take into account a spectrum of different sorts of X-events that it may experience.

As an X-event itself is, by definition, rare and surprising, it's a pretty tricky business creating the infrastructure needed to be resilient against all such contingencies. In fact, it's impossible. Just like buying insurance, you can protect yourself against some types of unknown unknowns, like heart attacks and stroke but not against Ebola fever or a rare blood disease. In fact, it's flat out impossible to buy insurance against every possible illness or accident that may befall you. So let's revisit yet again, but briefly, the notion of an X-event and examine different aspects for building in protection against one.

5.1.1
DISCUSSION QUESTION:
RESILIENCE ON ALL SCALES

> *Resilience is all about being able to overcome the unexpected.*
> *Sustainability is about survival. The goal of resilience is to*
> *thrive.*

Jamais Cascio

1 Identify examples of resilience in psychology, economics, biology, ecology, organizations, societies, and geopolitics.
2. Can you associate each of the four As with each example?

5.2
RESILIENT AGAINST WHAT?

Conventional risk analysis typically proceeds by identifying all the different sorts of shocks that a system might experience, calculating the probabilities of each of these shocks, subtracting each of these numbers from 1, and then (assuming the shocks are independent!) multiplying the resulting numbers together to obtain the likelihood that no shocks will occur. If that number is too small, steps then should be taken to reduce one or another of the initial probabilities to get the final result down to an acceptable level. Of course, this is a caricature of the actual process of everyday risk analysis. But it already underscores many of the problems in using such an analysis to address resilience.

First of all, individual shocks are seldom, if ever, independent. For instance, the Fukushima incident in Japan in 2011 showed the earthquake and the tsunami that shorted out the nuclear reactors were far from independent. Moreover, the electrical supply to drive the water pumps to prevent the reactor from overheating was totally dependent on the height of the retaining wall that was supposed to protect the pumps. And so on and so forth.

Furthermore, there simply did not exist a database of past earthquakes that would have enabled analysts to forecast the probability of the magnitude 6.9 earthquake that actually occurred, since it was larger than any previously recorded quake. So, in fact, almost all the factors necessary to do a conventional risk analysis were absent. The end result was what is currently estimated to be the costliest disaster of all time, one that the World Bank estimates to ultimately be about $235 billion.

The 2011 Japanese earthquake shows that not only are X-events rare and surprising, but that the event itself is generally a cascade of smaller events that ultimately creates the X-event that we want to be resilient against. For instance, the damage was not caused directly by either the earthquake or the tsunami. The nuclear power plants were well-positioned to withstand both of these "sub" X-events. The problem was farther downstream residing with the retaining walls that were designed to protect the water pumps. The walls were too low and the pumps were located beneath the level of the wall. So any water that breached the retaining wall was sure to flood the pumps. Thus, the X-event that caused the damage was a cascade of the earthquake, the tsunami, and the low height of the retaining walls. If any of these sub-events had not occurred, Fukushima would not be a word known anywhere outside Japan.

So when it comes to resilience against an X-event, we have to abandon the notion that the "event" is a single entity; rather, it is almost always a sequence of sub-events that are later gathered together under one label. But the actions taken to be resilient to that headline event must take into account the entire sequence. Thus, when we speak about the Japanese earthquake, we should bear in mind not just the earthquake itself, but the events that follow from the earthquake and their compound impact on the nuclear power plants at Fukushima. This very same story applies to all the X-events of concern to businesses, governments, other social organizations, and communities. It's the interconnected systems that matter, not stand-alone problems.

Another element entering into the resilience equation is time. X-events will happen regardless of how much energy, effort, and money we put in to prevent them. This means that there are two types of planning required in order to be able to absorb the shock of the event and come back stronger than ever. One is the planning done for protection before the X-event occurs, mitigation if you like. The other is planning how to restructure and reconfigure the system after the event has run its course. Each of these factors merits its own slice of our attention.

◆ ◆ ◆

In his book *The Edge of Disaster*, security expert Stephen Flynn speaks of a panoply of threats to our safety and well-being: a breakdown in the power grid, stoppages in the global food supply chain, a chemical accident in a major urban area, damage to urban water supplies, and so forth. In Flynn's world of terror, the most likely threat is a terrorist attack that pushes panicked legislators to overreact by doing something stupid, such as tearing up the Bill of Rights!

Flynn notes that the tendency in government, especially in the post World War II era, has been to try to eliminate such threats. But the historical record for the past 60 years does not look too kindly on the approach of reducing risk to zero. No amount of science, money, or energy has managed to win the wars on cancer, drugs, poverty, crime, terrorism, or any other existential threat to humankind. What's needed instead, Flynn argues, is not to try to do the impossible and reduce risk to zero. Rather, go the other direction and make American society more robust, so that it's able to absorb these shocks and keep on running. He notes that a very big part of this approach is the reorientation of people's attitudes toward risk. Society must take in the message that there's no such thing as a risk-free world. As we put it a moment ago, you can't buy insurance against everything. Stuff happens. What you need to do is to accept that as an operating principle and be ready to roll with the punches and come back fighting. Resilience is the core element for this program.

Implementing a resilience-based program won't be easy, though. Most government officials, particularly those in the security end of things, regard the whole idea of resilience as "defeatist." Flynn remarks, "They believe our job is to prevent these things from happening. What we have seen is that we keep having big events that are profoundly disruptive and that we are woefully underprepared to deal with." Like a lot of other lessons that are "obvious," there's little, if any, hope of converting such officials to a new way of viewing the world. They have too much at stake in protecting the old ways to even consider a change of such magnitude. Rather, one has to begin the process by educating those whose minds are not already cast in concrete. Enter Thomas Homer-Dixon.

Homer-Dixon is a professor of international affairs at the University of Waterloo in Canada and a keen observer of the way complexity has entered into the way the world now works. He says that when he lectures to audiences of even educated people—businessmen, civil servants, and social scientists—the audience has a tendency to believe that systems always tend toward an equilibrium and that small causes give rise to only small effects. This is the very type of thinking that comes from classical physics, a la Newton. It is also the type of thinking that the world is just risky, not inherently uncertain. To combat this view of the way things work, we require a sea change in attitudes and teaching of the principles of complex systems early on in the academic curriculum.

If you're going to think big like Homer-Dixon, then you may as well go all the way. And he does just that. His program for resilience is organized around the "creative destruction" ideas of the Austrian-American economist Joseph Schumpeter. We will say more about that a bit later. But for now it suffices just to note that Homer-Dixon argues that the very source of resilience rests in the process of creative destruction. Our political and economic systems are resilient then because they operate on the basis of the Schumpeterian principle by undergoing constant cycles of ruin and reinvention. So it is this process itself that gives rise to resilience; the resilience comes from systems that have reinvented themselves continually over a long period of time, learning in the process how to survive in the face of unknown—and probably unknowable—adversities.

In terms of our Four As concept of resilience sketched earlier, this before-the-fact planning corresponds to the first two As: Awareness and Assimilation. Now let's go to the other side of the coin and examine the after-the-fact rebuilding of the system once the X-event has run its course. How should we prepare to take advantage of the X-event, not be destroyed by it?

◆ ◆ ◆

A number of years ago, one of us (JC) was invited to Hamilton, Bermuda to speak to a group of reinsurers on the theme of what the world of science might contribute to the global catastrophe-insurance industry. This was at a time when Wall Street was vacuuming up every unemployed physicist they could find, so I guess the reinsurers realized that they were the only industry that had more money than the banks and that they should try to get in on the action. Anyway, the panel of speakers consisted of JC, a system theorist/modeler from the Santa Fe Institute, and three climatologists. This mix suggested immediately that the reinsurance industry thought that the best thing science could do for them was to provide a sure-fire, can't-fail method for predicting the time, location, and severity of hurricanes. Oddly, it doesn't take much thought to realize that any such model/program that could do that would be the worst thing that ever happened to the reinsurance industry, not the best, as it would put them out of business almost overnight. After all, the essence of insurance is risk. So if you remove the risk, you eliminate the need for the industry. At the other end of the scale, if you have no knowledge whatsoever about any aspects of where or when the next hurricane will occur, that's pretty bad, too. In that case, you have no rational way to price your product. Logically, it then follows that there is some sweet spot between full knowledge and no knowledge at which a given reinsurance company is most healthy. In his presentation, JC asked precisely this question, arguing that the best way to discover that sweet spot (and it's not the same spot for every company) would be to construct the world of reinsurance inside a computer and use that world as a laboratory to investigate the question.

It's probably fair to say that the vast majority of the audience found this argument literally incomprehensible, going as it did against the grain of the conventional wisdom in the corridors of power in Hamilton at that time. Fortunately, though, a handful of far-sighted executives and researchers approached JC afterwards and inquired about how that magic computer simulation might be created. After several months of back-and-forth between the scientists in Santa Fe and the insurers from not only Bermuda, but also England, Switzerland, and the United States, a consortium was formed to provide the funding and expert knowledge required to get Insurance World, the world-of-reinsurance-in-a-box, put together.

As a first approximation, the insurance industry can be regarded as an interplay among three components: firms, which offer insurance, clients, who buy it, and events, which determine the outcomes of the "bets" that have been placed between the insurers and their clients. In Insurance World, the agents consist of the managers of a set of primary casualty insurers and a set of reinsurers, which are the firms that insure the insurers, so to speak. The events are natural hazards, such as hurricanes and earthquakes, as well as various external factors like government regulators and the global capital markets.

Insurance World is a laboratory for studying questions of the following sort:

Optimal Uncertainty: What is that sweet spot at which an organization can operate most effectively? Does it vary across firms? Does it vary between reinsurers, primary insurers, and/or end consumers?

Industry Structure: In terms of the standard metaphors used to characterize organizations—a machine, a brain, an organism, a culture, a political system, a psychic prison—which type(s), if any, most accurately represents the insurance industry? And how is this picture of the organization shaped by the specific "routines" used by the decision-makers in the various components making up the organization?

The simulator calls for the management of each firm to set a variety of parameters having to do with their desired market share in certain regions for different types of hazards and level of risk they want to take on, as well as to provide a picture of the external economic climate (interest rates, likelihood of hurricanes/earthquakes, inflation rates, and so forth). The simulation then runs for ten years in steps of three months, at which time a variety of outputs can be examined. For instance, Figure 5.1 shows the market share for Gulf Coast hurricane insurance of the five primary insurers in this toy world, under the assumption that the initial market shares were almost identical—but not quite. In this experiment, firm #2 has a little larger initial market share than any of the other firms, a differential advantage that it then uses to squeeze out all the other firms at the end of the ten-year period. This is due to the "brand effect," in which buyers tend to purchase insurance from companies that they have heard about.

Returning now to the idea of planning for after-the-fact X-events, the events in *Insurance World*, a hurricane or an earthquake, certainly qualifies as an X-event. In the simulator, the managers of the insurance companies accept the fact that nature will throw these events at them from time to time. So they ask themselves, What is the right thing for me to do now, in order that my firm not only survives the event, but is positioned to benefit from it? There is no one-size-fits-all answer to this question. In fact, the correct answer is, the right thing to do depends on what everyone else is doing, including Nature.

And since one never knows what everyone else is doing, but have at best limited information of this type, you have to experiment. That's what Insurance World allows you to do. You can make assumptions about what everyone else is doing, as well as arrange for Nature to give you a Force 5 hurricane in the Gulf Coast and see what happens when you do this, that, or something else. In this manner, you can develop some intuition about how to act under a variety of circumstances, as well as discover what kind of information is most useful in creating strategies that enable your firm to ride out the vast majority of unknown X-events waiting to jump out of the closet.

So agent-based simulation is one way to deal with the second half of the Four As, Agility and Adaptation. You can survey the landscape created by the X-event and see where opportunities present themselves for you to deploy your resources. You may then actually deploy those resources (Adaptation) and see the consequences of those actions.

Before throwing the baby out with the bathwater and abandoning completely the conventional wisdoms of trying to prevent X-events from happening in the first place, let's take a little longer look at how these events might at least be either reduced in damage and severity or at least anticipated through a judicious use of our ideas on complexity mismatches and overload.

Market Share, Gulf Coast, Hurricane

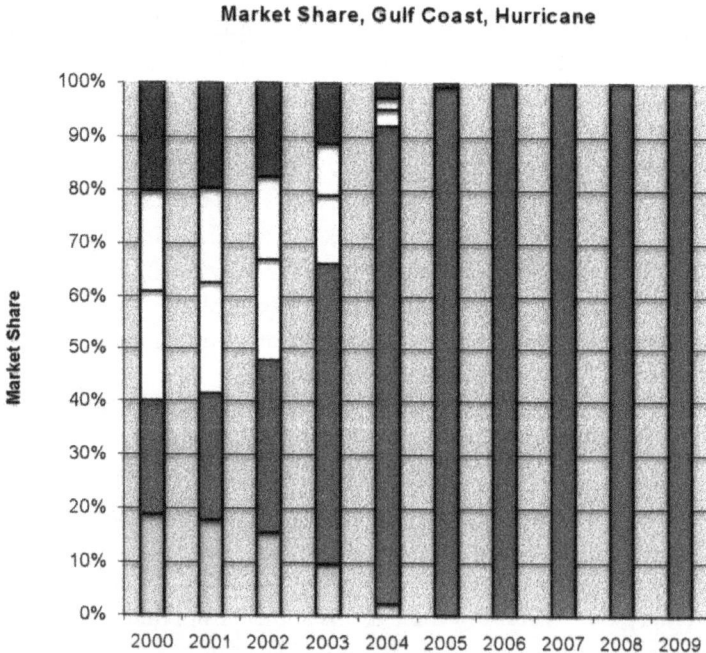

Figure 5.1 Market Share for the Gulf Coast Hurricane Market. Five companies are represented. Company 2 has slightly more market share initially that the other companies, yet it captures the entire market.

5.2.1
EXERCISE: INSURANCE WORLD

There is no problem that doesn't have some underlying need for more optimism, stamina, resilience, and collaboration. And games are, I believe, the best platform we have for providing that.

Jane McGonigal

Create a simple simulation of the reinsurance industry. Test the simulation against X-events. What do you conclude?

5.3
PLANNING FOR THE UNIMAGINABLE

One of the threads running through this book is the notion that there can be no human progress without X-events. Of course, here we are speaking of the kind of "progress" that's revolutionary in character, not evolutionary. This is progress in which visible, meaningful change happens rapidly enough that we can often see the change taking place before our very eyes. The argument we've given for the claim that X-events are a necessary condition for this type of progress is that revolutionary change requires that existing social, economic, and/or political structures that have outlived their usefulness be swept away. But if there is anything the power structures in modern society—mostly politicians, banks, and megacorporations— want, it is to maintain the status quo. So the only thing that can overcome that sort of power-induced stasis is an "act of god," i.e., an X-event, something that the existing power structure is powerless to prevent.

When presenting this line of argument in public, reactions often take the form: do you mean we should deliberately go out and destroy the social structures that most of us depend upon for our daily lives, in order to open up niches for these new structures that you say constitute "progress"? Well, not quite. We're not advocating total and complete anarchy here. Throwing out the baby with the bathwater doesn't really benefit anyone, especially the baby. What we do advocate, though, is that humans be a bit more imaginative and devote a lot more thought into seeing how to create controlled X-events that will clean out the Augean stables without destroying the horses in the process. In other words, we should deliberately promote experiments that will not kill the experimenter. In fact, we already engage in such activities, albeit without labeling them "X-events" (yet!). Here are a couple of examples.

If left unattended, forests will continue to grow until the trees fill up all available space for expansion. This means that there are way too many trees clustered too close together, so that when the inevitable lightning strike or insect infestation occurs, it spreads literally like wildfire through the forest and destroys everything. The forest is effectively leveled and the entire growth process must start again from its original (and literal) ground state. This is especially bad since the growth of a forest to maturity takes place on a times-cale measured in decades, if not centuries.

To prevent this type of calamity, forestry managers introduced the idea of a controlled burn to clear out dead trees, over-crowding and other conditions that interfere with the forest's ability to resist attacks from insects, lightning, and other such existential threats. Logic and intuition argue that thinning out the forest in this way will help protect it from a catastrophic collapse. The US Forest Service, which manages 200 million acres of public land, believes it and contracts with logging companies to take out large and small trees using pre-scribed types of small fires.

The Forest Service approach is based upon tree ring studies, and is an attempt to reconstruct the forests of the western United States to their state before the twentieth century. But recently ecologists and environmentalists began to argue that such a procedure of controlled X-events rests upon shaky science and is actually environmentally harmful. They argue that tree ring records do not tell the whole story, and that forests have historically suffered much more severe fires than the rings would argue.

These counter-arguments to controlled burns imply that the ecology of forests depends on fires of many different degrees of scale and intensity— including what we would see today as catastrophic fires. In short, the argument is that large fires can actually stimulate biodiversity rather than destroy it. Of course, this is an argument of degree, not kind. Everyone agrees that burns are helpful. What seems to divide the Forest Service from the academic ecologists is the type of burns they advocate. The ecologists say that the matter should be left to nature to provide the scope and scale of the burns needed to promote diversity, and not left to managed burns created on the basis of incomplete science and human intuition. And it does not appear that either side would advocate burns that completely destroy the forest! So the question is, just how controlled is "controlled"? There is simply no uniform answer, as the forest burn issue illustrates.

Before leaving this point, let us note that the very same principle is at work in many other areas besides forests. When we go out to our backyard garden and start pulling weeds, we are thinning the vegetation in a way that we believe will help our tomato and cucumber plants have a better chance to produce something for the dinner table than if we'd left the garden alone. It's clear that you don't have to eliminate every single weed to end up with a nice home-grown salad. But it's equally clear that you can't let the weeds take over the garden either. A similar story can be told about raising cattle or sheep. We cull the herds so as to remove animals that are injured, genetically weak, or otherwise using resources that could be put to better use by more healthy animals in the herd. And in another direction entirely, we often pump water into earthquake fault zones to deliberately promote small, tension-relieving quakes to reduce the stress on tectonic plates that could otherwise rupture in the Big One.

As a last remark, let's talk for a moment about humans instead of weeds or stragglers in a herd. Does introducing humans into the picture change the picture? Probably the first thought that comes to mind is that any public talk about "weeding out" humans would be akin to political suicide, evoking dark thoughts about genocides, social Darwinism, and the like. While in many cases that may well be the case, here is an example of how things may go in just the opposite direction.

About 20 years ago, the state of Oregon got fed up with the foot-dragging at the federal level in putting together a decent healthcare program of the sort everyone takes for granted in much of the rest of the industrialized world. So they decided to do it themselves. Here is a rather potted version of how it worked out. The details can be found on the Wikipedia page under "Oregon Health Plan."

Basically, the state had a certain level of funds available to support the health plan. So they assembled a long list of medical conditions, procedures, drugs, and the like that their citizens might require for maintaining their health. The state then estimated how much it would cost to service each of these medical conditions and simply ordered these costs in some way. They then went down the list adding up the expenses until they ran out of available funds. At that point, a line was drawn and the state declared that they could not service any condition that fell below the line. This meant that many people with rare and/or extraordinary expensive medical conditions would not receive benefits from the state health plan. As just noted, one might have expected this procedure to generate a huge outcry from the state's residents in general, and those with conditions below the line in particular, with declarations of social injustices and bias heading the list of grievances. But, in fact, even though there were grumblings here and there, no such massive outcry emerged. Why not?

While it's difficult to give a full and complete explanation for why the residents didn't call for impeachment of the governor and other legislators and initiate a flurry of lawsuits against the state for various types of biases, here are two of the main reasons: (1) the process of deciding what conditions did and did not fall below the line was a public process, and (2) everyone had an opportunity to voice their opinion about the process. Consequently, the process was perceived as being fair even though it generated winners and losers in this healthcare lottery. In essence, the residents of Oregon realized that there was simply not enough money to go around to protect everybody against everything. Some choices had to be made, and the process for making them was seen as fair.

What we have been describing as a controlled burn is nothing more than a reframing of the general issue we've spoken about before. That is the idea of a complexity gap that cannot be allowed to grow to the point where the stresses in the system must be relieved by a dramatic and devastating X-event. This message is important enough for us to revisit it here within the context of system resilience. Let's start by re-examining the Oregon Health Plan.

From a systemic standpoint, we can view the Oregon Health Plan as two systems in interaction. One system is the Residents of the state with their accompanying health needs. If we consider the healthcare needs of an individual resident and then add these needs together for every single resident as a measure of the complexity of the Residents, that system has a huge complexity level somewhere in the many millions. The other system is the State, with its resources available to attend to these healthcare requirements. Suppose we measure the State's complexity by the number of healthcare needs that it can actually finance. As already noted above, this complexity is considerably less than the needs of the Residents. So there is a gap, the difference between the needs of the Residents and the State's ability to service those needs.

As long as that gap remains relatively small, there is no problem. Most of the needs of most of the people can be met and the dynamic balance between the two systems is sustainable. But as is almost always the case in such matters, the Residents begin asking for more of their needs to be serviced. But the State cannot raise money fast enough to keep up with these requests. So the complexity of the Residents grows at a faster pace than that of the State. Eventually, this gap widens to the point where either the State has to raise more healthcare revenues or the Residents have to reduce their demands. The usual situation is that neither of these remedies can be applied, with the inevitable result that the cohesion between the two systems snaps and there is a collapse. And while the Oregon Plan has not yet collapsed, it has undergone major changes over the past decade or so in order to close this gap. And at the moment the gap seems to have been reduced to a level that allows the two systems, Residents and State, to co-exist.

Many other examples from earlier in the book can be seen as illustrations of this same principle, so we won't repeat them here. The point is that a resilient system would be able to anticipate that these dangerous gaps will arise, as well as have developed procedures for monitoring the change in complexity levels so as to be able to seen when the systems are entering the "yellow zone" where a collapse starts to become imminent. Finally, the resilient system would already have a plan in place to reduce the gap in order to stave off, or at least reduce, the impact of the resulting X-event.

The final question that usually arises in discussions of resilience is a simple one to ask, but fiendishly difficult to answer: how do we measure the resilience of a system? As with "complexity," another very useful everyday word used differently in the scientific world than in ordinary life, what constitutes resilience and how it is measured probably has as many answers as there are researchers and scholars who are studying the problem. Earlier, we gave one partial answer when we argued for a definition of resilience in terms of the Four As. So let's return to that definition and look at it now from the perspective of attaching a numerical measure to it in a given situation.

5.3.1
DISCUSSION QUESTION: OREGON HEALTHCARE

Nature works with five polymers. Only five polymers. In the natural world, life builds from the bottom up, and it builds in resilience and multiple uses.

Janine Benyus

Discuss the Oregon healthcare plan in the context of the healthcare discussion in Chapter 4.

5.4
HOW RESILIENT ARE YOU?

The first item on the road to a measure of resilience is to remember that resilience is a context-dependent systemic property. It depends on the type of X-event you want to be resilient against. This point must be kept uppermost in mind, since it does no good to build resilience against a terrorist bombing when what happens is a hurricane or an Internet crash. So to set the stage for our Four As resilience measure, let's assume we want to be resilient to an Internet failure. So that's our target X-event. But even that's not enough. We have to specify a few more details about the failure before we start measuring how well our protection is working. These details include whether it's a purely in-house IT failure of a server or some other part of the local information-processing infrastructure or the failure goes outside your own organization. In the latter case, we then must ask if it's local in the sense that the failure rests in your local ISP or if it's global in the sense that the failure extends beyond simply your own provider. We can further subdivide the problem. But this is probably enough to get the general idea, which is that you have to have a very good idea of what you're trying to be resilient against before you can even begin to put protection in place.

Once the matter of exactly what X-event is of concern is settled, we can bring out the Four As: Awareness, Assimilation, Agility, and Adaptivity and assign an integer from 0 to 10 to each category, reflecting how well-prepared we are for the X-event in the activities described by that category. So if our X-event is an in-house internet failure, we can first look at whether we had in place any kind of procedure for giving an early-warning signal for that particular event. In other words, how was our Awareness of an in-house failure? If we had a good early-warning of the failure, then we'd give a high mark, say 9 or 10, to Awareness; if we had no warning at all, then for Awareness we would assign a low value, say 0 or 1.

We now continue to Assimilation and ask how well we were prepared to survive the Internet failure and still keep at least a skeletal system going. Again, a high number means we did pretty well, a low number says we did poorly. We then continue with Agility, our ability to examine the situation after the Internet failure and look for opportunities that the failure created. Finally, we consider how Adaptive we are in the sense of being able to move into a new way of carrying out our in-house computing created by the failure.

In this manner, we obtain a set of four numbers (A1, A2, A3, A4) characterizing how resilient our system is to an Internet failure. If all of these numbers are large, great. The system is very resilient. But if even one of the numbers is small, then we have a potential problem and our resilience level is low. So perhaps the risk-averse way to measure resilience against an in-house Internet failure is to just take the smallest of the four numbers A1, A2, A3, A4. Or maybe the average of these numbers. Or even the variance of the four numbers. Which is the best way to reflect the resilience against this type of X-event also depends very much on the specific system we're managing and the details of the hypothetical X-event.

Now recall that so far we've spoken about just one specific X-event. But there may be many more that concern the system manager. And for each of these X-events of concern, there is another set of four numbers characterizing how prepared we are for that X-event using the Four As categories. In the end, if we have N X-events, we'll end up with a collection of N sets of four numbers. We then have to somehow combine that set of 4-tuples into a single number that reflects our estimate of the overall resilience of our system. Again, there are many ways to create that single measure, ranging from taking the minimum of all the other minima to some kind of statistical measure like an average. What works best is an empirical question that's currently under investigation.

5.4.1
EXERCISE: MEASURING THE FOUR AS

The biggest risk is not taking any risk. . . In a world that is changing really quickly, the only strategy that is guaranteed to fail is not taking risks.

Mark Zuckerberg
That which does not kill us makes us stronger.

Friedrich Nietzsche

1. Identify an X-event. Imagine you are responsible for an organization that will be affected by the X-event. Design a system based on the four As to prepare and manage through the event.
2. Are you comfortable with the approach? What are the strengths and weaknesses?

5.5
CLIMATE CHANGE: AN EXAMPLE OF MANAGING THE FOUR AS

Climate change is a possibly pending X-event. We can use climate change as an exercise in the four As: Awareness, Assimilation, Agility, and Adaptivity.

Awareness: What are the early warning signs of an impending climate-change X-event?

Assimilation: What survival mechanisms are available to get through significant climate change?

Agility: What tools are available to survey the post X-event landscape in order to deploy resources?

Adaptivity: What might be the potential opportunities of climate change?

We will work through the four As for climate change in the next few sections. The next section, on awareness, will address the question if man-made climate change is real and how the evidence does and does not support the forecast of a climate-change X-event.

5.5.1
BUILDING ON THE HURRICANE EXAMPLE

We used the hurricane in Chapter 1 as a metaphor for a social X-event. We introduced the concept of complexity mismatch as measured by the difference in temperature between two locations. We saw that a simple temperature difference can lead to exotic and complex phenomena such as convection zones, weather patterns, hurricane formation, and beta gyres. The transition from one level of complexity to a greater level of complexity was sudden—an X-event. Moreover, as the temperature gradient increased, the complexity became more and more localized, from the global convection zones for small temperature gradients to localized hurricanes for higher temperature gradients. As the complexity became more localized, the concept of random trigger emerged. For complex hurricanes, a random low-pressure center in the ocean served as a *nucleation site* for the formation of the hurricane. The temperature gradient formed a long-lived structure in the form of the hurricane that only disappeared when the heat the hurricane was carrying was dissipated into its cooler surroundings. The hurricane is an example of complexity mismatch (the temperature gradient) creating order (the hurricane). In this example, X-events create order.

The order of the hurricane interacts with the order of social infrastructure. Hurricanes flood roads, destroy bridges and buildings, interrupt power and other services, and displace people. Hurricanes are not the only effects of global heating. Ice melts; oceans rise; salt content changes in the seas; salt gradients lead to other orderly oceanic structures; local climate changes; rain patterns change, carbon dioxide levels change; and plant growth changes. The effects of global heating can be plentiful and strange.

5.5.2
BELIEFS AND MOOD ON CLIMATE CHANGE

One concept in the book did not appear in the treatment of hurricane formation—social mood. Social mood does not affect hurricane formation—or does it? Hurricanes form as a consequence of temperature gradients, or excessive local heating. If excessive heating is due to man-made climate change, then social mood certainly does affect hurricane formation—and much more. No proper treatment of X-events can give short shrift to climate change. If real, climate change will lead to outcomes that we cannot currently predict or imagine. This is a true and proper X-event. How are we to be resilient? The first thing we need to do is to understand the threat as much as possible; to understand the nature of landscape in which we find ourselves. We will walk through the climate-change evidence carefully in order to convince ourselves there is or is not truly a real threat. If we decide the threat is real, then the question remains: how does the human race remain resilient through the X-event?

Climate scientists are nearly unanimous that the earth is heating and that we should see more consequences of climate change. They also agree that humans play a major role in the heating process. The general public, however, is more divided on man-made climate change. This has become (2015) a political issue in the US. In fact, the serious back-and-forth among the parties in the debate is worthy of late-night comedy. This, however, is not really an issue for the Earth. After all, the sun will rise tomorrow and tomorrow and tomorrow for some time to come. The Earth is resilient. This is only an issue for the future of human beings and the biosphere in which they live, perhaps less resilient than the planet itself.

5.6
CLIMATE CHANGE: AWARENESS

The sun also ariseth, and the sun goeth down, and hasteth to his place where he arose.

Ecclesiastes 1:5

MACBETH:
She should have died hereafter.
There would have been a time for such a word.
Tomorrow, and tomorrow, and tomorrow,
Creeps in this petty pace from day to day
To the last syllable of recorded time,
And all our yesterdays have lighted fools
The way to dusty death. Out, out, brief candle!
Life's but a walking shadow, a poor player
That struts and frets his hour upon the stage
And then is heard no more. It is a tale
Told by an idiot, full of sound and fury,
Signifying nothing.

William Shakespeare, *Macbeth*, Act 5, Scene 5

Is man-made climate change real? Is it a threat? If it is a threat, how big is the threat? On what time scales would an event take place?

In this section we will work through the scientific arguments of climate change to provide a baseline for the climate-change conversation. We will look for weaknesses in the argument. Then, for those people convinced of the science, we will look at climate change in the context of a resilient response to the threats.

In December 2014 the Royal Society in the UK along with the National Academy of Sciences in the US published a concise synopsis of the evidence for climate change available for download. In the opening flash page, they state the current scientific consensus on climate change.

> Climate change is one of the defining issues of our time. It is now more certain than ever, based on many lines of evidence, that humans are changing Earth's climate. The atmosphere and oceans have warmed, accompanied by sea-level rise, a strong decline in Arctic sea ice, and other climate-related changes.
>
> Greenhouse gases such as carbon dioxide (CO_2) absorb heat (infrared radiation) emitted from Earth's surface. Increases in the atmospheric concentrations of these gases cause Earth to warm by trapping more of this heat. Human activities—especially the burning of fossil fuels since the

start of the Industrial Revolution—have increased atmospheric CO_2 concentrations by about 40%, with more than half the increase occurring since 1970. Since 1900, the global average surface temperature has increased by about 0.8°C (1.4°F). This has been accompanied by warming of the ocean, a rise in sea level, a strong decline in Arctic sea ice, and many other associated climate effects. Much of this warming has occurred in the last four decades. Detailed analyses have shown that the warming during this period is mainly a result of the increased concentrations of CO_2 and other greenhouse gases. Continued emissions of these gases will cause further climate change, including substantial increases in global average surface temperature and important changes in regional climate. The magnitude and timing of these changes will depend on many factors, and slowdowns and accelerations in warming lasting a decade or more will continue to occur. However, long-term climate change over many decades will depend mainly on the total amount of CO_2 and other greenhouse gases emitted as a result of human activities.

These are quite simple declarations. Science rarely states a case so definitively. There must be caveats. In fact, the preamble to the document contains some backtracking.

The evidence is clear. However, due to the nature of science, not every single detail is ever totally settled or completely certain. Nor has every pertinent question yet been answered. Scientific evidence continues to be gathered around the world, and assumptions and findings about climate change are continually analyzed and tested. Some areas of active debate and ongoing research include the link between ocean heat content and the rate of warming, estimates of how much warming to expect in the future, and the connections between climate change and extreme weather events.

I do not know about you, but the caveats make me (RDJ) more comfortable. Science is not supposed to be dogmatic. Science can only state truths with some probability, but not definitely. A proper scientist will not state with 100 percent confidence that the sun will rise tomorrow. He or she will only state that it is very, very likely that the sun will rise tomorrow. Scientists will leave it to the author of Ecclesiastes to state that the sun will definitely rise tomorrow. Let's take a closer look at the data and the interpretations to see if there are any showstoppers that would negate the conclusions of the Royal Society and the National Academy of Sciences.

The format of the report is a list of 20 questions with answers from the scientists. Let's go through these questions one by one. First the question is stated. Then the scientist's response. Finally, we ask our own questions about the data.

5.6.1
IS THE CLIMATE WARMING?

> **Yes. Earth's average surface air temperature has increased by about 0.8°C (1.4°F) since 1900, with much of this increase taking place since the mid-1970s . . . A wide range of other observations (such as reduced Arctic sea ice extent and increased ocean heat content) and indications from the natural world (such as poleward shifts of temperature-sensitive species of fish, mammals, insects, etc.) together provide incontrovertible evidence of planetary-scale warming.**

The report presents five charts to support this claim: global average surface temperature as compared with the average temperature measured from 1961 to 1990; Arctic sea ice minimum and maximum extents; decrease in snow cover in the Northern Hemisphere; global average upper ocean heat content; and global sea-level rise. All five of these charts show strong indications for temperature rise over the last hundred years. The weakest chart may be the snow cover chart. An obvious question one might have looking at these charts is about the length of time of the measurements. Humans have been on the planet a few million years. What did the temperature look like in earlier times? One can address this question if one is able to identify that recent human activity is causal to the temperature change over the last hundred years.

5.6.2
DISCUSSION QUESTION: MEASURING ANCIENT TEMPERATURES

A Harvard Medical School study has determined that rectal thermometers are still the best way to tell a baby's temperature. Plus, it really teaches the baby who's boss.

Tina Fey

Is there some way to measure temperatures to high accuracy as long ago as a million years? Can temperatures be seen in geological evidence? In paleontology evidence? Can the remains of ancient organisms be seen moving toward the poles or away from the poles over time?

5.6.3
HOW DO SCIENTISTS KNOW THAT RECENT CLIMATE CHANGE IS CAUSED BY HUMAN ACTIVITIES?

Scientists know that recent climate change is largely caused by human activities from an understanding of basic physics, comparing observations with models, and fingerprinting the detailed patterns of climate change caused by different human and natural influences.

Okay, this is a bit vague. Let's dig deeper. It turns out that CO_2 is a key culprit in global warming. We (I, RDJ, include myself among physicists) know this because of the way that CO_2 and sunlight interact. CO_2 behaves like glass; it is transparent to visible light, but opaque to longer-wavelength infrared light. A layer of CO_2 therefore behaves like a greenhouse, hence the name "greenhouse gas." The visible light passes through the CO_2 layer on its way to the Earth's surface. At the surface, the light interacts with water and solids. Light is re-emitted by the surface in the form of infrared light, which is trapped in the atmosphere by the CO_2 layer. The infrared light heats the surface of the Earth as the light is further absorbed. Physics models can quantify the amount of heating to expect based on the material and light properties.

The report points out that measurements of CO_2 trapped in ice indicate that CO_2 levels have increased 40% between 1800 and 2012. Isotopes are forms of atoms that have the same number of protons in the nucleus but different numbers of neutrons. Different isotopes of CO_2 are produced in different industrial processes. The amounts of the various isotopes of CO_2 are consistent with the timing of industrial processes from 1900 on. We will go into more detail on this topic in the answer to the next question.

CO_2 is not the only greenhouse gas that has increased in this period due to industrial behavior. Methane and Nitrous Oxide have also increased and are quantitatively correlated with human activities.

Temperature and CO_2 levels are not the only independent variables that can be used to validate and provide confidence in the physics models. The report goes on to say, "The observed patterns of surface warming, temperature changes through the atmosphere, increases in ocean heat content, increases in atmospheric moisture, sea-level rise, and increased melting of land and sea ice also match the patterns scientists expect to see due to rising levels of CO_2 and other human-induced changes."

But do human activities outweigh natural effects that might increase green-house levels? The report indicates the answer is no.

Natural causes include variations in the Sun's output and in Earth's orbit around the Sun, volcanic eruptions, and internal fluctuations in the climate system (such as El Nino and La Nina). Calculations using climate models . . . have been used to simulate what would have happened to global temperatures if only natural factors were influencing the climate system. These simulations yield little warming, or even a slight cooling, over the 20th century. Only when models include human influences on the composition of the atmosphere are the resulting temperature changes consistent with observed changes.

This seems to be a striking result.

5.6.4
DISCUSSION QUESTION: CO_2

We can't conclusively say whether man-made carbon dioxide emissions are contributing to climate change.

Tony Abbott, 28th Prime Minister of Australia

I cannot imagine any objective finding that CO_2 is a pollutant. If that is true, God is a polluter.

Joe Barton, R-Texas

Carbon dioxide is portrayed as harmful. But there isn't even one study that can be produced that shows that carbon dioxide is a harmful gas.

Michele Bachmann, R-Minnesota

CO_2 in my opinion is not a pollutant. God gave us CO_2 to grow plants, for us to exhale, everything else.

John Wood, R-Florida

Ultimately, society must recognize that science is not a democracy in which the side with the most votes or the loudest voices gets to decide what is right.

Gregory Poland and Robert Jacobson, *New England Journal of Medicine*, January 2011

1. Are there weaknesses in the CO_2 and greenhouse gas argument? In the argument that correlates increased amounts of greenhouse gas with human activity?
2. Why is there such disagreement between scientists and many politicians on the role of CO_2 in climate change?

5.6.5

CO_2 IS ALREADY IN THE ATMOSPHERE NATURALLY, SO WHY ARE EMISSIONS FROM HUMAN ACTIVITY SIGNIFICANT?

Human activities have significantly disturbed the natural carbon cycle by extracting long-buried fossil fuels and burning them for energy, thus releasing CO_2 to the atmosphere.

Okay, let's dig deeper into the report. CO_2 is constantly moving about the biosphere. The atmosphere is constantly exchanging CO_2 with plants and animals through photosynthesis, respiration, and decomposition. The atmosphere and the ocean exchange CO_2 through natural physical processes like those that cause a glass of soda to release its CO_2 into the atmosphere and go flat. This process can also go the other direction if there is an excess of CO_2 in the atmosphere. There is a tiny amount of CO_2 released into the atmosphere in volcanic emissions. There is an equivalent tiny amount that is absorbed in the weathering of rocks. And finally, there is release of CO_2 into the atmosphere as a consequence of burning fossil fuels, which is a human activity.

How do we distinguish CO_2 generated from the hydrocarbons in fossil fuel from the normal CO_2 passing through the atmosphere, biomass, and the oceans? The answer is that carbon bound in fossil fuels has a different distribution of isotopes than carbon in the atmosphere. The atmosphere is bombarded with cosmic rays. These rays strike a normal nitrogen ^{14}N, which has seven protons and seven neutrons for an atomic number of 14. A certain number of isotopes of carbon, ^{14}C, that have extra neutrons are created by this bombardment. These isotopes decay back to ^{14}N. This happens in several thousand years for ^{14}C. The result is that carbon atoms trapped underground in fossil fuels do not see cosmic rays because they are shielded by earth. Therefore, underground carbon isotopes decay back to ^{14}N, but the isotopes are not created from ^{14}N. Carbon in fossil fuels that has been underground much longer than 10,000 years has no isotopes of ^{14}C, just ^{12}C. A collection of CO_2 molecules that are missing ^{14}C have a portion of their molecules of CO_2 that was released from fossil fuels. This little piece of physics allows scientists to measure how much CO_2 in the atmosphere has come from burning fossil fuels. This allows scientists to say that most of the 40 percent increase in atmospheric CO_2 since 1800 comes from the burning of fossil fuels. Comparison with CO_2 levels found in ice cores indicate this is the highest CO_2 level in 800,000 years.

5.6.6
DISCUSSION QUESTION: HYDROCARBONS AND MUCH MORE

> I would point out that if you're a believer in the Bible, one would have to say the Great Flood is an example of climate change and that certainly wasn't because mankind had over-developed hydrocarbon energy.

Joe Barton, R-Texas

> It can scarcely be denied that the supreme goal of all theory is to make the irreducible basic elements as simple and as few as possible without having to surrender the adequate representation of a single datum of experience.

Albert Einstein

- How would you respond to Mr. Barton's comment? Would the conversation include a discussion of ^{14}C? Is there a complexity mismatch between Mr. Barton's picture of climate change and the scientific picture that has been presented so far? Should the comparison use the same type of language? Compare Mr. Barton's mythical picture with the mythical language we developed in Chapter 1 for the creation of hurricanes. We claimed that the mythical language of Chapter 1 was scientifically accurate. Hurricanes are just one aspect of climate change, but a comparison can still be made between the complexity of Mr. Barton's internal model and the scientifically accurate mythical model of Chapter 1.

- How would you relate this mismatch to the inequality gap discussed in Chapter 3? It was argued that the inequality gap was also a complexity gap. People at the low end of the spectrum had fewer options than people at the higher end. Therefore, people at the lower end were forced into less complex lives, while people at the higher end were only limited in complexity by their multitude of options. Does the inequality gap, then, affect the complexity of the internal models that people use to understand the world about them? Does the inequality gap amplify the differences in the way people understand the world?
- A requirement for a scientific theory is that it obey *Occam's Razor*; that it is the simplest theory that explains the observations. This puts a lower limit on the complexity of a scientific description. Is the scientific theory for temperature and CO_2 emission presented so far the simplest theory that explains the observations?

5.6.7
WHAT ROLE HAS THE SUN PLAYED IN CLIMATE CHANGE IN RECENT DECADES?

The Sun provides the primary source of energy driving Earth's climate system, but its variations have played very little role in the climate changes observed in recent decades. Direct satellite measurements since the late 1970s show no net increase in the Sun's output, while at the same time global surface temperatures have increased.

There are variations of about 0.1 percent in the Sun's energy output that are correlated with the 11-year *sunspot* cycle. These variations can have an effect on the stratosphere, the atmospheric level above the weather patterns, during the 11-year cycle. This may have a small effect on surface temperature also during this 11-year cycle. However, the Sun's output has not increased on longer timescales, while the surface temperature has. Heating does not seem to be due to increased solar output.

5.6.8
EXERCISES: SUNSPOT CYCLE

> *It was one of those March days when the sun shines hot and the wind blows cold: when it is summer in the light, and winter in the shade.*

Charles Dickens

1. What causes the sunspot cycle?
2. How do sunspots interact with Earth?
3. What is the role of the Earth's magnetic field in interaction with sunspots?
4. What are *Northern Lights*?
5. Does the Earth's magnetic field move? Change polarity? How often?
6. Are magnetic field changes of the Earth likely to affect the arguments about the effect of solar output on timescales of a hundred years?

What do changes in vertical atmospheric temperature—from the surface, up to the stratosphere—tell us about the causes of recent climate change?

The observed warming in the lower atmosphere and cooling in the upper atmosphere provide us with key insights into the underlying causes of climate change and reveal that natural factors alone cannot explain the observed changes.

Physics simulations indicate that, in the case of man-made global warming, the lower atmosphere will increase in temperature while the upper atmosphere will decrease. If the warming were due to increases in the Sun's output, the simulations indicate that warming would occur throughout the atmosphere including the upper layers. This result is intuitive. The CO_2 layer lies in the lower stratosphere just above the troposphere. The CO_2 layer traps heat in the troposphere, thus heating the troposphere at the expense of the stratosphere. Without the greenhouse layer, the heating will be more uniform, and the stratosphere will be warmer.

5.6.9
CLIMATE IS ALWAYS CHANGING. WHY IS CLIMATE CHANGE OF CONCERN NOW?

All major climate changes, including natural ones, are disruptive. Past climate changes led to extinction of many species, population migrations, and pronounced changes in the land surface and ocean circulation. The speed of the current climate change is faster than most of the past events, making it more difficult for human societies and the natural world to adapt.

It is instructive to look at the effects of recent ice ages. Ice ages are caused by slow changes in the Earth's orbit that redistribute the Sun's output on the surface of the Earth. The surface temperature increases since the last ice age is about 4–5°C. This has happened over a period of 7,000 years starting 18,000 years ago. By contrast, CO_2 has increased by 40 percent in the last 200 years leading to a temperature increase of 0.8°C. This is 10 times faster than the warming at the end of the last ice age. Physics modeling indicates that this rate will be sustained as long as CO_2 levels remain increasingly high.

5.6.10
EXERCISE: ICE AGES

Some say the world will end in fire, some say in ice.

Robert Frost

Dig deeper into the science of ice ages. What is the role of greenhouse gases during an ice age? How long do ice ages last? Why?

5.6.11
DISCUSSION QUESTION: TIME SCALES

I love to compare different time frames. Poetry can evoke the time of the subject. By a very careful choice of words you can evoke an era, completely throw the poem into a different timescale.

Robert Morgan

It is dangerous to compare two trends that are on different time scales. Fluctuations localized in time can have a much higher rate of increase than a long-term trend. Here we are comparing a trend over 7,000 years with a trend over 200 years. If that were the only information we had, it would not be convincing. How does the physics modeling increase our confidence that the difference in rates between warming after an ice age and warming due to greenhouse gases is significant?

5.6.12
IS THE CURRENT LEVEL OF CO_2 CONCENTRATION UNPRECEDENTED IN EARTH'S HISTORY?

The present level of atmospheric CO_2 concentration is almost certainly unprecedented in the past million years, during which time modern humans evolved and societies developed. The atmospheric CO_2 concentration was however higher in Earth's more distant past (many millions of years ago), at which time palaeoclimatic and geological data indicate that temperatures and sea levels were also higher than they are today.

The report displays a dramatic chart of the CO_2 concentration over the last 800,000 years. These measurements come from ice cores. The recent dramatic rise in CO_2 over the last 200 years is clearly an outlier.

5.6.13
IS THERE A POINT AT WHICH ADDING MORE CO_2 WILL NOT CAUSE FURTHER WARMING?

No. Adding more CO_2 to the atmosphere will cause surface temperatures to continue to increase. As the atmospheric concentrations of CO_2 increase, the addition of extra CO_2 becomes progressively less effective at trapping Earth's energy, but surface temperature will still rise.

This has been confirmed by laboratory measurements as well as satellite and surface observations of the emission and absorption of infrared energy by the atmosphere.

5.6.14
EXERCISE: ABSORPTION BANDS

If you can't stand the heat, get out of the kitchen.

Harry S. Truman

What are absorption bands? What are the absorption bands of CO_2? CO_2 has a strong absorption band. What is the role of the weaker absorption bands in atmospheric heating at higher CO_2 concentrations?

5.6.15
DOES THE RATE OF WARMING VARY FROM ONE DECADE TO ANOTHER?

Yes. The observed warming rate has varied from year to year, decade to decade, and place to place, as is expected from our understanding of the climate system. These shorter-term variations are mostly due to natural causes,

and do not contradict our fundamental understanding that the long-term warming trend is primarily due to human-induced changes in the atmospheric levels of CO_2 and other greenhouse gases.

The warming trend is modulated by various natural factors such as volcanic eruptions and oceanic circulation and mixing that occur on several natural time scales.

Even with these modulations, the long-term increasing temperature trend is evident.

5.6.16
EXERCISE: MODULATIONS

Look more closely at the natural and human-induced modulations in temperature and CO_2 concentrations. Do you feel the answer to this question is justified?

5.6.17
DISCUSSION QUESTION: FROGS IN A POT

One of the big questions in the climate change debate: are humans any smarter than frogs in a pot? If you put a frog in a pot and slowly turn up the heat, it won't jump out. Instead, it will enjoy the nice warm bath until it is cooked to death. We humans seem to be doing pretty much the same thing.

Jeff Goodell

Discuss Mr. Goodell's observation about frogs in a pot. How does this relate to trend following? How does this relate to the survival of businesses such as Kodak?

5.6.18
DOES THE RECENT SLOWDOWN OF WARMING MEAN THAT CLIMATE CHANGE IS NO LONGER HAPPENING?

> No. Since the very warm year 1998 that followed the strong 1997–98 El Nino, the increase in average surface temperature has slowed relative to the previous decade of rapid temperature increases. Despite the slower rate of warming the 2000s were warmer than the 1990s. A short-term slowdown in the warming of Earth's surface does not invalidate our understanding of long-term changes in global temperature arising from human-induced changes in greenhouse gases.

The report gives several reasons why the heating rate has been slower over the last decade and is simply a fluctuation. I (RDJ) was left with an unsatisfied feeling upon reading this section of the report. There are many interacting pieces to this puzzle. I think this question deserves a deeper dive with an exercise.

5.6.19
EXERCISE: WARMING OVER THE LAST DECADE

> *It is the greatest scam in history. I am amazed, appalled and highly offended by it. Global Warming; it is a scam. Some dastardly scientists with environmental and political motives manipulated long term scientific data to create an illusion of rapid global warming.*
>
> John Coleman, Founder of the Weather Channel
>
> What are the causes of the slowdown in global warming over the decade 2005–2015?

5.6.20

IF THE WORLD IS WARMING, WHY ARE SOME WINTERS AND SUMMERS STILL VERY COLD?

Global warming is a long-term trend, but that does not mean that every year will be warmer than the previous one. Day to day and year to year changes in weather patterns will continue to produce some unusually cold days and nights, and winters and summers, even as the climate warms.

We can answer this question from what we have learned so far in this book. As we saw in the hurricane example, differential heating can cause exotic atmospheric phenomena to occur. These phenomena tend to equalize the temperature across the planet. These exotic phenomena cause differential behavior in wind, rainfall, temperature, and heating. In other words, the complexity mismatch of differential heating causes all types of weather. The intensity of the weather increases as the heating increases. This is consistent with the observation that the average temperature of the planet is increasing.

5.6.21

DISCUSSION QUESTION: SECOND LAW OF THERMODYNAMICS

There has been evidence throughout history of cycles when the earth gets warmer and cycles when the earth gets colder. We should always be wise stewards of the earth and all of our natural resources. But as a policymaker, I won't be guided by the global warming propaganda machine. Al Gore—we need you to return your Nobel Peace Prize!

Raul Labrador, R-Idaho

The *Second Law of Thermodynamics* states that **a closed system** will always become more and more random until it reaches a state of maximum disorder—of maximum *entropy*. The end state of every closed system is a random uniform soup or heat bath of constant temperature. This is a dismal prediction. It predicts that the universe will end its life as a cosmic featureless broth. With this kind of forecasting it is no wonder that more pleasant predictions based on personal religions are more popular than predictions based on physics.

But wait. The Second Law does not jive with our personal experience. We live on a planet in which order is spontaneously created every day. Hurricanes, for instance, are orderly flows of wind and heat that are created out of the random heat baths of ocean and atmosphere. We get order from nothing. We could go into the orderly creation of life, but we won't. That would require more pages than are available in this book.

How do we reconcile what we see on Earth with a very established law of physics, the Second Law? The answer is that the Earth is not a closed system. Objects and energy are flooding the planet from outer space every day. The most important of these is light originating from the Sun. The universe is a closed system, but any subcomponent of the universe, like our planet, is an open system. Open systems can create spontaneous order driven by the external energy that is flowing into the systems. This is what we saw in detail when we examined hurricanes. The energy flow from the Sun created a differential heating of the surface of the Earth, which led to the creation of a hurricane. The Sun's heating created local order on the Earth. The Sun itself, however, lost energy and is becoming more disorderly. Its entropy is increasing. In fact, the sum of the Earth's entropy and the Sun's entropy is increasing consistent with the Second Law.

Order creation in open systems is the source of fluctuations in measurable quantities like temperature and CO_2 concentration. As heating increases, we would expect that the fluctuations will also increase.

5.6.22
EXERCISE: AUTOCATALYTIC REACTIONS

Biology is far from understanding exactly how a single cell develops into a baby, but research suggests that human development can ultimately be explained in terms of biochemistry and molecular biology. Most scientists would make a similar statement about evolution.

Kenneth R. Miller

Read the Wikipedia article on *Autocatalytic Reactions*. Describe the order created by these reactions. What is the complexity mismatch that drives the creation of this order?

5.6.23
WHY IS ARCTIC SEA ICE DECREASING WHILE ANTARCTIC SEA ICE IS NOT?

Sea ice extent is affected by winds and ocean currents as well as temperature. Sea ice in the partly-enclosed Arctic Ocean seems to be responding directly to warming, while changes in winds and in the ocean seem to be dominating the patterns of climate and sea ice change in the ocean around Antarctica.

Sea ice is interestingly sensitive to temperature. The white ice reflects most sunlight. This prevents the light from melting snow efficiently by direct radiation. But the dark ocean absorbs sunlight very well and is more easily heated. There is an instability from this effect. Sunlight heats the ocean, which melts the ice floating in the ocean. The melting ice exposes more open water that is heated more effectively, and even more ice is melted, leading to a vicious cycle of melting. There seems to be unequivocal evidence for heating in the Arctic. The loss of ice has been dramatic.

This is not true in the Antarctic. Most of the Antarctic is land mass covered by snow and ice. The report claims that the melting in the Antarctic is dominated by winds and currents, rather than by heating by sunlight. I think this demands a deeper dive in an exercise.

5.6.24
EXERCISE: ICE MELT IN THE ANTARCTIC

The thing that is most beautiful about Antarctica for me is the light. It's like no other light on Earth, because the air is so free of impurities. You get drugged by it, like when you listen to one of your favorite songs. The light there is a mood-enhancing substance.

Jon Krakauer

Why is the ice melt in the Antarctic different than the ice melt in the Arctic? What is the Ozone Layer? What effect might it have on Antarctic ice melt?

5.6.25
HOW DOES CLIMATE CHANGE AFFECT THE STRENGTH AND FREQUENCY OF FLOODS, DROUGHTS, HURRICANES, AND TORNADOES?

Earths lower atmosphere is becoming warmer and moister as a result of human-emitted greenhouse gases. This gives the potential for more energy for storms and certain severe weather events. Consistent with theoretical expectations, heavy rainfall and snowfall events (which increase the risk of flooding) and heatwaves are generally becoming more frequent. Trends in extreme rainfall vary from region to region: the most pronounced changes are evident in North America and parts of Europe, especially in winter.

We went into some detail on this question with our hurricane example of Chapter 1.

5.6.26
HOW FAST IS SEA LEVEL RISING?

Long-term measurements of tide gauges and recent satellite data show that global sea level is rising, with best estimates of the global-average rise over the last two decades centered on 3.2 mm per year (0.12 inches per year). The overall observed rise since 1901 is about 20 cm (8 inches).

This is a simple and straightforward measurement.

5.6.27
EXERCISE: FLORIDA

The impact on the level of the sea . . . is equivalent to the difference in this piece of paper. For me, that is not good science. That is not a good reason to implement this provision on the people of Florida.
John Wood, R-Florida

What is the average and maximum altitude of Florida? At the measured rates of rise in sea-level, when will Florida be under water? When will Manhattan?

5.6.28
WHAT IS OCEAN ACIDIFICATION AND WHY DOES IT MATTER?

Direct observations of ocean chemistry have shown that the chemical balance of seawater has shifted to a more acidic state (lower pH). Some marine organisms (such as corals and some shellfish) have shells composed of calcium carbonate which dissolves more readily in acid. As the acidity of sea water increases, it becomes more difficult for them to form or maintain their shells.

CO_2 that is absorbed into the sea is slightly acidic. This will change the ecological balance in the seas starting with shellfish and coral that have slightly basic shells. The report displays a chart of ocean pH that shows an unmistakable increase in acidity. This is a natural consequence of increased CO_2 levels.

5.6.29

HOW CONFIDENT ARE SCIENTISTS THAT EARTH WILL WARM FURTHER OVER THE COMING CENTURY?

Very confident. If emissions continue on their present trajectory, without either technological or regulatory abatement, then warming of 2.6 to 4.8 °C (4.7 to 8.6 °F) in addition to that which has already occurred would be expected by the end of the twenty-first century.

I paraphrase from the report, "The size of the warming that will be experienced depends largely on the cumulative amount of greenhouse gases. If the total cumulative emissions since 1870 are kept below about 1 trillion tons of carbon, then there is a two-thirds chance of keeping the rise in global average temperature since the pre-industrial period below 2 °C (3.6 °F). However, over half this amount has already been emitted."

5.6.30

DISCUSSION QUESTION: THERE IS TIME, BUT SO WHAT?

It is change, continuing change, inevitable change, that is the dominant factor in society today. No sensible decision can be made any longer without taking into account not only the world as it is, but the world as it will be.

Isaac Asimov

We have now worked through 16 of the 20 questions in the Royal Society/NAS report. As a scientist, I (RDJ) would have to say that the case for global warming seems quite strong. That is not to say that all the questions have been answered completely, but the evidence is dramatic. We will work through the last few questions from the report, but, at this point, I would say the case has been reasonably made. There will continue to be unbelievers, but I challenge them to present their arguments with at least the same rigor that we have seen here. It is time to start thinking about how to respond to a coming X-event. We will address this in the next section, but let's take a moment and stick our heads up and take a quick glance at the landscape.

The managers at Kodak rode their company all the way into the tarmac, even though the danger to their market was clear and obvious. Is that what will happen in the case of climate change? Let's leave that question in the back of our heads as we work our way through the remaining questions in the Royal Society/NAS report.

5.6.31
ARE CLIMATE CHANGES OF A FEW DEGREES A CAUSE FOR CONCERN?

Yes. Even though an increase of a few degrees in global average temperature does not sound like much, global average temperature during the last ice age was only about 4 to 5 °C (7 to 9 °F) colder than now. Global warming of just a few degrees will be associated with widespread changes in regional and local temperature and precipitation as well as with increases in some types of extreme weather events. These and other changes (such as sea level rise and storm surge) will have serious impacts on human societies and the natural world.

5.6.32
WHAT ARE SCIENTISTS DOING TO ADDRESS KEY UNCERTAINTIES IN OUR UNDERSTANDING OF THE CLIMATE SYSTEM?

Science is a continual process of observation, understanding, modelling, testing, and prediction. The prediction of a long-term trend in global warming from increasing greenhouse gases is robust and has been confirmed by a growing body of evidence. Nevertheless, understanding (for example, of cloud dynamics, and of climate variations on centennial and decadal timescales and on regional-to-local spatial scales) remains incomplete. All of these are areas of active research.

5.6.33

ARE DISASTER SCENARIOS ABOUT TIPPING POINTS LIKE "TURNING OFF THE GULF STREAM" AND RELEASE OF METHANE FROM THE ARCTIC A CAUSE FOR CONCERN?

Results from the best available climate models do not predict abrupt changes in such systems (often referred to as tipping points) in the near future. However, as warming increases, the possibilities of major abrupt change cannot be ruled out.

5.6.34

IF EMISSIONS OF GREENHOUSE GASES WERE STOPPED, WOULD THE CLIMATE RETURN TO THE CONDITIONS OF 200 YEARS AGO?

No. Even if emissions of greenhouse gases were to suddenly stop, Earth's surface temperature would not cool and return to the level in the preindustrial era for thousands of years.

The atmospheric/oceanic system is resilient, but only stable on long time scales.

5.7
WHAT ABOUT OTHER X-EVENTS SIMULTANEOUS TO CLIMATE CHANGE?

We have completed the walk-through of the Royal Society/NAS report. It looks like the case is strong for man-made global climate change. One assumption of the report is that this is the only major X-event that is occurring. What if another X-event occurs simultaneously that affects the outcome of the climate-change event? What about Peak Oil? What is Peak Oil? Would a drop in hydrocarbon emissions due to reduced oil supplies have a significant effect on climate change? Is this likely?

Will climate change interact with the demographic-transition X-event discussed in Chapter 2?

5.8
CLIMATE CHANGE: ASSIMILATION

Confront them with annihilation, and they will then survive; plunge them into a deadly situation, and they will then live. When people fall into danger, they are then able to strive for victory.

Sun Tzu

Can a climate-change X-event be averted? The Royal Society/NAS report indicates that there is time to act, but that does not answer the question. Is the human population likely to act? The answer to that question is probably "no." We point again to the Kodak example. The managers could see the future, but did not act effectively to avert the X-event. This point can be made more personal. Would you make the decision to forgo your education or the education of your children in order to avert a climate-change X-event in 75 years? I think many or most people would choose education now rather than safety three generations from now. The goal seems to be to survive a climate-change X-event rather than count on averting it.

5.8.1

DISCUSSION QUESTION: HOW BAD IS IT LIKELY TO BE?

Success breeds complacency. Complacency breeds failure. Only the paranoid survive.

Andy Grove

For what severity should we prepare? The report indicates that major tipping points in which the climate undergoes a phase change seems unlikely. We should not expect to see events such as turning off the Gulf Stream or significant release of methane from the Arctic. Therefore, we do not expect climate change to trigger events as large as the asteroids of Chapter 1.

We might expect events at the agricultural, economic, social, and political level. There will be significant agricultural disruption. The geographical distribution of fresh water will change. Crops that grow in one geography may no longer grow there because of changes in temperature and water distribution. As an example, citrus that only grew in southern Florida 50 years ago is now growing in northern Florida as well. Weather will become more volatile. The number and severity of hurricanes will increase. Pine trees cannot withstand hurricane force winds. The increase in hurricanes will affect the pulp and paper industry in the southern US. Late winter storms will affect crop risk. Food supplies will be affected.

Much of the population lives on the coast. The locations of many current cities will be underwater when ice melts. The ecology of the oceans will change as the seas become more acidic. Gradients in ocean salinity due to ice melt will change the behavior of the currents.

The changing geographical gradients in resources will create political pressures. Global economies will shift. We may see increased levels of warfare.

What else should we expect?

5.8.2
DISCUSSION QUESTION: HOW DO WE IDENTIFY OUR OPTIONS FOR SURVIVAL?

No institution can possibly survive if it needs geniuses or supermen to manage it. It must be organized in such a way as to be able to get along under a leadership composed of average human beings.

Peter Drucker

What resources do we have at our disposal that can be used to promote survival?

Technology and Medicine: We should not expect big science to bail us out. This did not work with the asteroids of Chapter 1. Perhaps science on a smaller scale can help. Would it be a good idea to develop genetically modified organisms (GMOs) to allow crops to survive in the new environment? Would this be a bad idea? Why? Will the structure of healthcare need to be modified for the new environment? Perhaps this might be necessary if the demographics of income change because of altered economics.

Economics and Infrastructure: The economics of agriculture will certainly change. The cities will need to move to higher ground.

Government and Military: What can be done with government subsidies, regulations, and tax breaks? How should the military adjust to a shifting warfare landscape?

How can these resources be applied to our survival?

5.8.3
DISCUSSION QUESTION: HOW DO WE EVALUATE OUR OPTIONS FOR SURVIVAL?

For humans, the Arctic is a harshly inhospitable place, but the conditions there are precisely what polar bears require to survive—and thrive. "Harsh" to us is "home" for them. Take away the ice and snow, increase the temperature by even a little, and the realm that makes their lives possible literally melts away.

Sylvia Earle

How do we evaluate the effect of our actions? We need to be able to understand how our actions interact with each other to yield certain outcomes. Climate scientists used physics and chemistry models to unravel the connections among various effects. We need something like those models for the social, political, and economic domain. We need "what if" tools, perhaps like Insurance World, to help us organize our plans.

5.8.4

DISCUSSION QUESTION: HOW DO WE IMPLEMENT OUR OPTIONS FOR SURVIVAL?

We shall require a substantially new manner of thinking if mankind is to survive.

Albert Einstein

The assumption is that, at this point, we are experiencing the X-event and that there is consensus in the population that something must be done to survive. The deniers have been convinced and are experiencing cognitive dissonance. We have developed the "what if" tools so that we are aware of the options and have a sense for potential outcomes. Now we must implement the plan for survival. Maybe we can take the lesson of the Oregon Health Plan. The process should be public, and everyone should have an opportunity to voice his or her opinion.

Is this picture realistic?

5.9
CLIMATE CHANGE: AGILITY

I don't think the human race will survive the next thousand years, unless we spread into space.

Stephen Hawking

How do we identify opportunities and the resources necessary to address the opportunities? How do we find the niches that have opened up during the X-event?

5.9.1
DISCUSSION QUESTION: WHAT ARE THE OPPORTUNITIES THAT MIGHT ARISE?

Irony is a clear consciousness of an eternal agility, of the infinitely abundant chaos.

Karl Wilhelm Friedrich Schlegel

Perhaps we can think like entrepreneurs and inventors. What will people need in a post climate-change world? Here are a few items in no particular order.

- Clean water
- Storm protection
- Crop insurance
- Weather derivatives
- Storm forecasting
- New construction on higher ground
- Storm water management
- Emergency management
- Storm insurance
- Reliable food supplies
- Greater protection from stressed countries and populations

What else?

5.9.2
DISCUSSION QUESTION: WHAT RESOURCES DO WE HAVE TO TAKE ADVANTAGE OF THE OPPORTUNITIES?

If opportunity doesn't knock, build a door.

Milton Berle

Many of the opportunities, such as storm forecasting and protection, fall under the auspices of the government. Some like crop insurance and new construction are well handled by the free market. Some opportunities may benefit from technology development. A new weather-derivative pricing model may be necessary to build a secondary market for weather derivatives and thus proving market liquidity. Technological advances may be necessary to develop a reliable food supply. What other resources do we have?

5.10
CLIMATE CHANGE: ADAPTIVITY

You have to be fast on your feet and adaptive or else a strategy is useless.

Charles de Gaulle

We know that change does not occur rapidly when a system is trend following. An X-event is required for rapid change. If our post-climate-change world is adaptive, then perhaps we should see a number of small X-events as the population adjusts to the new reality. These small X-events would be similar to aftershocks following an earthquake. If that is the case, then we should see adaptive X-events in government, business, and technology in the new world. These would be very natural.

5.11
DISCUSSION QUESTION: VENICE, ITALY

> *Venice is like eating an entire box of chocolate liqueurs in one go.*

Truman Capote

Venice is certainly one of the sublime achievements of the human race. It is a city built in a shallow lagoon on millions of wooden pilings that were driven four meters through the mud until they rested on a layer of compressed clay. Hundreds of years of contact with sea water petrified the pilings. Venetians built beautiful architecture on this foundation that borrowed liberally from Islamic, Byzantine, and Gothic influences. The buildings are filled with the music and art of Vivaldi, Tintoretto, and Titian. The Venetian Marco Polo opened Eastern Asia to trade with Europeans. The Venetians created a great empire and, in a less sublime moment, sacked Constantinople. Six hundred years ago, the Venetians diverted two rivers, thus deepening the lagoon. This provided extra protection from potential invaders.

Today, Venice is home to about 50,000 inhabitants, down from 200,000 a few hundred years ago. Millions of visitors experience Venice every year.

In the early twentieth century local industry on the mainland drilled wells to support production. This lowered the water table and the city began to sink. Drilling was banned in the 1960s and it appears that the sinking has stabilized. Still, the city is plagued by flooding about a dozen times a year in what is known as the *Acqua Alta*. The MOSE Project, an array of 78 flood gates designed to address the problem of *Acqua Alta*, will be completed in 2016. The project is controversial. Many people feel the project threatens the lagoon and changes the environment of the city detracting from just what makes the city a treasure.

Venice will be among the very first cities affected by rising seas due to global climate change. It will be one of the first tests of resilience to climate change.

- Discuss the Four As as they relate to climate change.
- What is an acceptable final state after a climate-induced X-event? What is important to save? Is it acceptable to have a city with only visitors and no inhabitants? Is that even a city? If so, how would the real Venice differ from the imitation Venice that is in Las Vegas? Is it acceptable to change the lagoon significantly to protect the city?
- There are many competing stakeholders: businesses built on tourism, the inhabitants, the visitors, fishermen, artists, art lovers. How should these interests be balanced?
- The opera house in Venice is named *La Fenice*, the Phoenix, because it burned three times and arose from the ashes each time. Is *La Fenice* and example of stability or resilience? Discuss.

5.12
DISCUSSION QUESTION: PUNCTUATED EQUILIBRIUM

Some people would claim that things like love, joy, and beauty belong to a different category from science and can't be described in scientific terms, but I think they can now be explained by the theory of evolution.

Stephen Hawking

One conceptual model within the domain of evolution is that of punctuated equilibrium postulated by Niles Eldredge and Stephen Jay Gould. The idea is that ecosystems undergo long periods of relative stability punctuated by occasional dramatic events that result in rapid change. The associated notion is that most evolution of species occurs in sudden bursts following a disruptive event. A typical example would be the one discussed at the beginning of this book: the asteroid impact that killed off the dinosaurs, which created the opportunity for mammals to evolve and dominate.

While the validity of punctuated equilibrium as a description of evolution is debated among biologists, it is often employed as an analogy in other areas such as social systems. One could argue that many of the examples discussed in this book fit the notion of punctuated equilibrium where the X-event provides the punctuation. In some cases, the X-event causes an organization to go extinct. In other cases, the X-event provides an organization the opportunity to adapt and thrive, and in other words, exhibit resilience.

- Do social systems (organizations, economies, nations) exhibit punctuated equilibrium? What is the evidence for and against?
- If punctuated equilibrium is an accurate description of social systems, should organizations attempt to change continuously or simply be prepared to change when an X-event occurs? Is this an argument in favor of being resilient rather than dynamic?
- What does punctuated equilibrium suggest about trend following among organizations?
- What was it about mammals that allowed them to survive the asteroid impact while the dinosaurs did not? Did these reasons have anything to do with a complexity gap? Are there any implications for organizations? What if the asteroid impact had not happened? Would dinosaurs still dominate? Does this suggest that there is no one right strategy and luck is always a major factor?
- If punctuated equilibrium is not an accurate description of social systems, then should organizations follow a different strategy? If so, what?

5.13
DISCUSSION QUESTION: HUMAN PROGRESS

If there is no struggle, there is no progress.

Frederick Douglass

One of the major themes of this book is that X-events are necessary for progress. In short, without major disruptive events, there would be no motivation to develop complex organisms, organizations, or societies. In a sense, complexity is necessary to deal with uncertainty. If there were little uncertainty, it would be inefficient to evolve complex biological and organizational structures. Consequently, if it were not for an uncertain world with occasional X-events, we would not exist, and no human progress would be made.

- Do you think that this line of reasoning is valid? If not, what would be a way that we could disprove it?
- In this chapter, we discussed that the typical philosophy of the government in the United States is that of risk elimination. While it is not possible to eliminate all risk, what are the implications for human progress if we could substantially reduce most risks?
- If risk is necessary for human progress, then is an approach that focuses on risk elimination counterproductive? I.e., does the attempt to eliminate some risks increase the exposure to other risks?
- There is a notion common in complexity science that life exists at the edge of chaos. Too little uncertainty and complex structures would not evolve. Too much uncertainty and complex structures would be destroyed. What does this suggest about risk management strategies? Should the objective of governments and corporations be to reduce the impact of X-events to manageable levels as opposed to eliminate them?
- Given the answers to the above, what can we say about resilient organizations?

5.14
DISCUSSION QUESTION: PATH DEPENDENCE

We understand tornadoes scientifically, but it still feels supernatural. The randomness makes it feel supernatural.

Michael Koryta

As has been discussed in this book, X-events result when a system enters a critical state such that an incidental trigger event can precipitate dramatic consequences. As a consequence, such scenarios exhibit path dependence. In other words, small changes in the sequence of events leading to the X-event can result in radically different outcomes.

- How does path-dependence affect the ability to predict specific scenarios?
- Would forecasting specific scenarios and preparing accordingly result in a resilient or fragile organization?
- Do you think it is possible to identify strategies that are effective against collections of scenarios?
- What are the implications of path dependence when deploying resources in anticipation of an impending X-event?

5.15
DISCUSSION QUESTION: SIMULATION

Do I believe, for example, that by using magic I could fly? No. How would you get around gravity? Impossible. Do I believe that I might be able to project my consciousness into a very, very vivid simulation of flying? Yeah. Yes, I've done that. Yes, that works.

Alan Moore

This chapter discussed the notion of exploring X-events via simulation. One of the challenges to simulating and predicting social phenomena is that the very complexity enables their survival. Just consider the difficulty of forecasting the economy! There are simply more relevant factors than can ever be captured in a simulation.

As a result simulations of social systems are often used to generate insights that can inform strategy as opposed to making specific predictions. The Insurance World simulation discussed in this chapter is one such example.

- How might one use simulation to explore possible strategies and evaluate organizational resilience?
- If resilience is enabled by fundamentally changing structure to accommodate new circumstances, then this implies that one would need to know how the model structure would change in response to an X-event in order to simulate adaptation and resilience.

Given the path dependence of X-events, how would one know exactly what the changes would be and under what circumstances they would occur? What are the implications for simulating adaptation and resilience to support strategic decision making?

- As noted in the discussion of the Insurance World simulation, the best strategy often depends on what everyone else is doing. How can agent based simulation be used to understand collections of actors employing different strategies? What types of insights might one be able to draw?

- The approach to simulation employed to model social systems is often very different than that used in physics and engineering. In particular, a well validated physics-based simulation can make very precise predictions, whereas the best we seem to be able to do with simulations of social systems is to gain insights. Is this difference fundamental? If so, why? How does the understanding of X-events inform this discussion?

- Given your answers to the above questions, what is the best way for an organization to employ simulation to support strategy development?

5.16
DISCUSSION QUESTION: CONTROLLED X-EVENTS

It is not light that we need, but fire; it is not the gentle shower, but thunder. We need the storm, the whirlwind, and the earthquake.

Frederick Douglass

In this chapter we discussed the notion of intentionally creating controlled X-events using the example of controlled burns in forests. Assuming that one wanted to follow such a strategy for an organization, how would one go about it? Unlike the forest fire example where we have relatively well understood mechanisms in play, the dynamics of social systems are often not fully understood. The first problem is determining the X-event that we should avert. As has been discussed in this book, forecasting such events is difficult, and they are often surprises. The second problem is that, assuming we know which category of X-events we wish to avert, how do we know when the system is in a state such that we should intervene with a controlled X-event? The last problem is, given that we successfully address the first two problems, what intervention would be appropriate and how would we go about it? There are no firm answers to these questions, if there are any at all. Consequently, we can only pose questions for further research.

- Are there general indicators that can be used to understand when a given system is in an unstable state?
- Are there ways to diagnose which aspects of a system are the most strained?
- What is the equivalent of a controlled burn for an organization?
- How would one know that the controlled X-event would not actually create more problems than it solves?

5.17
THE BURKIAN GAME

We learn the rope of life by untying its knots.

Jean Toomer

We would like to take this final section to bring the various threads of the book together.

5.17.1
CONNECTIONS

I love those connections that make this big old world feel like a little village.

Gina Bellman

In 1978, the BBC produced *Connections*, a television series written and hosted by the science historian James Burke. Burke's thesis was the "*gestalt* of the world was the result of a web of interconnected parts." History was a consequence of interactions among multiple agents that were working on their own independent interests. This has led to the state of human progress we see today. Among the questions that Burke poses is the very interesting question of how the human race can adapt to the fast change that an accelerating process of innovation generates. That is the concern of this book.

Let's take Episode 2 of the series as an example of the workings of Burke's mind. Burke starts with the discovery, in ancient Greece, of the touchstone, a stone for identifying and assaying precious metals. Precious metals leave an identifying mark on the touchstone. This tool standardized currency and stimulated trade between Greece and Persia. This led to the construction of a huge commercial center in Alexandria—with a library that contained Ptolemy's star tables. This was the beginning of a revolution in astronomy that enabled navigators in the Age of Discovery several centuries later. But navigators noted that compass needles did not point true north. This led to investigations on magnetism, which led to the discovery of electricity. Investigations of atmospheric electricity led to the invention of the cloud chamber, which led to the development of radar and nuclear weapons. And there you have it.

We like to call this type of extended causal chain the *Burkian Game*. We can tie many of the the topics and principles in this book together in our own version of the Burkian Game. This will create an example of the "*gestalt* that can help an individual anticipate and manage X-events" that was promised in the Preface. Since we are imagining a web of influence rather than the customary linear description of history, we can start the game anywhere. Let's start our game with Louis Pasteur and then move on to death rates, fertility, the population explosion, economics, women's education, fossil fuels, global climate change, and finally to hurricanes and deadly tornados. In our story we will talk about context, including complexity mismatch and social mood/beliefs; random triggers; timescales; and resilience—the principles in this book.

5.17.2
GERM THEORY OF DISEASE

A child who is protected from all controversial ideas is as vulnerable as a child who is protected from every germ. The infection, when it comes—and it will come—may overwhelm the system, be it the immune system or the belief system.

Jane Smiley

Let's start our Burkian Game with the story of Louis Pasteur, the great French chemist and microbiologist. Pasteur invented the process for treating milk and wine to stop bacterial contamination—a process known as *pasteurization*. His work led to a deeper understanding of vaccination and fermentation, which were both known in ancient times. (At this point we could branch off and explore how beer saved the world, but let's save this conversation for when the reader takes the authors out for single-malt whiskey.) Pasteur's discoveries established the germ theory of disease, which states that microscopic organisms are responsible for many common diseases. The clinical application of Pasteur's discoveries, along with improved sanitary living conditions, significantly reduced the death rates in humans. In particular, childhood deaths dropped.

Serendipity, of course, played an important role in the story of germs. There is the well known tale of Alexander Fleming and the discovery of penicillin. Fleming had returned to England from World War I anxious find a method to prevent infections, which he had seen take the lives of more people than artillery. Fleming's laboratory was not the tidiest, and he accidentally discovered the agent penicillin that killed bacteria among unwashed Petri dishes in his sink. Although he published the results, they were ignored until 1938 when a team at Oxford stumbled across Fleming's paper and rekindled the research and demonstrated the efficacy of the drug in lab animals. This was the beginning of World War II, and the need for an antibacterial agent was acute. The problem became producing enough penicillin. Researchers and capitalists in the US took up the challenge. Penicillin production went from a cumulative of 400 million units produced by the spring of 1943 to 650 *billion units per month* in 1945.

There is more to the story of penicillin. Ernest Duchesne, a PhD student at Ecole du Service de Sant Militaire in Lyons, made the same discovery they did independently 31 years later in England. Unfortunately for Duchesne—and for many infected soldiers in World War I—the document was ignored by the 10-year-old Pasteur Institute. Pasteur, himself, had died two years earlier. The dissertation did not reach the academic community until just recently.

There are some items to note in the story of penicillin. First, the story is filled with random triggers, both effective and ineffective: the discovery by the untidy Fleming of mold that kills bacteria; the fortuitous rediscovery of Fleming's paper by a member of the Oxford group; the failure of the scientists at the Pasteur Institute to appreciate or possibly even read Duchesne's dissertation; and the recent rediscovery of Duchesne's dissertation. The first two random triggers, Fleming's discovery and the rediscovery by the Oxford group, were timed in such a way that the context was ready for an X-event. World War I and II provided the complexity mismatch and the social mood/ beliefs. Fleming's discovery and the Oxford rediscovery were the random triggers that sent the world to a new state of equilibrium. The last two random triggers, Duchesne's discovery and his recent rediscovery, occurred at a time when the context was not prepared for change. And change did not happen.

5.17.3
CHILDHOOD DEATHS AND FERTILITY

When we talk about mortality, we are talking about our children.

Christopher Hitchens

The human population began rapid growth during the Industrial Revolution. This was discussed in some detail in Chapter 2. The world's population increased from 1 billion in 1800 to 1.6 billion in 1900 to 7 billion today. The growth is due to a mismatch between death rates and birth rates. Many more people are being born and surviving to procreate than are dying in childhood. This can be attributed to a mismatch in timescales between the processes of mortality and fertility. Childhood death rates dropped very rapidly during the Industrial Revolution, in large part due to the medical discoveries of Pasteur, his predecessors, and colleagues. Fertility, on the other hand, remained high during the Industrial Revolution. As discussed in Chapter 2, there are forces that drive the fertility down such that the distribution in ages in a population is somewhat evenly distributed across age, but these processes are slow compared with the sudden drop in mortality. It appears that these forces will cause the population to level off. Current estimates place this new population size at about 9 billion people. The transition from less than a billion people on the planet to approximately 9 billion in just a few hundred years is the *Demographic Transition*.

The Demographic Transition is an example of resilience of the size of the population to the complexity mismatch between medical advances and the health of the population. The population size moves from one stable state of less than 1 billion people to a completely new stable state of about 9 billion people. The sudden drop in childhood deaths acts as the trigger for the transformation. Social mood/beliefs affect the timescale in which the fertility responds to the mismatch in birth and death rates.

5.17.4
ECONOMIC RESPONSE

The curious task of economics is to demonstrate to men how little they really know about what they imagine they can design.

Friedrich August von Hayek

All the new people on the planet need to be fed, housed, and clothed. This has driven demand. Abundant fossil fuels have driven supply. Fossil fuels have been used to power transportation, heat, cool, preserve foods, extract mined materials, create fertilizers, power farm machinery, power irrigation, create plastics, create synthetic fabrics, and much more. Without fossil fuels, the economy would not be able to keep up with the demands of an increased population. Without fossil fuels, the demands of increased population would need to be met by an unmechanized agricultural economy powered by the Sun.

The forces of economics drive production efficiency. Increased productivity leads to social polarization as discussed in Chapter 3. This complexity mismatch in social systems leads to social X-events such as revolutions and wars.

A consequence of an active economy is that medical technology has improved. This was discussed in detail in Chapter 4 where we examined forces driving X-events within healthcare. Improved medical technology serves as a positive feedback loop to population growth by lowering mortality, thus increasing growth.

Economic growth supports women's education. This feeds back on fertility, lowering population growth.

Another consequence of an active economy is that the burning of fossil fuels has increased differential heating on the planet leading to climate change as discussed in this Chapter 5.

Unfortunately, or perhaps fortunately, fossil fuels are being depleted. Therefore, there is a competition between high demand of population growth and diminishing supply due to reduced inventories of fossil fuel. This is a serious complexity mismatch. We leave this branch of the causal chain for future discussions.

Economics changes on faster timescales than demographics has historically changed. Economics, therefore, has been able to track demographic changes fairly well. This does not mean that economics behaves smoothly in response to external demographic forces. It means that economics experiences X-events in response to smooth demographic changes on economic timescales.

5.17.5
CLIMATE CHANGE

Saving our planet, lifting people out of poverty, advancing economic growth . . . these are one and the same fight. We must connect the dots between climate change, water scarcity, energy shortages, global health, food security, and women's empowerment. Solutions to one problem must be solutions for all.

Ban Ki-moon

This brings us to climate change. Burning of fossil fuels leads to increased differential heating of the planet's surface as discussed in this Chapter 5. Rising seas follow along with increased numbers and intensities of storms as discussed in Chapter 1. Hurricanes and tornadoes become more of a problem.

Climate change is a feedback loop to the economy. Location of coastal cities, agriculture, fresh water supplies, food supplies, transportation, risk management, and markets are all affected. Similarly, climate change feeds back to the health and mortality of populations.

The complexity mismatch in climate change is due to the differential and increased heating patterns on the surface of the Earth. The mood/beliefs determine how much effort will be socially acceptable in reducing the impact of climate change by reducing carbon emissions. The timescales for climate change are longer than economic timescales. This probably means that economic concerns will prevail over climate concerns on the shorter timescales. Finally, as heating becomes more intense, atmospheric responses such as storms become more localized as described in Chapter 1. As storms become more localized and intense, random triggers such as small pressure fluctuations become more important. As randomness increases, predictability fails, leading to more difficult risk management.

5.17.6
DISCUSSION QUESTION: ARE HUMAN BRAINS BIG ENOUGH?

The human brain has 100 billion neurons, each neuron connected to 10 thousand other neurons. Sitting on your shoulders is the most complicated object in the known universe.

Michio Kaku

This brings us back to the question that James Burke proposed about "how the human race can adapt to the fast change that an accelerating process of innovation generates." In this section we posited a plausible causal chain that links the discoveries of Louis Pasteur with wars, epidemics, floods, storms, market collapses, mortality, women's education, and the cost of fresh tomatoes. Who could plan for this? According to Ashby's Law of Requisite Variety discussed in Exercise 1.2.2, if we want to control our future, we must be more complex than that which we wish to control. Is that feasible?

BIBLIOGRAPHY

"Returning to Simplicity (Whether We Want To or Not)." http://gregor.us/alternative-energy/returning-to-simplicity.

"Fleming Discovers Penicillin." http://www.pbs.org/wgbh/aso/databank/entries/dm28pe.html.

Oregon Health Plan. http://en.wikipedia.org/wiki/Oregon_Health_Plan.

"How Beer Saved the World," 2011. http://www.history.co.uk/shows/how-beer-saved-the-world.

James Burke. *Connections*. New York: Simon and Schuster, 1978, 1995, 2007.

Duchesne, Ernest. *Antagonism Between Molds and Bacteria*. PhD thesis, 1897. English translation by Michael Witty. Fort Myers, 2013. ASIN B00E0KRZ0E and B00DZVXPIK.

Eldredge, Niles, and S. J. Gould. "Punctuated Equilibria: An Alternative to Phyletic Gradualism." In *Models in Paleobiology*, edited by T.J.M. Schopf. San Francisco: Freeman Cooper, 1972 (82–115).

Flynn, S. *Edge of Disaster*. New York: Random House, 2007.

Francart, P. L. "What Does Resilience Really Mean?" *La Revue Géopolitique*, February 2010.

Gunderson, L., and C. S. Holling, editors. *Panarchy*, Washington, D.C.: Island Press, 2002.

Holling, C. S. "Resilience and Stability of Ecological Systems." *Ann. Rev. Ecology and Systematics* 4 (1973): 1–24.

Homer-Dixon, T. *The Upside of Down*. Washington, D.C.: Island Press, 2006.

Michel-Kerjan, E. "How Resilient is Your Country?" *Nature*, November 2012.

Robbins, J. "Forest Fire Research Questions the Wisdom of Prescribed Burns." *New York Times*, September 2012.

Royal Society and NAS. "Climate change: Evidence and causes." 2014. https://royalsociety.org/policy/projects/climate-evidence-causes/.

Walker, B., and D. Salt. *Resilience Thinking*. Washington, D.C.: Island Press, 2006.

INDEX

Academics   99, 152

Ackerman, Diane   68

Adaptation   72, 193, 242, 260, 303, 304

Adaptivity   254, 266, 267, 298

Affordable Care Act   229, 244

Africa   90, 94, 129, 130, 141

age distribution   115, 121, 126, 127, 129, 134, 139, 140, 141

age of mammals   19

age ratio   126, 127, 130

Agility   52, 254, 260, 266, 267, 297

Aging   95, 96, 108, 117, 121, 128–131, 140–143

aging populations   117, 140, 141

Ahmadinejad, Mahmoud   96

Allen, Paul   53

Allen, Woody   106, 243

Alterman, Eric   166

Alvarez, Luis   19

Alvarez, Walter   19

analog technology   195

anger   85, 97

Antarctic   287, 288

Apple   53, 54, 192, 194, 195, 202, 211

Arab Spring   32, 100

Arctic   270–272, 287, 288, 292, 294, 295

Aristotle   109, 212

Armageddon   21, 78

Ashby's Law of Requisite Variety   38, 78, 150, 311

Asia   86, 88, 90, 94, 95, 299

Asimov, Isaac   290

Assimilation   52, 254, 258, 266, 267, 293

Asteroids   19, 20, 22, 24, 28, 73, 78, 79, 294, 295

Attenborough, David   133

Attractor   82, 216

Augean stables   261

Aurelius, Marcus   100

Australia   130, 132, 141, 275

availability cascade   104

availability heuristic   104

Avon   193

Awareness   52, 254, 258, 266–269

Bachmann, Michele   275

Bahrain   129, 130

Bailout   198

Banks   75, 153, 162, 200, 258, 261

Bargaining   85

Barton, Joe   275, 277

Bayesian probability   101

Beach   234, 235

Beer Game   212–214, 216–219, 222–224

behavioral driver   33, 36

beliefs   33, 40, 43, 44, 46, 47, 76, 102–104, 106, 132, 157, 168, 181, 184, 185, 269, 306, 308, 309, 311

Benyus, Janine   265

Berk, Bradford   230

Berle, Milton   203, 298

Berry, Wendell   139

beta gyres   67, 78, 268

Bhutto, Benazir   134

birth rate   106, 108, 114, 117, 118, 124, 125, 129, 133, 134, 136, 139, 140, 149

Black-Scholes method   207, 208

Blackberry   201, 202

Boisot, Max   78

Bongaarts, John   129

Box, George E.P.   106

Brazil 130, 132

Brownian motion 101

Brunei 129

Brynjolfsson, Erik 162, 163

bubbles and crashes 103–105

bump 23, 25, 28, 29, 69

Burberry 202

Burch, Tom 15

Burke, James 305, 311

butterfly effect 65

calderas 26

Cambrian explosion 55

Campbell, Joseph 156

Canada 252

Canary Islands 199

Canon 194

Cap, Ferdinand 78

Capital 27, 85, 162, 167, 198, 207, 208, 259

Capote, Truman 299

Carbon 268, 270, 275, 276, 290, 311

Carbon Dioxide 268, 270, 275

Cascio, Jamais 77, 255

causal relationships 47, 107, 139–141

central limit theorem 103

Ceres 22

Chad 132

Chattopadhyay, Sahana 179

Chechnya 30

chemical energy in one barrel of oil 28

Chicxulub 19, 20, 33

childhood death 106–108, 114, 117, 118, 124, 126–128, 130, 136, 138–141, 307–309

childhood death rate 106, 108, 117, 124, 126–128, 138–141, 308

China 88, 91, 97, 129, 132, 158

Cliff 31, 33, 89, 201, 237

Climate 26, 51, 62, 82, 84, 87, 133, 259, 267–275, 277–280, 282–285, 287, 288, 291–294, 296–300, 306, 310, 311

climate change 84, 87, 133, 267–271, 273, 275, 277–280, 283, 284, 288, 291, 293, 294, 297–300, 306, 310, 311

clinical trials 236, 241, 242

closed system 49, 62, 117, 285, 286

cluster 20, 84, 128–130, 141, 172

cognitive dissonance 160, 168, 181, 296

Colgate 193

commercial collapse 86

commodities 84, 86, 204, 207, 227, 228, 235

commoditization 235

communication 32, 79, 89, 94, 103, 192, 199, 212, 214, 215, 223

complexity 33–39, 45, 48, 56–59, 61, 63, 66, 68, 70, 72, 83–90, 94, 96, 97, 100, 101, 103, 105, 110, 139, 148, 149, 151–153, 155, 157, 158, 161, 163, 181, 182, 184, 185, 187, 195, 199, 200, 202, 203, 205, 206–208, 210, 212, 218–220, 222–224, 226, 229, 232–234, 236, 240, 241, 244, 247, 248, 257, 260, 264, 265, 268, 277, 278, 285, 287, 301–303, 306, 308–311

complexity factor 35, 36

complexity gap 33–36, 48, 83, 84, 86, 88, 89, 94, 100, 149, 151, 153, 155, 158, 163, 187, 223, 247, 248, 264, 278, 301

complexity measurement 36

complexity mismatch 36, 38, 45, 56, 57, 61, 88, 96, 100, 139, 148, 157, 161, 181, 182, 184, 185, 202, 203, 208, 219, 220, 222–224, 232–234, 244, 260, 268, 277, 285, 287, 306, 308–311

complexity of the rock 37

complexity overload 34, 35, 85–87, 90, 97, 195, 199

context 28, 31–33, 35–41, 43, 45, 47–49, 54, 69, 76, 82–87, 89, 123, 131, 138, 141, 149, 184, 212, 254, 264, 265, 270, 306, 308

context-dependent factors 83

context-free drivers 83, 86, 87

control 30, 38, 50, 88, 117–120, 131–
134, 138, 140, 151, 164, 181, 183, 200,
209, 228, 236, 241, 244, 252, 311
controller responsiveness 120
Core Model 108–110, 121–125, 127,
129–132, 136, 138–143
Corgan, Billy 198
Coriolis force 63, 64, 66 - 68
Coriolis threshold 63–65
Corruption 99, 100
crashes and bubbles 103–105
creative destruction 54, 196 198,
211, 257
creativity 154, 167
Crestor 235
critical point 31, 82, 84
cultural collapse 86

Dawkins, Richard 150
death rate 106, 108, 114, 115, 117, 118,
124, 126–129, 132–136, 138–141,
306–309
Delta Airlines 42
Democratic Party 183, 185
demographic transition 106–109, 113,
118, 121, 123 , 124, 127, 128, 130, 131,
133, 135, 137–143, 181, 293, 309
demographic variables 108, 121, 124,
126, 127, 131, 140, 141
demographics 84, 87, 107, 120–122, 131,
139, 142, 181, 184, 185, 295, 310
demography 107, 120, 185
denial 85
density of air at sea level 25
density of water 25
Department of Homeland Security 34
Depression 26, 53, 85, 88, 159, 161, 167
Diabetes 235, 237
Diamond, Jared 87
Dickens, Charles 279
digital photography 194, 210, 211
dinosaurs 18–21, 25, 55, 300, 301
domain boundary 170

Douglass, Frederick 301, 304
Dow Jones Industrial Average 46, 89,
91, 92, 148, 183
downward mobility 160, 163
drivers 31, 33, 48, 55, 61, 81–88, 90–100,
102, 104, 106, 108, 110, 112, 114, 116,
118–120, 122, 124, 126, 128, 130, 132,
134, 136, 138, 140–142, 149, 218, 226
Drucker, Peter 295
Dryden, John 242
Duchesne, Ernest 307
dynamical system theory 82, 83, 217, 252

Earle, Sylvia 296
Earth's rotation 63
Earthquakes 18, 71, 74, 255, 259
Ecclesiastes 269, 272
eco-niches 31, 55, 196
ecology 51, 196, 252, 253, 255, 262, 294
ecosystems 50, 300
Edelman, Richard 97
Edges 49, 50, 70, 138
Edison, Thomas A. 186
Efficiency 38, 207, 236, 246, 310
Egypt 32, 89
Einstein, Albert 44, 124, 187, 277, 296
Eldredge, Niles 300
emergency doctor 232
Emerson, Ralph Waldo 168
Energy 20–23, 25–29, 37, 60, 62, 68, 69,
107, 120, 142, 252, 256, 257, 276–278,
282, 286, 288, 310
Energy Flux 29, 69
Enron Corporation 40
Enterprise Transformation 245
Entropy 39, 44, 45, 285, 286
Equation of State (EOS) 126, 137, 141
Equilibrium 55, 59, 60–62, 117, 118,
121, 127–129, 132, 134, 228, 229, 252,
257, 300, 301, 308
Erdös, Paul 239
Erdogan, Tayyip 96
Euler equations 68

Europe 88, 90, 91, 94–98, 141, 252, 288

Evans, Mason 151, 153

Evidence 19, 20, 38, 47, 94, 119, 148, 181, 184, 240, 268–273, 285, 287, 290, 292, 301

expected life span 107, 124, 125–127, 129

experiment 58, 96, 109, 110, 158, 215, 229, 238, 239, 259 - 261

extinction 21, 25–27, 96, 115, 280

Extreme Value Theory 71–74

Facebook 99, 153, 164

Failure 51, 187, 193–195, 199, 200, 215, 245–248, 265, 266, 294, 308

Feedback 43, 44, 72, 74, 76, 104, 111, 138, 166, 209, 210, 310, 311

feedback loop 43, 44, 72, 74, 76, 104, 138, 210, 310, 311

Ferguson, Niall 83, 97

Ferrel Cells 62 - 64

Fertility 91, 93–95, 106, 108, 115–121, 124, 126, 129, 131, 132, 136, 138–141, 306, 308–310

Fey, Tina 273

Feynman, Richard P. 22

financial collapse 40, 85, 86

financial services 34, 35, 90

Five Stages of Grief 85

fixed point 128, 130, 174–177, 220

Fleming, Alexander 307

Floods 71, 288, 311

Florida 275, 289, 294

Flynn, Stephen 256

Ford, Henry 204

Forest Service 262

Forests 20, 262, 304

fossil fuels 270, 276, 277, 306, 309, 310

Founder Effect 196

Four As 52, 254, 255, 258, 260, 265–268, 300

Francart, Loup 253

France 129, 132

Franchises 53

Frankfurter, Felix 179

Franklin, Ben 212

Fromm, Erich 121

Frost, Robert 280

fruit seller 32

Fujitsu 195

Fukushima 255, 256

Fukuyama, Francis 158

Futures 102, 205–207

Garcia, Jerry 122

Garden 109–118, 120, 262, 263

Gardiner, Chauncey 109

Gates, Bill 53, 188

Gaussian distribution 103

gedanken experiment 109, 110

General Electric 202

General Motors 42

Genocide 96, 263

Germany 91, 94, 130, 132

Gerrymandering 185

Gestalt 306

Giridharadas, Anand 151

global warming 197, 273, 279, 284, 285, 290, 291

globalization 84, 87, 88, 89, 91, 100

goats and cars 238, 239

Goodell, Jeff 283

Goldman, David P. 96

Gould, Stephen Jay 55, 300

Gracie, Royce 148, 150

Grapes of Wrath 164

Great Degeneration 97

Greeley, Horace 98

greenhouse gases 270, 271, 280, 281, 283, 284, 288, 290, 292

Greer, Germaine 139

Groupthink 169, 173, 178, 179

Grove, Andy 294

Gubbio, Italy 19

Hadley Cells 62, 64, 66, 68

Hamilton, Bermuda 258

Hamlet   150, 151

Hawking, Stephen   117, 297, 300

Hawn, Goldie   142

health outcomes   229

healthcare   38, 90, 95, 107, 120, 139, 140, 224, 225–236, 239, 241–244, 263–265, 295, 310

healthcare costs   226–228, 234, 242

heat   23, 24, 28, 29, 57, 58, 60–70, 268, 270–274, 279, 282, 283, 285–287, 309

herding   102, 104, 196

Hero's Journey   156, 157

Heuristics   104, 173

high pressure   57

Hinckley, Gordon B.   211

Hiroshima   19–22, 29

Hirschman, Albert O.   98

historical change   83–85, 97

Hodgkinson, Tom   165

Holling, C.S. ("Buzz")   50, 52, 252, 253

Holsapple, Keith A.   23

Homer   156, 257

Homer-Dixon, Thomas   257

Homophily   169, 179

hot-dog vendor   234

House Banking Scandal   99

Huffy Bicycles   35

human brains   311

human progress   261, 301, 302, 306

hurricane rotation   66

hurricanes   56–59, 65–70, 258, 259, 268, 269, 277, 286, 288, 294, 306, 311

hydrogen bomb   21

hyperlipidemia   235, 237, 238

ice   29, 79, 82, 268, 270, 271, 272, 274, 277, 280, 281, 287, 288, 294, 296

identity   96, 152, 153

Idestam, Fredrik   192

Ignatieff, Michael   158

International Institute for Applied Systems Analysis (IIASA)   50, 252

Immolation   32

Incumbent   48, 184

India   19, 91, 129, 130, 132

Inequality   149, 156, 158, 159, 162, 163, 165–168, 178–180, 182–184, 189, 278

inflation-adjusted family income   153

information management   226, 233, 234, 238, 241, 244

innovation   31, 54, 84, 87, 194, 197, 198, 211, 229, 231, 246, 306, 311

insurance   38, 136, 229, 237, 242, 243, 244, 254, 257–261, 296–298, 303, 304

Insurance World   258–261, 296, 303, 304

Internal Energy   28, 29

Intuition   113, 127, 154, 260, 262

investment decisions   73, 103

iPhone   53, 54, 192, 202

Iran   91, 94–96

Iridium   19

Irrigation Model   110, 119–121, 123

irrigation system   109, 112, 113, 115–119

Internal Revenue Service (IRS)   37

Jacobson, Robert   275

Japan   95, 97, 132, 148, 198, 252, 255, 256

Jeopardy   240

Joad, Tom   164

jobless recovery   88, 165, 167

Jobs, Steve   53, 54

Jones, Daniel J.   164

Jung, Carl G.   178

Kahn, Herman   187

Kamen, Dean   227

Katz, Jon   38

Keats, John   208

Kennedy, John F.   182

Kennedy, Robert   180

Kentucky Fried Chicken   53

Kenya   132

Kim, Thomas   195, 196

Kinetic Energy   25, 28, 29, 69

Klein, David   230

Kodak   194–196, 210–212, 230, 283, 291, 293

Koryta, Michael   302

Krauss, Lawrence M.   121

Kubler-Ross, Elisabeth   85

Kuper, Simon   152

Kuwait   129, 132

Labor   153, 154, 159, 167, 223

Landscape   31–33, 52, 54, 74–77, 83, 94, 152, 163, 219, 222, 254, 260, 267, 269, 291, 295

Lane, David   15

Latin America   90, 141

Lava   26

least-squares regression   107

Leave it to Beaver   151

Lewis, Thomas   180

Libya   129

life span   110, 124, 126, 131, 142

likelihood   30, 32, 33, 42, 44, 68, 83, 163, 180, 255, 259

Lindbergh, Charles   75

Linklater, Richard   151

Lipitor   235, 238

liquid water   29

Littlewood, J.E.   113

lognormal probability distribution   103

Lord Kelvin   113, 141, 142

Luddites   153

Magma   26

Manifold   94, 127, 128, 130, 138, 141

Mariotti, John   35

market index   46–48, 102

Marx, Groucho   182

mass driver   24

McGonigal, Jane   261

McNichols Sports Arena   148

Meadows, Donella   119

median age   115, 117, 118, 124, 126, 127, 129, 131, 135, 136, 142

Medicaid   225, 228, 236, 243

Medicare   38, 225, 228, 236, 243

Metaphor   31, 56, 57, 59, 61, 63, 65, 67, 69, 74, 83, 155, 259, 268

Meteor   18, 20, 22

Mexico   18, 93, 103, 129, 130, 132, 238

Microsoft   53, 54, 192, 211

middle management   208–211

Miller, Kenneth R.   286

Mitchell, Joni   115

Model   49–51, 53, 72, 82, 83, 101, 103, 106–110, 119–132, 135, 136, 138–143, 168–170, 173, 178, 179, 186, 200, 201, 209, 212, 214, 216, 217, 220, 223, 224, 238, 247, 252, 258, 273, 274, 277, 278, 292, 296, 298, 300, 303, 304

Molyneux, Stefan   128

Massive Open Online Courses (MOOC)   166

Mood   33, 36, 38, 39, 40, 42–44, 46–48, 68, 76, 77, 83–87, 89–91, 97, 100, 102–106, 132, 148, 149, 151, 160, 163, 164, 165, 168–170, 173, 178–185, 195, 203, 205–207, 218, 220–224, 244, 269, 288, 306, 308, 309, 311

Moon   20, 310

Moore, Alan   303

Mount Everest   19, 20

Mount Fuji   26

Mount St. Helens   26

mountain peaks   31

Mubarak regime   32

Muslim countries   91, 95, 96

NASA   19–21

National Academy of Sciences   252, 270, 272

natural sciences   49, 57, 61, 82, 107

natural selection   107, 134

neoclassical economics   102

new artisans   155, 156

New York   20, 34, 83, 149, 151, 164, 201, 229–231

Newton's Third Law   24

Nietzsche, Friedrich 267
Nightingale, Florence 232
Nikon 194
Nimoy, Leonard 72
Nin, Anaïs 71
Nocera, Joe 201
Nodes 49, 50, 70, 138, 173, 174, 177,
  226, 237
Nokia 192
normal distribution 103
North America 90, 192, 288
nuclear bomb 20–22
nuclear holocaust 96

Occam's Razor 43, 278
ocean acidification 289
Organisation for Economic Cooperation
  and Development (OECD) 128–130,
  141
Oil Cluster 129, 130
Oregon Health Plan 263, 264, 296
organizational inertia 245
Orlandella, Dante 200
Orlov, Yuri 85
oscillatory behavior 121
Oxford 307, 308

paint it black 24
paleobiologists 19
Pallas 22
Palmer, Richard 103
parabolic mirror 24
Pasteur, Louis 306, 307, 311
Patent 194, 195, 225, 227, 234–237
patent cliff 237
path dependence 302–304
Peak Oil 293
Penicillin 307, 308
Pensions 90, 95, 96
Permian-Triassic extinction 25
Perry, Rick 230
personalized medicine 226, 238, 241
Pew Research Center 98, 149, 153, 181

pharmaceutical industry 224, 234, 235,
  237, 238
phase transition 82
photography 194, 210–212
physician compensation 231, 244
physicians 38, 225, 228, 231, 232, 238
physicists 273
physics 21, 45, 46, 57, 82, 110, 170,
  209, 257, 273, 274, 277, 279–281,
  286, 296, 304
Piaget, Jean 49
Piketty, Thomas 162
Pizza 231 - 233
Poland, Gregory 275
Polar Cells 61, 62
Polarization 162, 168, 180, 182, 185, 310
political collapse 86, 87
political systems 84, 87, 97
politicians 94, 99, 100, 161, 166, 203,
  261, 275
politics 124, 134, 166, 172, 182, 184, 185,
  194, 202, 253, 255
Pompeii 26
population dynamics 90, 94, 107
population explosion 116, 133, 134, 306
Potential Energy 22, 23, 28, 29
Power 21, 29, 30, 32, 33, 42, 47, 51, 62,
  69, 73, 85, 86, 96, 142, 149, 157, 185,
  194, 197, 229, 246, 248, 256, 258, 261,
  268, 309
Powers, Kevin 73
pre-existing condition 243, 244
predictability 65, 68, 105, 241, 311
Presidential Elections 47, 103, 183
Probability 33, 39, 45, 71–74, 76, 82, 83,
  101–105, 168, 188, 189, 239, 240, 271
probability distribution 45, 71–74, 83,
  103, 189
problem solving 154
productivity 85, 97, 100, 141, 142, 153,
  154, 165–167, 310
Prospect Theory 187–189
punctuated equilibrium 55, 300, 301

Qatar   129, 132
Quinn, James   85

random triggers   32, 48, 56, 69, 151, 244, 306, 308, 311
rational expectations hypothesis   102, 103
Rayleigh–Bénard convection   60, 61
Reason, James   200
Recession   149, 163, 167
Reed, Jack   207
Regulators   34–36, 42, 166, 225, 259
Reinsurance   258, 261
Religion   120, 160, 181, 286
repetitive jobs   166
Republican Party   183–185
research and development   237
resilience   48, 50–53, 55, 77, 189, 195, 195, 198, 208, 210, 211, 224, 252–258, 261, 264–266, 299–301, 303, 304, 306, 309
resilience revolution   252
revolutions   84, 225, 310
Research in Motion (RIM)   201
Risk   31, 33, 34, 71, 74, 75, 83, 85, 86, 96, 101, 157, 163, 169, 186–189, 196, 203–208, 231, 236, 237, 245, 247, 248, 253, 255, 257–259, 266, 267, 288, 294, 302, 311
risk analysis   33, 255
Rochester   230, 231
Rossby number   63
Rossman, Gabriel   196
Royal Society   270, 272, 290, 291, 293
rubber band   34, 155
Rubbermaid Office Products Group   35
Russell, Bertrand   181
Russia   95, 130, 132, 158
Rutherford, Sir Ernest   142
Rutter, Brad   240

Salinger, J.D.   150
Samsung   193–195, 202
Samuelson, Robert J.   160

Sanders, "Colonel" Harland   53
Santa Fe Institute   103, 258
Saudi Arabia   130, 132
Schopenhauer, Arthur   135
Schumpeter, Joseph   54, 196, 257
scientific method   43
Scientifically Accurate Poetry   57
Schrödinger wave function   83
sea level   25, 66, 270–272, 274, 281, 288, 289, 291
Second Chechen War   30
Second Law of Thermodynamics   62, 285
Sen, Amartya   119
September 11, 2001   34
Seuss, Dr.   224
Shakespeare, William   56, 150, 270
Shannon entropy   39, 44, 45
Shaw, George Bernard   223
Siberia   20, 24, 25
Simon, Herbert   36
Simon, Koren   194
Simulation   174, 177, 217–219, 239, 258–261, 274, 279, 303, 304
Singapore   129, 132
single-malt whiskey   150, 307
single-point failures   200
Sivananda, Swami   224
Smiley, Jane   307
social collapse   34, 86, 87
social Darwinism   263
social mood   33, 36, 38–40, 42–44, 46–48, 76, 77, 83–87, 89–100, 102–105, 148, 149, 160, 163–165, 168, 179, 183, 184, 195, 205, 244, 269, 306, 308, 309
Sony   195, 202
Soros, George   127, 235
Soviet Academy of Sciences   252
Soviet Union   158, 194
special relativity   107, 109
Springsteen, Bruce   164
Stabenow, Debbie   116

Stability   50, 51, 75–77, 95, 152, 177, 196, 208–211, 243, 252, 253, 300
stationary state   128
statistics   33, 82, 83, 207, 241
status   94, 152, 158, 159, 178, 197, 246, 247, 261
status quo   94, 197, 246, 247, 261
steady state   119, 139, 140
Stein, Gertrude   113
Steinbeck, John   164
Stibel, Jeff   195
Stills, Stephen   163
stock index   46
stock market   33, 41, 42, 47, 48, 103–105, 131, 183, 184
stock prices   47, 101, 103
storm surge   291
structural complexity   34
subjective probability   101, 102, 105
Sudden Complexity Shifts   61
Sumatra   26
Sunstein, Cass   179
super-volcanoes   26, 27
supermanagers   163
surprise   19, 55, 99, 104, 105, 162, 305
Sweden   132
Swiss Cheese Model   200, 201, 247
Switzerland   258
System   20, 24, 25, 29, 34–38, 43, 45, 49–52, 54–59, 61, 62, 65, 67–70, 72–77, 82–89, 94, 97, 102, 107, 109, 112, 113, 115–121, 127, 132, 137–139, 142, 148, 158, 161, 164, 166, 169–174, 177, 196–198, 200, 203, 207, 213–218, 223, 226, 227, 230, 231, 233, 240, 247, 248, 252–259, 264–267, 274, 278, 282, 285, 286, 291, 292, 298, 300–305, 307, 310

Tainter, Joseph   33, 189
Tampere, Finland   192
Tapscott, Don   167
technological innovation   84, 87

technology   103, 153–155, 162–164, 187, 192, 194, 195, 201, 202, 226, 227, 229–232, 234, 238, 242, 245, 295, 298, 310
temperature   18, 20, 26, 29, 45, 46, 57–62, 65, 67–70, 268, 269, 271–274, 278–287, 290–292, 294, 296
Tenerife   199, 200, 223
Terrorism   189, 257
Texas   21–23, 29, 184, 185, 230, 231, 275, 277
Texas politics   184, 185
theory of evolution   107, 125, 300
thermal conduction   59, 69
thermal transport   57
thermodynamic entropy   45
thick-tailed distributions   103
Thompson, Hunter S.   201
Thompson, S.P.   113
Thornton, Billy Bob   21
Timescale   19, 42, 43, 46, 55, 84, 96, 105–107, 124, 132, 142, 262, 278, 279, 281, 292, 306, 308–311
tipping point   292, 294
Toba   26, 33
Toomer, Jean   305
Tornadoes   288, 302, 311
Total Energy   23, 25, 29
Traf-O-Data   53
Transparency International   100
Trend   33, 47, 48, 52–55, 59, 82, 83, 90, 96, 100, 101, 104, 106, 151, 163, 194, 195, 201, 206, 281, 283, 285, 288, 291, 298, 301
Triceratops   18
Truman, Harry S.   282
trust in governments   97, 99, 161, 162
tsunamis   18, 27
Tunguska 20, 22, 24
Tunisia   32, 89
Turkey   88, 91, 95, 96
Twain, Mark   203
Twitter   47, 153
Tyson, Neil deGrasse   125

U.K.   129, 132

U.S.   21, 26, 27, 42, 86, 88, 94, 95, 130, 132, 141, 149, 158, 159, 162, 180, 181, 184, 198, 228, 258, 262, 302

Ueshiba, Morihei   71

ultimate fighting (UFC)   148

unemployment   88, 149, 159, 160, 167, 183, 210

unfriending the trend   52

uniform age distribution   117

University of British Columbia (UBC)   50, 252

United Arab Emerates   129

unkown unknowns   82, 251, 252, 254, 256, 258, 260, 262, 264, 266, 268, 270, 272, 274, 276, 278, 280, 282, 284, 286, 288, 290, 292, 294, 296, 298, 300, 302, 304, 306, 308, 310

urbanization   93, 120, 132, 140

US Air   42

Utility   186–189, 242

van Zanten, Jacob   199

Vaneigem, Raoul   165

Venice   234, 299, 300

Vesta   22

Vesuvius   26

Vienna   50, 51, 252

visual arts   212

vital ratio   126, 127, 130

volcanoes   18, 26–28

vos Savant, Marilyn   239

Waldman, Ayelet   180

Wang Laboratories   201, 202

Wang, An   201, 202

War   19, 28, 29, 30, 33, 35, 74, 157, 158, 160, 161, 182, 197, 256, 257, 307, 308, 310, 311

water vapor   29

Watson, James D.   238

Welch, Jack   202

what-if world   109

White, Jack   76

Wildfire   262

Will, George   131

Willis, Bruce   21

wisdom of crowds   102

Wittgenstein, Ludwig   13

women's education   119, 120, 132,138, 140, 306, 310, 311

World Trade Center   34

World War   160, 161, 197, 256, 307, 308

WorldCom   42

Wright, Will   119

Wrigley   193

X-events   28, 30, 31–34, 52, 53, 55, 72, 74, 77, 82, 83, 102, 123, 150, 151, 156, 179, 181–183, 185, 187, 189, 196, 212, 218, 224, 236, 244, 254, 256, 259–262, 266, 268, 269, 293, 298, 301–306, 310

Xerox   230

Yellowstone National Park   27

young population   121, 126, 129

Yucatan peninsula   18, 19

Zakaria, Fareed   178

Zimbardo, Philip   157

Zuckerberg, Mark   267